THE LETTERS OF SIR JOSHUA REYNOLDS

THE LETTERS OF SIR JOSHUA REYNOLDS

EDITED BY

JOHN INGAMELLS AND JOHN EDGCUMBE

PUBLISHED FOR THE PAUL MELLON CENTRE FOR STUDIES IN BRITISH ART

BY

YALE UNIVERSITY PRESS

2000

Designed in Adobe Garamond by Guilland Sutherland
Printed in Great Britain by Biddles Ltd, Guildford and Kings Lynn

Library of Congress Catalog Card Number 00-109240
ISBN 0-300-08733-0

A catalogue record for this book is available from the British Library.

CONTENTS

ILLUSTRATIONS

PREFACE

We read Reynolds's letters not for their literary style, but for the additional light they shed on his remarkable career. He was not a natural letter writer. 'If I felt the same reluctance in taking a Pencil in my hand as I do a pen', he once told Boswell, 'I should be as bad a Painter as I am a correspondent' (Letter 107). He was, of course, a very good and ambitious painter, whose dedication is constantly apparent. 'Whoever is resolved to excel in painting', he told James Barry, 'must bring all his mind to bear on that one object, from the moment he rises till he goes to bed' (Letter 22). So much so that Reynolds could send a scruffy note to the greatest English writer of his day, his friend Dr Johnson, explaining that he had 'a sitter waiting so you must excuse the Blots' (Letter 87).

Reynolds would never have anticipated an edition of his letters, but they are now of the greatest interest. They emphasise his eminent friendships with Burke, Johnson and Garrick; they underline his ambition and reveal both his erudition and his accommodating temperament. He could politely discuss Hebrew verse with Bishop Lowth, ideas of truth and imagination with James Beattie, or a Latin epitaph with Samuel Parr. But in the end it is his pride in his profession and achievement which will most intrigue the reader. In the grim summer of 1779, for example, when a French invasion seemed imminent, he was able, in his professional isolation, to tell Lord Ossory that he had been as busy 'in my little way as the rest of the world have been in preparing against the invasion: from the emptiness of the town I have been able to do more work than I think I ever did in any summer before' (Letter 84). Yet he could be bullish enough concerning foreign artists: those French Academicians engaged in 'furnishing Europe with bauble' (Letter 30); Dutch seventeenth-century painters seeing nature 'just as it is seen in a Camera Obscura' so that 'after having seen the best of each master one has no violent desire of seeing any more' (Letter 96), or the pre-eminent German master Mengs whose works, he thought, had 'a plausible appearance but I think discover no great vigour of mind' (Letter 35). As the first President of the new Royal Academy Reynolds was proud to tell Sir William Hamilton that 'we have as good Artists in every branch of the art as any other nation can boast' (Letter 21).

It must be emphasised that there is always an element of chance in the survival of eighteenth-century letters. While the majority of Reynolds's letters to the Duke of Rutland are preserved, making the Duke his most frequent correspondent, letters to other correspondents have certainly been lost. Of the dated letters printed here, more than half belong to the final decade of his life, and only twenty-five date from before 1769 when, at the age of forty-six, he became President of the Royal Academy.

John Ingamells
August 2000

ACKNOWLEDGMENTS

Since Hilles first assembled the letters of Reynolds in 1929 their number has increased by almost two thirds. A revised edition was first envisaged some twenty years ago by Brian Allen, now Director of Studies at the Paul Mellon Centre in London, and John Edgcumbe, a collateral descendant of Joshua Reynolds. They found themselves independently gathering new Reynolds material and from 1985 they conferred as their other considerable commitments allowed. The contents of this volume is entirely founded on their labours.

John Edgcumbe is anxious to acknowledge the great kindness with which he has invariably been received in the course of his pursuit of letters by Reynolds in both America and England. The late Frederick Whiley Hilles and his wife, Susan Morse Hilles, gave generous encouragement. Hilles had continued to annotate his 1929 edition and he acquired new letters which he bequeathed in 1975 to the Sterling and Beinecke Libraries and to the Yale Center of British Art. Mary Hyde, now Viscountess Eccles, gave every facility for invaluable study at Four Oaks Farm. Much help was given by Fritz Liebert, Louis Martz, James Osborn, Steven Parks and Mrs Marjorie Wynne at Yale; Hugh Amory, Lou Donovan and Joan Nordell at Harvard; and Duncan Robinson, Elizabeth Fairman and Betty Muirden at the Yale Center. John Riely supplied copies of letters from the Rutland collection and Caroline Treffgarne negotiated the Duke's permission for their publication. Many other owners of letters were generous in providing access: Lady Lucas, Lady Salisbury, Lord Crawford, Lord

Grantham, Lord Iddesleigh, J.C.R. Comyn, and John Edgcumbe's collateral descendants: Mrs A.T. Copland Griffiths and her son and grandson; Major E.A. Hadow; Geoffrey Snagge; and Pamela Fairclough. Librarians have been both knowledgeable and helpful: at the Royal Academy of Arts, Sidney Hutchinson, Mary Anne Stevens and Nicholas Savage, and E.B. Nurse at the Society of Antiquaries. Many members of the Johnson Club of London have over the years freely provided specialist knowledge, notably Basil Barlow, E.S. de Beer, James Clifford, David Fleeman, Kenneth Garlick, W. Ketton-Cremer, Peter Laslett, Roger Lonsdale, James McLaverty, Pat Rogers and Kai Kim Yung. Special thanks are owed to Brian Allen who has been constantly supportive and generous with his time. To Teryll, his wife, and to his children, Jane and Richard, he offers his very grateful thanks for their support.

John Ingamells's acknowledgments are essentially to printed sources. With characteristic generosity David Mannings, who discovered several new letters, permitted consultation of the proofs of his Reynolds catalogue, as did Martin Postle, who catalogued the subject-pictures in that great volume and also discovered the important 1753 letter to Wilton. Richard Wendorf and Hugh Belsey also furnished welcome advice. Particular use has been made of Harry Mount's edition of Reynolds's *Journey to Flanders and Holland* (1996), Francis Broun's comprehensive doctoral dissertation 'Sir Joshua Reynolds's Collection of Paintings' (1987), and the catalogue of the Royal Academy Reynolds exhibition of 1986, compiled principally by David Mannings and Nicholas Penny.

At the Paul Mellon Centre in London Emma Lauze and Guilland Sutherland have been indispensable in the production of the book.

LOCATIONS OF LETTERS

Listed alphabetically by Country; followed by the numbers of the Letters

FRANCE
Paris: Collection Frits Lugt, Fondation Custodia (nos.104, 165, 219, 239)

IRELAND
Dublin: National Library of Ireland (no.184)

UNITED KINGDOM, INSTITUTIONS:
Aberdeen: Special Libraries and Archives, King's College, University of Aberdeen (nos.101, 223, 228)
Aylesbury: Buckinghamshire Record Office (no.27)
Bedford: Bedfordshire and Luton Archives and Records Services (nos.30, 35, 40, 65, 66)
Bristol: Record Office (no.122)
Cambridge: Fitzwilliam Museum (nos.45, 61, 64, 252), by permission of the Syndics of the Fitzwilliam Museum to whom rights in this publication are assigned
Edinburgh: National Library of Scotland (nos.118, 224, 267)
Lichfield: Johnson Birthplace Museum, Lichfield City Council (no.220)
Liverpool: Record Office, Liverpool Libraries and Information Services (no.126)
London:
British Library (nos.12, 36, 46, 48, 49, 88, 102, 111, 117, 175, 185)
British Museum (nos.168, 169, 170, 205, 264, 265, 274), by courtesy of the Trustees of the British Museum
Foundling Hospital (no.100)
National Art Library, Victoria and Albert Museum (no.80)
Royal Academy of Arts (nos.1, 2, 3, 19, 195, 196, 197, 199, 229)
Society of Antiquaries (no.53, 249)
Manchester: John Rylands University Library (no.201)
Oxford: Bodleian Library (nos.159, 214)
New College (nos.62, 66, 69, 137, 273)
Plymouth: Cottonian Collection (no.32)

Sheffield: Wentworth Woodhouse Muniments, Sheffield Archives (nos.18, 96, 121, 131, 187, 213, 276), with permission from the Head of Leisure Services, Sheffield City Council, and the Trustees of the Rt Hon Olive, Countess Fitzwilliam's Chattels Settlement
Windsor: Royal Archives (nos.285, 286, 287)

UNITED KINGDOM, PRIVATE COLLECTIONS:
Belvoir MSS, Belvoir Castle (nos.103, 106, 124, 134, 135, 136, 139, 140, 141, 142, 143, 147, 149, 150, 151, 152, 154, 157, 160, 162, 164, 171, 172, 283)
Castle Howard Archives (no.52), by kind permission of The Hon Simon Howard
Devonshire MSS, Chatsworth, Compton Place MSS (nos.268, 269)
Woburn MSS (no.260)
Anonymous Private Collections (nos.9, 10, 23, 24, 38, 63, 71, 81, 82, 89, 93, 97, 113, 114, 116, 163, 189, 208, 212, 227, 247, 248, 256, 275, 288)

UNITED STATES, INSTITUTIONS:
Boston, Mass.: Boston Public Library (no.51), by courtesy of the Trustees of the Boston Public Library
Cambridge, Mass.: Houghton Library of the Harvard College Library (nos.8, 44, 57, 85, 144, 271), by permission of the Houghton Library, Harvard University
Haverford, Pa.: Charles Roberts Autograph Letters Collection, Magill Library, Haverford College (no.1)
New Haven, Conn.: Beinecke Rare Books & Manuscript Library (nos.8, 13, 14, 15, 25, 28, 50, 54, 55, 58, 67, 70, 78, 79, 92, 105, 107, 123, 125, 133, 190, 193, 203, 210, 233, 234, 237, 238, 240, 241, 242, 251, 257, 270, 278)
Yale Center for British Art (nos.5, 21, 60, 90, 91, 95, 108, 127, 145, 146, 153, 156, 161, 167, 174, 179, 191, 192, 198, 200, 207, 211, 215, 231)
New York. N.Y.: Pierpont Morgan Library (no.37, 119, 180, 182)
Philadelphia, Pa.: Historical Society of Pennsylvania (nos.7, 120, 206)
Princeton, N.J.: Princeton University Library, Manuscripts Division, Department of Rare Books and Special Collections (nos.75, 236), published with permission of the Princeton University Library
San Marino, Calif.: The Huntington Library (nos.33, 209, 243, 245)
Washington, D.C.: Library of Congress (no.74)
Folger Shakespeare Library (nos.43, 132, 290)

UNITED STATES, PRIVATE COLLECTION
Hyde Collection (nos.16, 20, 41, 72, 76, 87, 110, 183, 186, 218, 253, 266, 289)

CHRONOLOGY

1723 16 July, born in Plympton, third son and seventh child of the Revd. Samuel Reynolds.

1740 Starts his apprenticeship under Thomas Hudson in London.

1744–49 Practises as a portrait painter in Devonport and London.

1749 11 May, sails with Commodore Keppel to the Mediterranean; stays in Minorca.

1750–52 Arrives in Rome by April 1750 and stays for two years; in April 1752 he visits Naples, returning to Rome the same month and proceeding to Florence in May; on 3 September, after he had left, elected an honorary member of the Accademia di Belle Arti, Florence; visited Bologna and Venice in July and August and Paris in September, before returning to London in October. Briefly visits his family in Devonshire.

1753 Established in London, first at St Martin's Lane,then in Great Newport Street.

1759 Publishes essays on painting in *The Idler* (29 September, 20 October and 10 November).

1760 Moves to Leicester Fields and builds a new studio.Exhibits with the Society of Artists each year to 1768.

1762 Accompanies Dr Samuel Johnson on a six-week tour in Devonshire (leaving London on 16 August and returning on 26 September).

1764 Founds The Club with Dr Samuel Johnson. Suffers a brief but severe illness.

1766 Elected to the Society of Dilettanti.

1768 Visits Paris (9 September–23 October) and elected first President of the Royal Academy on 14 December.

1769 Reynolds delivers his first *Discourse* on the opening of the Royal Academy on 2 January. He would henceforward deliver regular *Discourses* at the distribution of prizes to the students, annually to 1772 and biennially thereafter.

Knighted on 21 April; exhibited at the first RA exhibition which opened on 26 April, and annually thereafter until 1790.

1771 Visits Paris (15 August–early September).

1772 September, elected Alderman of the Borough of Plympton, Devonshire.

1773 Hon. DCL at Oxford on 9 July; elected Mayor of Plympton in September, being sworn in on 4 October.

1775 On invitation, sends his *Self-portrait* to the Accademia di Belle Arti, Florence.

1779 The first seven *Discourses* collected and published in May.

1780 RA moves the annual exhibition to Somerset House, marked by the *Ninth* and *Tenth Discourse* given there on 16 October and 11 December 1780.

1781 Tour to the Netherlands with Philip Metcalf (24 July–14 September).

1782 Elected a Steward of the Foundling Hospital.

1783 January, recovering from a violent inflammation of the eyes.

1784 1 September, succeeds Allan Ramsay as Painter in Ordinary to the King.

1785 Second tour of the Netherlands with Philip Metcalf (20 July–August).

1789 July, obscuring of one eye. Visits the Sussex coast in August. Vision lost in the afflicted eye in October.

1790 11 February, resigns as PRA following a dispute over the appointment of a Professor of Perspective, but withdraws his resignation on 16 March. Exhibits for the last time at the RA on 25 April. On 16 October he is described as having almost stopped painting. Delivers his final *Discourse* to the RA on 10 December.

1791 November, nearly totally blind.

1792 23 February, dies of a malignant tumour on the liver. He lies buried in St Paul's where a monument by John Bacon was unveiled in 1814.

EXPLANATION

SELECTION

The selection of letters differs slightly from that previously followed by Hilles.

Official letters, written as President of the Royal Academy, are omitted (Hilles nos.xv, cxx, cxxvii, cxxviii, clvi and clvii); they are impersonal and belong more properly to a history of the Royal Academy.

Receipts and Letters concerning payments made to Reynolds appear in a separate section (nos.255–289). Of these, one concerns the *Discourses*, one an inheritance, and two give instructions to his bankers (nos.266, 271, 280 and 289); the remainder concern pictures painted by Reynolds.

Untraced Letters (nos.290–308) are the equivalent of Hilles Appendix I, ('Letters not included in this edition'), but seventeen of the letters he listed now appear in the main body of letters (nos.16, 52, 58, 67, 74, 178, 179, 180, 183, 186, 193, 195, 197, 199, 204, 227, 284). Memoranda to write letters appearing in Reynolds's pocket-books, cited by Hilles, are here omitted.

No letters to Reynolds are printed (Hilles, Appendix III, cited fifteen). Where letters from Reynolds are responses to known letters from his correspondent, these are noticed in footnotes.

EDITING

Where the original letter has not been seen the Source quotes the Hilles number (together with Hilles's source). Where the original letter has been seen, the text is reproduced as faithfully as possible. Strike-throughs, amendments and insertions are preserved and the following symbols are used:

< > insertion

[ ] enclosing illegible or deleted word[s] or indicating lacunae as a result of a damaged manuscript

[*italics*] indicates a word or phrase supplied by the editor

Abbreviations, repetitions and mis-spellings are preserved and the temptation to follow each by [*sic*] has generally been resisted. Reynolds consistently wrote 'immediatly' and 'tast' (for 'taste'). Other inaccuracies appear to be those of the distracted correspondent, as 'caoch' for 'coach', and occasionally it seemed essential to point up solecisms (e.g. 'contrivanec' for 'contrivance' in Letter 106).

APPENDICES

Following the letters will be found two biographical Appendices, the first concerning Reynolds's relations, the second his correspondents. All other persons mentioned in the letters are identified in footnotes.

ABBREVIATIONS

Allen and Dukelskaya	B. Allen and L. Dukelskaya eds., *British Art Treasures from Russian Imperial Collections in the Hermitage*, 1996
BL	British Library
BM	British Museum
BMPL	British Museum, Print Room Library
Boswell	James Boswell, *Life of Samuel Johnson*, ed. G. Birkbeck Hill and L.F. Powell, 6 vols., 1934–50
Broun 1987	F. Broun, 'Sir Joshua Reynolds' Collection of Paintings,' PhD diss. Princeton, 1987, 2 vols.
Burke *Corr.*	*The Correspondence of Edmund Burke*, ed. T.W. Copeland *et al.*, 10 vols., 1958–70
Burl. Mag.	*Burlington Magazine*
cat.	catalogue
Commons	*The History of Parliament, The House of Commons, II, 1754–90*, ed. L. Namier & J. Brooke, 1964
Cormack	M. Cormack, 'Reynolds's Ledgers', *Wal. Soc.*, XLII, 1970, pp. 105-69
cos.	cousin
Cotton 1856	W. Cotton, *Sir Joshua Reynolds, and his works, gleanings from his diary, unpublished manuscripts, and from other sources*, 1856
Cotton 1859	———, *Sir Joshua Reynolds' Notes and Observations on Pictures … extracts from his Italian Sketch books … also the Rev. W. Mason's Observations on Sir Joshua's method of colouring*, 1859
CP	G.E.C., *The Complete Peerage*, 6 vols., 1982 (1st pub. 13 vols. 1910–59)
d.	died
[date]	estimated date
dau.	daughter
Discourses	Joshua Reynolds, *Discourses on Art* [1st complete ed. 1797], ed. R. R. Wark, 1997 [reference is made to the *Discourses* by number and line as in Wark's edition]
DNB	*Dictionary of National Biography*
exh.	exhibited or exhibition

Farington 1819	Joseph Farington, *Memoirs of the Life of Sir Joshua Reynolds*, 1819 [reprinted in Malone 1819, pp. cxxv–ccciii, the page numbers being each 120 higher than in Farington 1819]
Farington Diary	*The Diary of Joseph Farington*, 16 vols., 1978–84 [index vol. 1998]
Fifer 1976	C.N. Fifer ed., *The Private Papers of James Boswell* (research edition), III, *The Correspondence of James Boswell with Certain Members of the Club*, 1976
Foster	J. Foster, *Alumni Oxonienses ... 1715–1886*, 4 vols., 1887–88
Garrick Corr.	D.M. Little and G.M. Kahrl eds., *The Letters of David Garrick*, 3 vols., 1963
GC	A. Graves and W.V. Cronin, *History of the Works of Sir Joshua Reynolds*, 4 vols., 1899–1901
GM	*Gentleman's Magazine*
Gwynn 1898	S. Gwynn, *Memorials of an eighteenth-century painter: James Northcote*, 1898
Hilles 1929	F. W. Hilles, *Letters of Sir Joshua Reynolds*, 1929
Hilles 1936	———, *The Literary Career of Sir Joshua Reynolds*, 1936
Hilles 1952	———, *Portraits by Sir Joshua Reynolds*, 1952
Hilles 1967	———, 'Horace Walpole and the Knight of the brush', in *Horace Walpole: Writer, politician, and connoisseur*, ed. W.H. Smith, 1967, pp. 141–66
Hilles 1969	———, 'Sir Joshua at the Hôtel de Thiers', *Gazette des Beaux-Arts*, LXXIV, 1969, pp. 201–10
Hilles 1970	———, 'Sir Joshua and the Empress Catherine' in *Eighteenth-Century Studies in honor of Donald F. Hyde*, Grolier Club, New York, 1970, pp. 267–77
Hilles, *Notes*	Annotations by F.W. Hilles in his own copy of Hilles 1929 (YCBA)
HMC Rutland	Historical Manuscripts Commission, 14th Report, Appendix, part 1, *The Manuscripts of the Duke of Rutland preserved at Belvoir Castle*, vol. III, 1894; vol. IV, 1905
Hudson 1958	D. Hudson, *Sir Joshua Reynolds, a personal study*, 1958
Ingamells, *Dictionary*	J. Ingamells, *A Dictionary of British and Irish Travellers in Italy 1701–1800*, 1997
Joshua's Nephew	S.M. Radcliffe ed., *Sir Joshua's Nephew, being letters written, 1769–1778, by a young man to his sisters*, 1930
Journey 1996	H. Mount ed., *Sir Joshua Reynolds, A Journey to Flanders and Holland*, 1996
JWCI	*Journal of the Warburg and Courtauld Institutes*
Kerslake 1977	J. Kerslake, *Early Georgian Portraits* (National Portrait Gallery, London), 1977
LT	C.R. Leslie and T. Taylor, *Life and Times of Sir Joshua Reynolds*, 2 vols., 1865
Lugt	F. Lugt, *Répertoire des catalogues de ventes publiques 1600–1825*, 1938 (reference is made to the numbered list of sales)
m.	married
Malone 1819	E. Malone, *The Literary Works of Sir Joshua Reynolds, Kt*, 3 vols., 5th ed., 1819. Farington's *Memoirs of the Life of Sir Joshua Reynolds* appears on pp. cxxv–ccciii (see Farington 1819)

Mannings	D. Mannings, *Sir Joshua Reynolds A Complete Catalogue of his Paintings* [the subject pictures catalogued by M. Postle], 2 vols, 2000 (refs. made to cat. nos.)
Mannings 1997	———, 'Reynolds and the Shaftos: three letters and a deposition', *Burl. Mag.*, CXXXIX, 1997, pp. 753–55
Northcote 1813	*James Northcote, Memoirs of Sir Joshua Reynolds, Knt.*, 1813
Northcote 1818	*ibid.*, 2nd ed. revised and augmented, 2 vols.
Northcote, *List*	unpaginated supplement to Northcote 1813 and Northcote 1818, II, pp. 346–56: 'List of the Historical & Fancy Subjects together with some of the Most Illustrious and Eminent Portraits executed by Sir Joshua Reynolds'
Pasquin 1796	Anthony Pasquin (John Williams), *An Authentic History of the Professors of Painting, Sculpture & Architecture, who have practised in Ireland; involving original letters from Sir Joshua Reynolds, which prove him to have been illiterate. To which are added Memoirs of the Royal Academicians*, 1796. References are made to the 1970 reprint.
Penny 1986	N. Penny ed., *Reynolds*, exh. cat., RA 1986
Postle 1995	M. Postle, *Sir Joshua Reynolds, the subject pictures*, 1995
RA	Royal Academy
Redford	B. Redford ed., *The Letters of Samuel Johnson*, 5 vols.; vols. I–III, 1992, vols. IV–V, 1994
RO	Record Office
s.	son
suc.	succeeded
Vases and Volcanoes	I. Jenkins, K. Sloan, *Vases and Volcanoes, Sir William Hamilton and his Collection,* exh. cat., British Museum, 1996
Venn	J.A. Venn, *Alumni Cantabrigienses … 1752–1900*, 6 vols. 1940–54.
Walpole Corr.	*Horace Walpole's Correspondence,* ed. W.S. Lewis *et al.*, 47 vols., 1937–83
Wal. Soc.	*Walpole Society*
Whitley 1928	W.T. Whitley, *Artists and their Friends in England 1700–1799*, 2 vols., 1928
Whitley 1930	———, *Art in England 1821–1837*, 1930
Woodforde 1951	C. Woodforde, *The Stained Glass of New College, Oxford*, 1951

LIST OF LETTERS

Incorporating a concordance with the Hilles edition

30	3 April 1772	Lord Grantham	*
31	16 August 1772	Anon	XIX
32	26 September 1772	Paul Ourry	XX
33	March–April 1773	Mrs Elizabeth Montagu	XXI
34	14 July 1773	Luke Gardiner	XXII
35	20 July 1773	Lord Grantham	*
36	16 October 1773	Lord Hardwicke	XXIII
37	1773	Benjamin West	XXIV
38	1773	E.-M. Falconet	*
39	22 February 1774	James Beattie	XXV
40	2 May 1774	Lord Grantham	*
41	2 August 1774	David Garrick	XXVI
42	4 September 1774	David Garrick	XXVII
43	9 September 1774	David Garrick	XXVIII
44	18 January 1775	Charlotte Lennox	*
45	25 January 1775	Dr Charles Burney	*
46	28 January 1775	Sir William Chambers	*
47	1 March 1775	Thomas Percy	XXIX
48	15 April 1775	Caleb Whitefoord	XXX
49	23 April 1775	Caleb Whitefoord	XXXI
50	9 August 1775	Henry Thrale	*
51	4 October 1775	Sir John Pringle	XXXII
52	2 November 1775	Lord Carlisle	*
53	23 November 1775	Dr Samuel Farr	XXXIII
54	26 January 1776	Giuseppe Pelli	XXXIV
55	13 July 1776	Giuseppe Pelli	XXXV
56	3 September 1776	James Northcote	XXXVI
57	9 October 1776	Charlotte Lennox	*
58	25 December 1776	George Macartney	Appendix
59	December 1776	Charles Smith	LXXIII
60	5 March 1777	Thomas Percy	XXXVII
61	1 July 1777	Harry Verelst	XXXVIII
62	5 July 1777	Joseph Warton	*
63	12 August 1777	Theophila Palmer	XXXIX
64	9 September 1777	Daniel Daulby	XL
65	1 October 1777	Lord Grantham	*
66	10 November 1777	Potter	*
67	?10 December 1777	Hannah More	Appendix
68	17 December 1777	Samuel Johnson	XLI
69	27 December 1777	John Oglander	XLII
70	9 January 1778	John Oglander	XLIII
71	21 April 1778	Sir William Forbes	*
72	15 September 1778	Mrs Hester Thrale	XLIV
73	18 September 1778	Lord Harcourt	XLV
74	4 November 1778	Robert Lowth	Appendix
75	7 November 1778	Robert Lowth	XLVI
76	11 December 1778	Joseph Banks	XLVII
77	12 February 1779	Lord Keppel	XLVIII

78	24 February 1779	George Michael Moser	XLIX
79	29 March 1779	Thomas Cadell	*
80	2 April 1779	Thomas Cadell	*
81	18 May 1779	Sir Robert Chambers	*
82	6 August 1779	Sir William Forbes	*
83	30 August 1779	Miss More	*
84	21 September 1779	Lord Ossory	L
85	13 October 1779	Thomas Evans	*
86	4 May 1780	Nicholas Pocock	LI
87	10 May 1780	Samuel Johnson	LIII
88	6 July 1780	Warren Hastings	*
89	29 July 1780	Sir William Forbes	*
90	[1780]	John Hely Hutchinson	*
91	17 January 1781	William Johnson	LIV
92	12 April 1781	James Boswell	*
93	30 June 1781	Mrs Theophila Gwatkin	LV
94	2 August 1781	Edmund Burke	LVII
95	10 August 1781	Edmund Burke	*
96	14–30 August 1781	Edmund Burke	LVIII
97	[29 September] 1781	Mrs Theophila Gwatkin	*
98	1781	Frances Reynolds	LVI
99	1 February 1782	Ozias Humphry	LIX
100	28 February 1782	Thomas Collingwood	LX
101	30 March 1782	James Beattie	LXI
102	13 May 1782	Thomas Warton	LXII
103	6 June 1782	Rutland's Agent	LXIII
104	17 June 1782	A Nobleman	*
105	12 September 1782	Bennett Langton	*
106	13 September 1782	Duke of Rutland	LXIV
107	1 October 1782	James Boswell	*
108	19 January 1783	William Johnson	LXV
109	12 February 1783	Thomas Percy	LXVI
110	4 March 1783	George Crabbe	LXVII
111	5 March 1783	Lord Hardwicke	LXVIII
112	6 May 1783	Valentine Green	LXIX
113	1 June 1783	Valentine Green	LXX
114	18 September 1783	Mrs Theophila Gwatkin	LXXI
115	18 October 1783	Sir William Forbes	*
116	28 November 1783	Joseph Palmer	*
117	5 December 1783	Lord Hardwicke	LXXII
118	16 February 1784	James Boswell	*
119	8 March 1784	Thomas Astle	LXXIV
120	8 April 1784	Stephen Fuller	LXXV
121	24 August 1784	Edmund Burke	*
122	31 August 1784	Bristol Corporation	*
123	2 September 1784	James Boswell	*
124	24 September 1784	Duke of Rutland	LXXVI
125	25 September 1784	Jonathan Shipley	LXXVII

222	25 May 1791	anon.	*
223	28 May 1791	James Beattie	*
224	May 1791	Joseph Farington	*
225	31 May 1791	Dr Samuel Parr	CLVIII
226	11 July 1791	Dr Samuel Parr	CLIX
227	19 July 1791	Thomas Barnard	Appendix
228	7 August 1791	James Beattie	*
229	10 November 1791	Benjamin West	CLXI
230	15 December 1791	John Boydell	*

UNDATED LETTERS

231		Mrs Abington	*
232	[24 June 1780]	Lord Barrington	LII
233		James Boswell	*
234		Mr Burney	*
235		Mr Burney	*
236		Thomas Cadell	*
237	[6 February 1789]	Sir William Chambers	CXXVI
238	[17 March 1790]	George Colman	*
239	[22 April 1789]	Richard Cosway	CXXIX
240	[24 December 1789]	Samuel Farr	*
241	[20 February]	William Hodges	*
242		Ozias Humphry	CLX
243		Mr Jerningham	*
244	[3 May 1782]	Samuel Johnson	*
245		Dr and Mrs Percy	Appendix
246		Dr Percy	*
247		Walter Radcliffe	*
248		Walter Radcliffe	*
249	[September 1777]	George Selwyn	XIV

UNDATED LETTERS TO UNKNOWN CORRESPONDENTS

250	[20 April 1791]	[Thomas Cadell]	CLV
251	[28 April 1791]	[Sir William Scot]	*
252			
253			*
254			*

LETTERS CONCERNING PAYMENTS

255	18 October 1755	Anthony Eyre	*
256	26 April 1757	James Buller	*
257	3 June 1758	Lord Brownlow Bertie	*
258	18 July 1759	Sir Thomas Harrison	*
259	20 August 1759	The Duke of Richmond	*
260	19 September 1759	The Duchess of Bedford	*
261	19 March 1761	Mrs William Lee	*
262	27 January 1762	Lord Granby	*
263	26 June 1762	Henry Fane	*

264	18 September 1765	Mrs Alvin	*
265	16 August 1766	Mrs Alvin	*
266	27 October 1769	John Palmer	*
267	6 May 1771	Lord Clermont	*
268	29 May 1771	Thomas Partington	*
269	17 June 1771	Thomas Partington	*
270	24 April 1778	John Gawler	*
271	27 November 1778	Thomas Cadell	*
272	6 August 1779	Sir William Forbes	*
273	16 June 1780	New College, Oxford	*
274	5 August 1780	Royal Academy	*
275	21 May 1781	Miss Camilla Shafto	*
276	2 July 1781	Lord Rockingham	*
277	18 October 1783	John Wauchope	*
278	July 1786	The Earl of Thanet	*
279	18 August 1786	The Earl of Thanet	*
280	6 September 1786	Thomas Coutts	*
281	10 October 1786	The Duke of Rutland	CVIII
282	23 December 1786	Charles Greville	CXIII
283	1787	The Duke of Rutland	*
284	22 April 1788	George Birch	CXXII
285	22 April 1788	Mr Robinson	*
286	24 April 1788	Mr Robinson	*
287	April 1788	Mr Robinson	*
288	16 January 1789	Mrs Adair	*
289	27 August 1790	Mr Antrobus	*

UNTRACED LETTERS

290	1750	Miss Weston
291	1750–52	Mrs Mary Palmer
292	1750–52	Mrs Elizabeth Johnson
293	July 1761	Joshua Sharpe
294	Spring 1767	David Garrick
295	1770	James Brunton
296	1772?	Lord Townshend
297	1773	Sir William Elford
298	15 April 1775	James Boswell
299	July 1775	John Robinson
300	March 1777	Prince Hoare
301	29 September 1780	Mr French
302	22 November? 1780	Jonathan Shipley
303	c.1781	Lord Temple
304	19 April 1782	Thomas Gainsborough
305	[after October] 1783	Princess Dashkov
306	April 1785	Thomas Warton
307	10 September 1785	Pieter de Gree
308	1787	Lord Cornwallis

DATED LETTERS

On 13 October 1740, at the age of seventeen, Reynolds came to London, bound apprentice for four years to the Devonian portrait painter Thomas Hudson (1701–79) then living at Lincoln's Inn Fields. In the summer of 1743 he left Hudson, amicably, to practise on his own in Devonshire. By April 1745 he was back in London, although his stay was not protracted and was probably ended by his father's death in December that year. From this period there survive only four extracts from letters written by Reynolds to his father and to Mr Cranch, an early Devonshire patron.

1

TO SAMUEL REYNOLDS [OCTOBER 1740]

Source: letter from Samuel Reynolds to Charles Cutcliffe, dated Plympton, 26 October 1740; copy, Royal Academy (REY/3/95)

. . . We see his wife[1] she says she will write to him about it, but I am at present at my Uncle's.[2]

1 i.e. Thomas Hudson's wife, the daughter of the painter Jonathan Richardson. Hudson was then in Bath (Cotton 1856, 47; LT, I, 19).

2 Probably the Revd. John Reynolds (Cotton 1856, 47n3), as subsequently accepted by Hilles (Hilles, *Notes*). Farington 1819, 18, alleged that when Hudson 'dismissed' JR in the summer of 1743 for failing to deliver a canvas promptly to Vanhaecken on a wet evening, he then stayed with an uncle 'who resided in the Temple'.

2

TO SAMUEL REYNOLDS [DECEMBER 1741]

Source: letter from Samuel Reynolds to Charles Cutcliffe, dated 1 January 1742; copy, Royal Academy (REY/3/95)

. . . On Thursday next, Sir Robert Walpole sits for his picture, master[1] says he has had a great longing to draw his picture, because so many have been drawn, and none like.[2]

1 i.e. Thomas Hudson.

2 No portrait of Walpole by Hudson survives, but on 20 April 1742 Samuel Reynolds told Cutcliffe that Hudson 'had finished the head of the Earl of Orford entirely to his satisfaction, and likewise to his own' (Cotton 1856, 51); Walpole was created Earl of Orford on 6 February 1742.

3

TO SAMUEL REYNOLDS [JULY 1742]

Source: letter from Samuel Reynolds to Charles Cutcliffe, dated 3 August 1742; copy, Royal Academy (REY/3/95)

. . . While I am doing this[1] I am the happiest creature alive. . . .

1 i.e. painting.

4

TO MR CRANCH [BEFORE MAY 1745]

Source: extract from a letter from Samuel Reynolds, dated Plympton, 24 May 1745; Cotton 1856, 62

I understand by a letter which Joshua has writ to Mr Craunch, that Joshua's Master[1] is very kind to him, he comes to visit him pretty often, and freely tells him where his pictures are faulty, which is a great advantage; and when he has finished any thing of his own, he is pleased to ask Joshua's judgment, which is a great honour.

1 i.e. Thomas Hudson.

In May 1749 Reynolds set out for Italy, sailing from Plymouth in The Centurion *as the guest of Commodore Augustus Keppel who had been charged with a diplomatic mission to the Bey of Algiers. They reached Lisbon on 24 May, Cadiz on 31 May and Gibraltar on 10 June; Keppel then sailed to the Bay of Tetuan, leaving Reynolds in Gibraltar. On his return they proceeded to Algiers, arriving on 20 July, and the next day Reynolds attended Keppel's audience with the Bey; on 18 August they reached Port Mahon in Minorca, where Reynolds stayed until 25 January 1750, when he sailed to Leghorn and proceeded to Rome.*

Joshua Reynolds, *Augustus Keppel;* engraving by Edward Fisher 1760

Dear Miss Weston December 10th 1749

My Memory is so bad that I vow I dont remember whether or no I writ you about my expedition before I left England, since, I am sure I have not, for I have writ to nobody. I saild from Plimouth so long agone as May 11th and am got no further yet than Port Mahon, but before you shall receive this expect to be on tother side the water; I have been kept here near two months by an odd accident, I dont know whether to call it a lucky one or not, a fall from a horse down a precipice which cut my face in such a manner as confined me to my room, so that I was forced to have

Letter to Miss Weston, Rome, 10/21 December 1749
Yale Center for British Art, Paul Mellon Collection

5

TO MISS WESTON 21 DECEMBER 1749

Source: Yale Center for British Art

December OS 10th 1749

Dear Miss Weston

My Memory is so bad that I vow I dont remember whether or no I writ you about my expedition before I left England, since, I am sure I have not, for I have writ to nobody. I saild from Plimouth so long agone as May 11th and am got no further yet than Port Mahon, but before you shall receive this expect to be on tother side the water; I have been kept here near ~~three~~ <two> months by an odd accident, I dont know whether to call it a lucky one or not, a fall from a horse down a precipice, which cut my face in such a manner as confined me to my room, so that I was forced to have recourse to painting [for my a]musement at first [but have][1] now finishd as many [pictures as] will come to a hund[red and] pounds[2] the unlucky [part of the] Question is ~~I have~~ <my lips are> spo[iled now for] kissing for my upper [lip was so] bruisd that a great p[art ~~of it~~ was] cut off and the rest [so disfigured?] that I have but a [ ] to look at, but in [<time> the hope you] wont perceive the d[ifference].

So far it has been P[*leasantest*] tour to me that can[*be imagined*] When we were at sea [, I employed] myself with reading [having the] use of a well chosen [library of] Books which belong'd to [the ~~Commodor who~~ <Captain>[3]I] was allways in his Cabb[in and eat]and dra<n>k with <him> so that [the whole] voyage did not cost m[e pounds]. There will be the more mony you know to spend at the Jubilee.[4] Whenever the Commodore went a shore at Cadiz ~~at~~ Lisbon ~~at~~ Gibralter he allways took me with him and even when he waited upon the Day or King of Algiers ~~he~~ I went with him and have had the honour of shaking him by the hand three several times, he Introduced me likewise to the Governour here General Blackney[5] in so strong a manner that the Governour insisted on my not being at any expence whilst I was ~~here~~ <on the Island> but to eat at his house and orderd his secretary to provide me a lodging. You may imagine I spend my time here very agreably, here are above thirty English Ladies [deletion] Balls continually at the Generals, and on Board the ships.

When I am settled at Rome I will write to you again to let you know how to direct to me in the mean time I shall be much obliged to you if you will call and see that my Goods are safe and not spoiling, I would write to him <who has them> could I think of his name. I should be glad if you had a spare place in your Garret <that> could they be at your house.

From your slave

J Reynolds

My compliments to Mr. Charlton[6] and Mr. Wilks[7] I hear the whole world is to be at the Jubilee I hope to see Mr. Charlton at least there/ At ~~Cad~~ Lisbon I saw a Bull fight and another at Cadiz which will be the subject of many conversations here <after>.

1 The second page of the letter is torn down the right-hand side (as it was first published in 1796, see under Weston, Appendix II). The missing text, here cited in square brackets, has been supplied (copied?) in an early-19th-century hand.

2 Between 1742 and 1748 JR charged 3 guineas for a head (30 x 25 in.), see Penny 1986, p.58. An Irish ex-commissary who had sat to JR in Minorca later told Fanny Burney that 'then [JR] knew how to taker a moderate price; but now, I vow, ma'am, 'tis scandalous – scandalous, indeed! to pay a fellow here seventy guineas for scratching out a head!' (Madame D'Arblay, *Diary and Letters*, ed. C. Barrett, 1904, 1, 301).

3 Annotated at the foot of the page 'Commodore Keppel'.

4 1750 was made a Jubilee, or Holy, year in Rome by Pope Benedict XIV who issued a bull to that effect on 3 March 1749; it was estimated that three million pilgrims came to Rome in 1750 (*Wal. Corr.*, xx, 43nn6, 7).

5 William Blakeney (1672–1761), major-general 1745; lieutenant-governor of Plymouth 1746–48, and of Minorca 1748–56; following his gallant but unsuccessful defence of Minorca against the French in 1756 when he was eighty-four, he was made KB and cr. Baron Blakeney of Castle Blakeney [I].

6 Unidentified; a Mr Charlton appears in the sitter-books on 15 August 1755 (with Mr Wilks) and in January and August 1757. Mrs Charlton appears in March and April 1757. A half-length portrait called Sir Francis Charlton by JR was sold Sotheby's, 12 July 1967 (116), presumably Sir Francis Charlton, 6th Bt. (d. 1784) of Lindford, Hereford, who d. unm. (see Mannings 350).

7 JR knew the three Wilkes brothers, John (1725–97), the celebrated radical (see Letter 206), Heaton (1727–1803) and Israel. Whitley 1928, 1, 103–04, 146, also suggested, less probably, that this may have been the 'Wilks' listed in the Art of Painting, 1748, among 'those painters of our nation, now living, many of whom have distinguished themselves and are justly esteemed eminent masters'.

6

TO RICHARD, 1ST BARON EDGCUMBE [AFTER MAY 1750]

Source: Northcote 1813, 26-28 (as 'the first sketch of [a letter] he sent to his friend and patron Lord E.')

[AFTER MAY 1750]

My Lord,

I am now (thanks to your Lordship) at the height of my wishes, in the midst of the greatest works of art that the world has produced. I had a very long passage, though a very pleasant one. I am at last in Rome,[1] having seen many places and sights which I never thought of seeing. I have been at Lisbon, Cadiz, Gibraltar, Algiers, and Mahon. The Commodore[2] staid at Lisbon a week, in which time there happened two of the greatest sights that could be seen had he staid there a whole year, – a bull feast, and the procession of Corpus Christi.[3] Your Lordship will excuse me if I say, that from the kind treatment and great civilities I have received from the Commodore, I fear I have even laid your Lordship under obligations to him on my account; since from nothing but your Lordship's recommendation I could possibly expect to meet with that polite behaviour with which I have always been treated:[4] I had the use of his cabin, and his study of books, as if they had been my own; and when he went ashore he generally took me with him; so that I not only had an opportunity of seeing a great deal, but I saw it with all the advantages as if I had travelled as his equal. At Cadiz I saw another bull feast. I ask your Lordship's pardon for being guilty of that usual piece of ill manners in speaking so much of myself; I should not have committed it after such favours. Impute my not writing to the true reason: I thought it impertinent to write to your Lordship without a proper reason; to let you know where I am, if your Lordship should have any commands here that I am capable of executing. Since I have been in Rome, I have been looking about the palaces for a fit picture of which I might take a copy to present your Lordship with;[5] though it would have been much more genteel to have sent the picture without any previous intimation of it. Any one you choose, the larger the better, as it will have a more grand effect when hung up, and a kind of painting that I like more than little. Though perhaps it will be too great a presumption to expect it, I must needs own I most impatiently wait for this order from your Lordship.

I am, &c.&c.

Joshua Reynolds

1 Leaving Minorca on 25 January 1750, JR reached Rome by 15 April.

2 i.e. Augustus Keppel (see Appendix II).

3 Corpus Christi was on 5 June 1749 NS, 25 May OS.

4 Lord Edgcumbe had introduced JR to Keppel.
5 Although JR made several copies in Rome (see Cotton 1859, 1; LT, 1, 40–41), he was later to describe copying as a 'delusive kind of industry' (*Second Discourse*, 135–42) and see Letter 22. JR's copy of Guido Reni's *St Michael* in the church of S.Maria della Concezione, Rome, made between 30 May and 10 June 1750, is now at Hampton Court (Mannings 2235).

7

TO MISS WESTON [LATE 1750]

Source: Historical Society of Pennsylvania (Gratz Collection)

Dear Miss Weston

I ~~k~~wonder I have not receiv'd an Answer to all the Letters I have sent you this is the third from Rome and one before from Mahon I suppose they have all miscarried so I take this opportunity of sending one by my good Friend Mr. Dalton[1] and a Worthy man he is, I hope he will deliver this Letter himself that you may be acquainted and when I return we shall have many agreeable jaunts together.

I shall set out from Rome immediatly after the next Lent or Carnival,[2] Give my service to Mr. Charlton & Mr. Wilks[3] and tell them that if it was possible to give them an Idea of what is to be seen here, the Remains of Antiquity the Sculpture, Paintings, Architecture &c. they would think it worth while, nay they would break through all obstacles and set out immediatly for Rome, then the Carnival of which I have heard so much that I am resolved to stay here to see the next which they say will exceed all the former since there has been none this Jubilee or Holy year[4] so the next they will make up for the old & the new, If they would set out so as to be here a Month or two before the Carnival after which Ashley[5] and I will accompany them <(as we intend to do otherwise)> to Venice and from thence to Paris seeing every thing between those two places that are worth seeing going ~~th~~now & then a little out of ~~our way~~ <the direct Road> and from thence to England or perhaps we shall go to Antwerp first.[6] I am not [deletion] <in jest> now but good earnest and wish they would really think of it Mr. Dalton will acquaint them with the time such a journey will take and the Expence, & the most expeditious way of traveling, I don't think they need be out of England above a year I wish them a good journey if they will write to me when they set out I will come as far as Florence to meet them.

send me a [deletion] all the new~~n~~s you know, not forgetting to say something about my Goods

I am My Dear Miss Weston

Yours

JReynolds

Don't forget to remember me to Mrs. Sutherland, Mr. Hart, and Mr. Price[7] if you ever see them & the Mr. Pines[8] not forgetting the little Girl at Westminster by the Park,[9]

write me immediatly immediatly[10] by the first post. Mr. Dalton will tell you how to direct.

Annotated: Addressed to Miss Weston of Great Queen St. / Lincoln's Inn Fields and written ~~from~~ at Rome in 1751.[11]

1 Richard Dalton (c.1713–91) was in Rome in March 1750 and had returned to England by April 1751; he became Librarian to George III 1760–91, surveyor of the King's pictures 1778–91, and antiquary to the RA 1770–84.

2 The Roman Carnival in 1751 was 12–24 February.

3 See Letter 5.

4 i.e. 1750, see Letter 5.

5 John Astley (1724–87), painter, a pupil of Thomas Hudson in London with JR, was in Rome 1750–51. Farington 1819, 35–36, characterised him as 'a tall, showy man' with 'high animal spirits, which inclined him to dissipation'.

6 This plan did not materialise; Astley returned to England by July 1752, JR in October.

7 Sutherland and Hart remain unidentified: Price was possibly, as Hilles suggested, William Price (d. 1765) the glass painter.

8 Probably the engraver John Pine (1690–1756) and his son the painter Robert Edge Pine (1730–88).

9 See Letter 8.

10 If not a solecism, perhaps, as Hilles suggested, in imitation of the Italian *subito subito.*

11 The context of the letter, however, clearly indicates that it was written in 1750, see note 4; it was probably received in London in 1751.

8

TO MISS WESTON 30 APRIL 1751

Source: Houghton Library

Rome. 30 April 1751

Dear Miss Weston

Your Letter I receiv'd with a great deal of Pleasure and as tis increasing a pleasure to comunicate it I read it to a great many English that were at the

Coffe house[1] but without mentioning the writer <(tho if I had, it would have been much to your honour)> for you must know when a Letter comes ~~from~~ from England we are all impatient to hear news, and indeed your Letter w~~h~~as full of it, and however it happend every person took the same pleasure in it as my self Mr. Lovelace Mrs. Pine were known to most of the painters, others knew Miss Hambleton and others Mr. More others Miss Gunnings indeed their fame had reachd here some time a~~b~~gone.[2] But nobody but me knew the westminster Girl alack alack she ~~is~~ has been brought to bed and tis a fine Chumning boy but who is Lord John?[3] ~~and indeed had would~~ <well who would> have thought it oh the nasty creature to have to do with a man. I [deletion] am sorry you have <been> at the expence of paying for my Goods[4] I shall take care to repay you with thanks when I return which will be infallibly this ~~June~~ <year> we set out in about two months time and take the tour of Venice and through Germany and let France alone ~~for ab~~ till next year since it lies so near England that I can take a trip there in a summer and back again ~~as I shall~~ my fellow traveller is Mr. Ashley who lived with Mr. Hudson.[5]

We are all extremly afflicted for the loss of the Prince of Whales[6] who certainly would have been a great Patron to Painters as he already was to Mr. Dalton[7] I feel an additional sorrow on his account I beg my compliments to him particularly and to all friends. I cannot form to my self any Idea of a person more miserable than the Princess of Whales must be, deprived at once of a Husband she loved and with him all thoughts of ambition,

Adiu I will not desire you to write any Answer to this Letter because I shall remove from Rome to Florence and other Parts of Italy[8] so that you wont know where to direct, but I shall not for that reason neglect writing to you Remember me to mama

Yours

JReynolds

To / Miss Weston

in Great Queen Street / Lincoln's Inn Fields / London

1 The English Coffee House in the Piazza di Spagna, Rome, a traditional gathering place for artists, where JR was staying.

2 Mr Lovelace is unidentified; Mrs Pine was possibly the wife of the engraver John Pine (see Letter 7n8). Mr Mores: probably Edward Moore (1712–57) the dramatist, whose *Gil Blas* was produced without success at Drury Lane between 2 and 12 February 1751 (G.W. Stone

jr., *The London Stage 1660–1800*, IV, 1962, 234–36). Miss Hambleton: probably Jenny Hamilton who m. Edward Moore in 1749. Miss Gunnings, the celebrated sisters Elizabeth (1733–90), later Duchess of Hamilton and Duchess of Argyll, and Maria (1733–60), later Countess of Coventry. JR also wrote 'Hambleton' for Hamilton in Letter 9.

3 Lord John unidentified (Lord John Cavendish, 1732–84, seems to have been rather virtuous).

4 See Letter 7.

5 See Letter 7.

6 Frederick, Prince of Wales, eldest son of George II, died suddenly on 20 March 1751 (or 31 March according to the Gregorian calendar which was used in Rome), aged forty-four.

7 See Letter 7n1. Dalton's connection with Frederick, Prince of Wales, is not otherwise established.

8 JR eventually left Rome on 3 May 1752 and came home via Florence, Bologna, Parma, Venice, Turin and Paris, reaching London on 16 October 1752.

Reynolds returned to London from his tour of Italy on 16 October 1752. He lived first in 'handsome apartments' at 104 St Martin's Lane, before moving to Great Newport Street later in 1753. His final move was to Leicester Fields in 1760.

9

TO JOSEPH WILTON 5 JUNE 1753

Source: Private Collection[1]

direct opposite Mays Buildings in St. Martins Lane[2]

Dear Wilton

I writ you a Letter from Venice and desired an answer directed to Paris but receiv'd none, I have delay'd writing to you since I been in England not on that account but 'till I might be able to inform you that I ha<d>~~ve~~ receiv'd from Ld. Edgcumb the mony for the Bustos which I did Yesterday, the sum of 50£ carriage &c included, which I shall give to your Father[3] the next time I see him which will probably be to morrow. My Lord is very well pleased with the Julius Caesar[4] and would be very glad if you could do to Busto's more for him I gave him to understand he was to take it as a favour if you undertook them, since you were determined only to finish what you had begun, The Busto's he fix'd on were the Caracalla and the Cicero in the Gallery[5] which I recommended as one of the best heads in the Gallery.

I should be very sorry if this should be the occasion of your staying at Florence even a month extraordinary I think it high time for you to begin a Reputation in London Rubiniac[6] has more business than he can make models for he is now besides other business about six Monuments in Westminster Abby[7] and some very considerable ones. whatever mony you can spare lay it out at Carrara the English are very curious in the whiteness of the marble and scruple no price for the best for the chimneys &c Your Father talks of building a house for you if he can agree about the Land in the the very best situation in all London if so, & as there is room enough he should build appartments for me and as the custom is I would take it for a term of years and give him so much for every hundred pounds he has layd out.

I dare say ~~or~~ I flatter myself at least that you are impatient for me to talk of myself and our old Roman acquaintances. ~~If you ever~~ <I hope you never will> mention again what I am going to say or I trust ~~that~~ at least you never will say from whence you owed your intelligence Mr. Alexander[8] is so very bad that he is a proverb as bad as Alexander. Mr. Hambletons[9] business is very near entirely gone from him he is in a very melancholy situation having engaged a house for three years at 120£ a year. Ashly[10] has run into the same dangerous experiment of making a great figure in his house and servants however he is 20£ more more [*sic*] modest in his house than Hambleton, both of them living at this great expence they were obliged to dispatch their Pictures as fast they could in order to receive the cash so that their first Pictures which were exposed and by which their reputation was to stand or fall were slight indigested and incorrect things Ashly by my persuasion ha~~d~~s finish'd one or two heads of his acquaintance in order to show which much superior to what he did before and I believe will rise in time if he is not <in> too great a hurry. I find I have but a little room left so must tell you as fast I can ~~who~~ of the principal <people that I> have drawn and leave you to conclude the rest I have finishd the head of the Duke of Devonshire[11] he himself and all the family say it is the only like picture he ever had of himself there are many copies bespoke, I have drawn a whole length of Ld. Anson[12] and another of Comodore Kepple and his brother Ld. Bury:[13] Ld. & Lady Kildare[14] who is thought the handsomest woman in England. Lord & Lady Carisfort[15] Mr. Fox the Secretary at war[16] ~~and~~ The Ld. Godolphin[17] and this week the Duke of Grafton[18] is to sit I am told that the Prince of

Whales[19] intends to come and see my Pictures. I ~~have~~ could mention more pictures but have no more room

Yours

J Reynolds

Giuseppe[20] is grown so intollerably proud that I fear we shall not keep long to gether he is above being seen in the streets with any thing in his hand

I have pay'd your Father

my compliments to all friends Mr. Hone I heard from his brother he's on the road homewards & with Miss Reed.[21] Lio~~r~~tard[22] is here and has vast business at 25 Guineas a head in crayons.

I beg you would present my duty to Mr. Man[23]

when will you send my pictures

A / Mons.Mons. Wilton[24] / chez Mons.Mons. Man / Resident di S.M. Britanique / en Florence

Endorsed: Pd 1s/3d

Annotated: Mr Joshua Reynolds,/from London June 5th /1753/ to me at Florence

1 Letter first published by M. Postle (*Apollo*, CXLI, 1995, 11–18), to whom the following notes are frequently indebted.

2 i.e. 104 St Martin's Lane, as recorded by J.T. Smith, *Nollekens and His Times*, 1829, II, 230–31.

3 William Wilton (d. 1768), ornamental plasterer and papier-mâché manufacturer; the success of this manufactory had enabled his son to go to Italy, see B. Allen, *Burl. Mag.*, CXXV, 1983, 199.

4 The busts supplied to Lord Edgcumbe are presumed to have been destroyed in 1941. In February 1752 Wilton had unsuccessfully sought permission from the marchese Casali to have a cast made of a bust of Julius Caesar (Ingamells 1997, 1009).

5 i.e. the Uffizi Gallery, Florence.

6 Louis-François Roubiliac (1702/5–62), sculptor, in Italy with Thomas Hudson, June–October 1752; on their outward journey they met JR crossing the Alps, and their tour was so brief that they returned from France with JR in October.

7 Roubiliac then had three monuments for Westminster Abbey in hand, for General James Fleming (completed in 1754), General William Hargrave (1757) and Sir Peter Warren (1757); he was also engaged on monuments for the Duke and Duchess of Montagu for Warkton Church, Northamptonshire (both 1754), and for Viscount Bolingbroke and his Countess for Battersea Old Church (September 1753), see D. Bindman & M. Baker, *Roubiliac and the 18th century Monument*, 1995, nos. 5, 8–11).

8 Cosmo Alexander (1724–72), Scottish painter, in Italy 1747–52.

9 Gavin Hamilton (1723–98), Scottish painter and archaeologist, had been in Italy 1748–50 and was to return in 1756 to Rome, where he died in 1796. In July 1751 in London it was suggested that he very often required a spur to industry. JR also wrote 'Hambleton' for Hamilton in Letter 8.

10 John Astley, see Letter 7n5.

11 William Cavendish, 3rd Duke of Devonshire (1698–1755); JR's three-quarter length portrait is at Chatsworth (Mannings 333).

12 George Anson (1697–1762), cr. Baron Anson 1747, following his naval victories over the French; JR's portrait was probably the three-quarter length portrait at Shugborough (Mannings 66).

13 'Comodore Kepple', i.e. Augustus Keppel, see Appendix II. Lord Bury was his older brother, George Keppel (1724–72), army officer, styled Lord Bury until 1754 when he suc. as 3rd Earl of Albemarle; JR's portrait is in a private collection (Mannings 1054).

14 Lady Emily Lennox (1731–1814), dau. of 2nd Duke of Richmond, m. 1747 James Fitzgerald, Earl of Kildare, cr. Marquess of Kildare 1761 and Duke of Leinster 1766; JR's three-quarter length portraits are in a private collection (Mannings 620, 624).

15 John Proby (1720–72), cr. Baron Carysfort 1752, m. 1750 Elizabeth, dau. of 2nd Viscount Allen; JR's portrait is in a private collection (Mannings 1493).

16 Henry Fox (1705–74), cr. Baron Holland 1763; m. Lady Caroline Lennox, sister of Emily (see note 14); JR's portrait remains untraced (see Mannings, p.206).

17 Francis Godolphin, 2nd Earl of Godolphin (1678–1766); JR's portrait remains untraced.

18 Charles Fitzroy, 2nd Duke of Grafton (1683–1757), Lord Chamberlain of the Household 1724–57; JR painted him several times in the 1750s and here refers, probably, to the untraced three-quarter length (Mannings 639).

19 The fifteen-year-old George, Prince of Wales (1737–1820), later George III, who first sat to JR in 1759 (Royal collection; Mannings 715).

20 Giuseppe Marchi, (1735–1808), painter and engraver; JR brought him back from Italy in 1752 as his studio-assistant and, apart from a short break c.1770, he stayed with him in London. The first of several portraits of him by JR was painted in 1752–53 (RA; Mannings 1219).

21 Samuel Hone (b. c.1726), Irish painter, brother of the better-known Nathaniel; JR and Astley had travelled with him from Rome to Florence. Katherine Read (1723–78), Scottish painter, in Italy 1751–53.

22 Jean-Etienne Liotard (1702–89), the French pastellist, who was several times in London between 1753 and 1755.

23 Horace Mann (1706–86), cr. Bt. 1755, KB 1768, diplomat and tireless correspondent of Horace Walpole; in Florence he was successively the British resident 1740–65, envoy 1765–82 and minister plenipotentiary 1782–86.

24 For this 'courteous French fashion' of address, see, for example, T. De Quincey, *Confessions of an English Opium-Eater*, 1948 ed., p.59.

10

TO ANNE, COUNTESS FITZWILLIAM 14 JULY 1754

Source: Private Collection

My Lady

I ask pardon for keeping Lady Charlot's Picture so long,[1] my time haveing been so much taken up in heads that I have scarce been able to do any drapery to any of my Pictures,[2] but Lady Charlots is now finish'd and will be fit to be sent away in threeweeks time as it will take that time before it is thoroughly dry so as to be sent away without danger. I hope it will meet with your Ladyships approbation as it has of every body that has seen it, and that I am very proud of it myself the request I am going to make your Ladyship will show, which is to beg the liberty of having a Mezzotinto Print from it, which will be finish'd whilst the Picture is drying, so that it will not be detain'd on that account. If your Ladyship has no objection to having a Print taken from it I shall beg the favour to know what is to be writ under the Print.[3]

I remain

Your Ladyships most humble
& most obliged servant
J Reynolds

Newport Street. July 14 1754

1 The Countess's second daughter, Lady Charlotte Fitzwilliam (1746–1833) who m. 1764 Sir Thomas, later Baron, Dundas; JR's half-length portrait belongs to the Executors of the 10th Earl Fitzwilliam (Mannings 531).

2 Giuseppe Marchi, see Letter 9n20, and George Roth, see Letter 199, were probably Reynold's only assistants during 1754, but there is no sitter-book or ledger for that year.

3 Engraved by James McArdell (1729–65), lettered: *J. Reynolds pinxt J. McArdell fecit. Lady Charlotte Fitz-William. Publish'd by J. Reynolds ... 1754.* One of the earliest prints of a JR portrait and the only one published by JR himself. Nollekens recalled JR turning over a number of McArdell's prints and remarking, 'By this man, I shall be immortalised' (J.T. Smith, *Nollekens and His Times*, 1829, II, 213).

There follows a seven-year gap, filled by nine receipts from Reynolds, see Letters 255–263. By the time Reynolds wrote his next surviving letter in 1765, he was well-established in Leicester Fields as a leading portrait painter and had published three letters on painting in Dr Johnson's Idler *in 1759.*

II

TO MRS ELIZABETH HUMPHRY [30 APRIL 1765]

Source: Charles Roberts Autograph Letters Collection, Magill Library, Haverford College

Madam

I am extremely obliged to you for the present you have favourd me with,[1] which I am no means entitle'd to, from any civility I may have shewn to your Son, his merit in his profession is so great that a man does honour to himself in recommending him; I have a picture in my possession of his Painting[2] which is superior to anything I ever saw antient or modern, It is with great pleasure I say this to you who are so nearly interested in his success

I am Madam

Your most humble and

obedient servant

J Reynolds

To Mrs Humphrys / at Honiton / near / Exeter

Postmark: 30AP

1 Mrs Humphry, a widow, ran a business in Brussels lace at Honiton in Devon; on 24 April 1765 she had written to JR thanking him for the attention he paid to her son the painter Ozias Humphry, see Appendix II, and enclosing something 'of our own manufacturing as a small Instance of gratitude' (Hilles 1929, 240; G.C. Williamson, *Life and Works of Ozias Humphry*, 1918, 9, 11, 16).

2 Humphry's copy of JR's *King Lear* of 1763 (Mannings 2100) was bought by JR for 5 gns. (cf. Williamson, at note 1, 24–26; Northcote 1819, II, 174–78).

12

TO THOMAS, DUKE OF NEWCASTLE 26 AUGUST 1765

Source: British Library (Add MSS 32969, f.195)

Mr. Reynolds presents his duty to His Grace and will be at Newcastle House tomorrow morning in order to see the Pictures put in the Frames[1]

Leicester fields 26th Aug 1765 / To His Grace The Duke of Newcastle

1 The Duke appears to have owned two portraits by JR: a reduced whole length of John, Marquess of Granby (1760?), and a kit-cat of Samuel Foote (1764–67), both Lincoln sale, Christie's, 31 March 1939, lots 46 and 47 (Mannings 656, 1197) but these need not have been the pictures in question.

13

TO MISS OLIVER 6 AUGUST 1766

Source: Beinecke Library (Osborn Collection)

Mr. Reynolds presents his Compliments to Miss Oliver[1] and is sorry to have detaind the Picture so long on account of the Print. the Engraver[2]did not succeed the first time which obliged him to begin entirely a new plate, he has sent an impression of the last for her approbation.

Leicester fields August 6th 1766

1 Unidentified; a Miss Oliver sat to JR in September 1765, but her portrait remains untraced (Mannings 1361). E. Hamilton, *Engraved Works of Joshua Reynolds*, 1874, 93, identified her, mistakenly, as the daughter of Alderman Oliver (i.e. Richard Oliver, 1735–84, MP for London 1770–80 and Alderman 1770–78; m. 1758 his cos. Mary Oliver); J.C. Smith, *British Mezzotinto Portraits*, , 1883, 916, suggested she was the sister of Silver Oliver of Limerick (Irish MP 1757–83), who m. Standish Grady of Eton.

2 Giuseppe Marchi, see Letter 9n20, whose plate, lettered *Miss Oliver*, was published on 15 September 1767 (three-quarter length, a drawing in her right hand, porte-crayon in her left).

14

TO THE REVD THOMAS MORRISON 16 AUGUST 1766

Source: Beinecke Library (Osborn Collection)

Dear Sir

The greatest compliment I have ever yet receiv'd for any fancied eminence in my profession has not been so flattering to my vanity as having had the honour to have so excellent a Poem[1] address'd to me ~~and~~ as this really is which I have now before me, and the consideration that this compliment is made me by Mr. Morrison makes me at a loss in what manner to express the obligation I feel myself under for so great a favour. I may truly say and without affecting much modesty that I am not worthy of the attention you please to honour me with.

As I have not had time yet to consider it as maturely as I intend to do, I can only say in general terms that I admire it exceedingly

I am quite ashamed to have kept this Letter so long, which proceeded from an expectation I dayly had of reading the Poem with Mr. Johnson[2] and Dr Goldsmith[3] but which I have not yet been able to accomplish.

The former Part of this Letter was wrote a few days after I had <the> pleasure of seeing your Son;[4] You have surely the greatest reason in the world to think me the most illmannerd as well as the most ingrateful person breathing in not returning my thanks sooner; and now that it is delay'd so long it has not answerd any end except that I have the pleasure of saying, I find no cause on a second and third reading to retract what I said in the former part of the Letter, my own opinion is worth but little, but I hope soon to have the pleasure of acquainting you with the approbation of those Critics which it is some honour to please.

With great acknowledgment for the distinction you have been pleased to honour me with

I am with greatest respect

your most obliged / humble servant

JReynolds

I beg my compliments to Miss & Mr. Morrison[5]

London 16 Augst 1766

1 'A Pindarick Ode on Painting. Addressed to Joshua Reynolds, Esq.', published in 1767 (according to the title page, but actually in May 1768), apostrophising JR and his *Lady Bunbury sacrificing to the Graces* (exh. SA 1765; Art Institute of Chicago; Mannings 279) and *Garrick torn between Tragedy and Comedy* (exh. SA 1762; private collection; Mannings 700) – 'Spare, Oh! Time, these colours; spare 'em, / Or with thy tend'rest touch impair 'em'.

2 Samuel Johnson, see Appendix II.

3 Oliver Goldsmith (1728–74) met JR in 1762 and they became close friends; a founder member of the Club in 1763; he published *The Vicar of Wakefield* in 1766 and his *Deserted Village* 1770 was dedicated to JR; professor of ancient history at the RA 1769; his half-length portrait by JR of 1769 is at Knole (Mannings 736; there are several versions); Goldsmith's early death was 'the severest blow Sir Joshua ever received' (J. Northcote, *Conversations*, 1949 ed., 112).

4 Hooper Morrison (1737–98), rector of Atherington, Devon.

5 Morrison's unmarried daughter Eleanora (b. 1736) who lived with her father and his only son Hooper Morrison (see note 4).

15

TO THE REVD THOMAS MORRISON 8 JANUARY 1767

Source: Beinecke Library (Osborn Collection)

London Jany. 8th 1767

Dear Sir

I am much obliged to you for the compliment you make me in thinking my approbation of any value,[1] to tell you the truth the reason of my setting so little value on it myself, proceeds, not so much from modesty, or an opinion that I cannot feel the powers of Poetry, or distinguish beauties from defects, but from a consciousness that I am unable to determine (as all excellence in comparative) what rank it ought to hold in the scale of Art; and this judgment can be possess'd I think by those only who are acquainted with what the world has produced of that kind.

I have lately had the pleasure of reading your Poem to several friends, who have spoke much in its commendation, and Mr. Johnson[2] who is as severe a Critic as old Dennis[3] approves of it very much, he thinks it superior to any Poem of the kind that has been publish'd these many years and will venture to lay a wager that there is not a better publish'd this year or the next.

The Characters of the several Masters mention'd in the Poem are truly drawn,[4] and the descriptions of the severyal kinds of History Painting shew great imagination and a thorough knowledge of the Theory of the Art, and that this is deliver'd in Poetry much above the common standard I have Mr. Johnson's word who concluded his commendation with Imprimatur meo periculo,[5] which order if you have no objection we will immediatly put in execution.

I have scarce left room to subscribe myself

Yours,

JReynolds

1 See Letter 14.
2 Although Samuel Johnson was not in general addicted to the Pindaric Ode.
3 John Dennis (1657–1734), critic, poet and dramatist.
4 Descriptions of paintings by Van de Velde and Claude were apparently based upon examples in JR's own collection (see F.W. Hilles, *Augustan Reprint Soc.*, no. 37, 1952, 'Postcript', n.p.)
5 i.e. 'let it be printed at my risk'; the poem was duly published in 1768, see Letter 14n1.

16

TO THE REVD THOMAS PERCY 13 JULY 1767

Source: Hyde Collection

Mr. Reynolds presents his Compliments to Mr. Percy and has sent the three Volumes[1] and is very much obliged to him for the favourable exchange which he intends him, but is quite ashamed to find them so much soil'd, it shews however they have been much read tho by dirty people.

To / The Revd. Mr Percy
Leicester fields July 13 1767

1 Possibly Percy's celebrated *Reliques of Ancient English Poetry*, published in three volumes in 1765, second edition 1767.

17

TO THE REVD THOMAS PERCY 2 APRIL [1768]

Source: Hilles 1929, x

Leicester fields 2d April[1]

Mr. Reynolds presents his compliments to Mr. Percy and will do himself the honour of waiting on him today at two o clock. Dr. Goldsmith[2] will likewise attend him.

1 '1768' has been added by another hand.
2 Oliver Goldsmith, see Letter 14n3.

*On 9 September 1768 Reynolds and William Burke, a cousin and exact contemporary of Edmund Burke, left London to visit Paris, where they stayed between 14 September and 18 October. On 10 October Burke told James Barry in Italy that 'Mr Reynolds and I make this scamper together, and are both extremely satisfied with our tour ... The collections here are wonderful and the magnificence of their furniture transcends ours by far' (*The Works of James Barry, 1809, I, 101–03*). A letter from William to Edmund Burke, Paris, 25 September 1768 (Sheffield City Libraries), mentioned visits to the Palais Royal and the Luxembourg where they had seen paintings by Claude Vernet. They were back in London on 23 October.*

18

TO EDMUND BURKE [POST 25] SEPTEMBER 1768

Source: Sheffield Archives (WWM Bk P 1/226)

Dear Sir

With all your flouting and your gibing you shall not laugh me out of my principles, The French stile is to be sure the most common in France, but take in other Countries and other ages – I am as little disposed to enter into that argument at present as you would be to read it, and at present my head is full of other ~~thi~~ <matters>.

Mr. Burk[1] has already given you an account of the particulars of our journey so that I have nothing left to discourse of but the general principles of things I shall leave till I come to England my opinion of the Ta Blews[2] as they call them in their damn'd lingo which by the by I cannot yet speak for my life tho' I have tried at it ever since I have been here. Sir I am convinced that most of our <late> Books of Travels were fabricated by writers for Booksellers who were never out of their own country and are borrow'd from books wrote ten years ago,[3] tho' they may represent the true state of things as they were at that time would be a very false representation of what they actually are at present. I am well acquanted with the opinion the English entertain in regard to the French, it is generally believed that the French are Ignorant in Philosophy and Bigots in Religion, that they wear nothing but wooden shoes, and have never a shirt in their whole country but instead of it were wrist bands with Ruffles and even <the> Ruffles are represented by the ingenious Mr. Hogarth as made of Paper[4] but it must be considerd that Mr. Hogarth is a satirest by Profession and I hold opinion with the illustrious Barretti[5] that there is great distinction to be made between the authority of a satirest and a grave relater of matter of fact which I profess myself to be, and I here solemnly declare that during the whole time I have been in France I never saw a single pair of paper ruffles, and as I lookd for them, I think, if they had been so common as they have been represented I should certainly have found them; and likewise their having no shirts is a great falsity or to speak in the most gentle terms a great exaggeration, I have seen many men working in the fields and in Paris with shirts some of which were blue and some orange colour, and more than that I am convinced ~~and I have~~ that many if not all the Quality in France were shirts of the finest holand, for tho' I never saw of them strip I have seen what is an equivalent proof, I have seen on the Bulwarks of Paris above twenty entire shirts hanging to dry that the best Gentleman in England might wear without disparagement.

The notion about the wooden shoes is as false as that of the shirts so far from being <so> common you will meet in Paris more people with Leather than wooden shoes; two to one, at least.

As to their bigotry, I will venture to say they have as much intellectual freedom as the English have political, we have been in company with some of their Witts, and it is amazing how impatient they are to ~~give you~~ <assure you that they> think for themselves, that they are not priest ridden in short that they have the honour to be ~~spir~~ *spriforts*[6] that is in English an Atheist however with all my partiality I cannot help thinking that they look <down> with too much contempt on those who still retain the early prejudices of education or have not that <strong> understanding which enables a man to shake them off, this is certainly very unreasonable, and very unphilosophical for I am of opinion a man may be a good member of society and even a man of sense in other things ~~not~~ tho' he may be weak enough to be a believer in – or even a Christian.

Je-hai le-honneur[7] / &

J. Reynolds

I beg to be rememberd by Mrs. Burk Mr. Dick &c.[8] We drink your healths every day.

1 William Burke (1729–98) MP, cousin and close friend of Edmund Burke.
2 *Tableaux.*
3 JR owned a copy of *A Voyage to the Ile de France* (Hilles 1936, 116) and he may also refer to *The Curiosities of Paris in nine letters*, by A.R., c.1760; he could have consulted, if his French allowed, the *Voyage pittoresque de Paris* (1757, 1765) and the *Voyage pittoresque des environs de Paris* (1755/1762/1768), both compiled by A.N. Dézallier d'Argenville.
4 Hogarth's *Calais Gate, Roast Beef of Old England* (Tate Gallery; engraved in 1749), shows a French soldier with paper ruffles.
5 Giuseppe Baretti (1719–89), born in Turin, came to London in 1751; he was soon part of the Johnson–JR circle and in 1760 published a *Dictionary of the English and Italian Language*; he returned to Italy in 1760–66; in 1769 he was made secretary for foreign correspondence at the RA and he assisted JR with Italian correspondence, see Letters 54 and 55, and translated JR's *Discourses* into Italian; his *Guide through the Royal Academy* describing Somerset House was published in 1781; his half-length portrait by JR of 1773 is in a private collection (Mannings 107). In his *Account of the Manners and Customs of Italy* . . ., 1768, I, 2, he referred to travel writers who filled pages with scurrilous narratives of pretended absurdities.
6 *esprits forts.*
7 *J'ai l'honneur.*
8 Jane Nugent, m. Edmund Burke in 1757; Richard Burke (1758–94), their son.

19

TO JOSHUA KIRBY 25 NOVEMBER 1768

Source: Royal Academy (SA/34/4)

Sir

I beg leave to return my thanks to yourself and the Gentlemen who have done me the honour of electing me one of the Directors of the Society of Artists.[1]

As I have for some years past entirely declined acting as a Director I must now request the favour of resigning that honour, the doing which I hope will not be understood as proceeding from any want of respect as I made the same request to the former set of Directors.

I am Sir

your most humble

and obedient servant

JReynolds

Leicester fields Novr 25 1768

To Joshua Kirby Esq / President of the Artists / Great-Briton

1 Kirby had been elected President of the Society of Artists on 18 October 1768. JR's refusal attracted bitter criticism from, for example, 'Fresnoy', see Whitley 1928, I, 251, and Whitley 1930, 322.

Reynolds last exhibited with the Society of Artists in September 1768. By this time the Society was fractious and Reynolds showed his discomfort in declining Kirby's offer of a directorship. In September and October, while Reynolds was abroad with Richard Burke, a number of artists, including William Chambers, Francis Cotes, Moser and West, framed the constitution of a new Academy, choosing Reynolds as their President without, it appears, his active participation in these preparatory negotiations. Membership was to be confined to forty Academicians, 'men of fair moral characters, of high reputation in their several professions, at least five and twenty years of age, resident in Great Britain, and not members of any other Society of Artists established in London'. The King signed the instrument for the foundation on 10 December 1768 appointing thirty-four Academicians.

The premises were those of Lamb the auctioneer in Pall Mall. On 2 January 1769 Reynolds delivered to his fellow academicians the first of his celebrated Discourses*: 'An Academy, in which the Polite Arts may be regularly cultivated, is at last opened among us by Royal Munificence. This must appear an event in the highest degree interesting, not only to the Artists, but to the whole nation'. Subsequent* Discourses *were given to the assembled academicians and students at the distribution of prizes in December, annually to 1772 and biennially thereafter, continuing until 1790. Reynolds was knighted by the King at St James's on 21 April 1769, before the opening of the Academy's first annual exhibition on 26 April.*

In January 1771 the Academy schools moved from Pall Mall to Old Somerset House which from 1776 was rebuilt according to the designs of Sir William Chambers (he had received a Swedish knighthood in 1770), the Treasurer of the Royal Academy. From 1780 both the RA schools and the exhibition were accomodated in the new rooms at Somerset House.

20

TO THE REVD THOMAS PERCY [17 DECEMBER 1768][1]

Source: Hyde Collection

Mr. Reynolds's Compliments to Mr. Percy, he was just going to write to him that he expected the honour of seeing him to day at three o'clock he shall see Mr. Chamberlain[2] this afternoon at the Academy.

Saturday

1 Written between the Foundation of the Royal Academy (10 December 1768) and 21 April 1769, when JR was knighted; on 17 December 1768 JR's sitter-book has: '4. Mr.Percy. 6. Academy'.

2 Mason Chamberlain (1727–87), portrait painter, foundation member of the RA.

21

TO THE HON. WILLIAM HAMILTON 28 MARCH 1769

Source: Yale Center for British Art

London. 28th March 1769

Sir

I ought to be ashamed to acknowledge the receipt of your kind Letter so many months since, but really my not answering it sooner proceeded rather from a mistake than neglect, ~~by~~ your saying I should receive another Letter from you soon I understood to imply that I should delay answering it till I had receiv'd the second, but as no second letter is arrived, I now suspect I was mistaken

I hope however you never will think that this delay proceeds from any want of proper attention or that I should be so different from other Artists as not to be allways proud of the honour of being remember'd by so great a Patron and judge of Arts as Mr. Hamilton.

I admire the work which is publishd under your Patronage exceedingly,[1] it is not only magnificent as it should be, being publishd with your name but it is likewise usefull to antiquarians and will tend to the advancement of the Arts, as adding more materials for Genius to work upon, the grace and genteelness of some of the figures are exquisite, particularly the Atalanta, and it is that kind of grace which I never observed before in the Antique, it is much more in the Parmegian stile.[2]

I hope you have been able to pick up some Capital Pictures as well as Etruscan Vases. I remember I saw in a Palace at Naples which had but few Pictures (I think it was that of Franca villa) a small Picture of Paulo Veronese[3] a gre[at][4] number of figures at a Table and Mary Magdalen wash[ing] Christs feet, I thought it the most brilliant Picture [of] the Master I had ever seen tho' perhaps they may be too [rich] to sell it, yet possibly it may be got at by exchange. I think it is worth at least a hundred Pounds.

I have the pleasure to acquaint you that the Arts flourish here with great vigour, we have as good Artists in every branch of the Art as any other nation can boast. and the King has very seriously taken them under his protection; he has establishd an Academy which opend the first of January. the Rooms that formerly belonged to Lamb the Auctioneer in Pall mall serve for the present till a proper building can be erected. It would take up too much room to give you our whole plan, when it is printed I will take the first opportunity to send it to you, however I cannot avoid just giving the outline. It is composed of forty and cannot exceed that number, out of which are chosen all the Officers, to the surprise of every body I have the honour of being President, and it is only honour for there is no salary annex'd to this dignity[5] Mr. Chambers[6] the Architect is the Treasurer 60£ per Ann. Secretary Mr. Newton[7] has likewise 60£, the Keeper Mr. Moser[8] 100£. we have four Professors Mr.Penny[9] of Painting Mr. Chambers of Architecture Mr.Wale[10] of Geometry and Perspective and Dr. Hunter[11] of Anatomy ~~wit~~ each gives six Lectures every year ~~from th~~ the salary 30£ per annum, we have nine Visitors who attend every evening for a month alternately, ~~they~~ he must be in the Academy two hours whilst the young men [make] a drawing for which he receives half a Guinea. Eight other members are appointed to form the laws, and it is this body which is calld the Councill who govern the Academy, the King interests himself very much in our success he has given an unlimited power to the Tresurer to draw on his Privy Purse for whatever mony shall be wanted for the Academy we have already expended some hundred pounds in purchasing books relating to the Arts. If you should think it proper to mention to the King of Naples ~~of~~ the establishment of a Royal Academy he would probably make a present of the Antiquities of Herculaneum.[12]

I am Sir Yours

J Reynolds

A Monsieur / Monsieur Hamilton[13] / Envoyè extraordinaire / et Plenipotentiaire de S.M.Brit. / a / Naples

Postmark: Germania. (F.O. ?) 1st – Wishart.

1 *Antiquités Etrusques, Grecques et Romaines, tirées du Cabinet de M. William Hamilton, Envoyé extraordinaire et plénipotentiaire de S.M. Britannique en Cour de Naples*, published late in 1767 (with a second volume in 1770 and a third and fourth in 1776), text by P.-F. Hugues (the baron d'Hancarville) with hand-coloured engraved plates; a sumptuous catalogue of Hamilton's remarkable collection of classical antiquities.

2 In fact the *Daughters of Leucippus*; the vase was included by JR in his whole-length portrait of Hamilton of 1777 now in the NPG. The 'Parmegian stile', in the style of Parmegianino, viz. Mannerist.

3 This Veronese was not acquired by Hamilton. JR had previously noticed the same subject by Veronese in Venice and Genoa (Cotton 1859, 29, 33–34; LT, I, 64). JR had already bought some pictures from Hamilton's first picture sale, 20 February 1761.

4 Sheet torn; missing words suggested in square brackets.

5 Three weeks after writing this letter JR was knighted.

6 See Appendix II.

7 Francis Milner Newton (1720–94), painter, secretary RA 1768–88.

8 See Appendix II.

9 Edward Penny (1714–91), painter, professor of painting RA 1769–83.

10 Samuel Wale (1721–86), painter and illustrator, professor of perspective RA 1768–86, and librarian 1782–86.

11 Dr William Hunter (1718–83), surgeon, anatomist and collector, professor of anatomy RA 1768–83.

12 *Le Antichità di Ercolano esposte*, five volumes of which had been published by 1767 (three more appeared in 1771, 1779 and 1792), published by Ferdinand IV, King of Naples (La Reale Accademia Ercolanese di Archeologia) to send as a gift to courts and cultural societies throughout Europe.

13 For this form of address see Letter 9n24.

22

TO JAMES BARRY[1] [BEFORE MAY 1769][2]

Source: The Works of James Barry, 1809, I, 84–86

London

Dear Sir,

I am very much obliged to you for your remembrance of me in your letter to Mr. Burke,[3] which, though I have read with great pleasure, as a composition, I cannot help saying with some regret, to find that so great a portion of your attention has been engaged upon temporary matters, which might be so much more profitably employed upon what would stick by you through your whole life.

Whoever is resolved to excel in painting, or indeed any other art, must bring all his mind to bear on that one object, from the moment he rises till he goes to bed; the effect of every object that meets a painter's eye, may give him a lesson, provided his mind is calm, unembarrassed with other subjects, and open to instruction. This general attention, with other studies connected with the art, which must employ the artist in his closet, will be found sufficient to fill up life, if it was much longer than it is. Were I in your place, I would consider myself as playing a great game, and never suffer the little malice and envy of my rivals to draw off my attention from the main object, which, if you pursue with a steady eye, it will not be in the power of all the Cicerones in the world to hurt you. Whilst they are endeavouring to prevent the gentlemen from employing the young artists, instead of injuring them, they are in my opinion doing them the greatest service. Whilst I was at Rome I was very little employed by them,[4] and that little I always considered as so much time lost: copying those ornamental pictures which the travelling gentlemen always bring home with them as furniture for their houses, is far from being the most profitable manner of a student spending his time. Whoever has great views, I would recommend to him whilst at Rome, rather to live on bread and water than lose those advantages which he can never hope to enjoy a second time, and which he will find only in the Vatican, where, I will engage no Cavalier sends students to copy for him. I do not mean this as any reproach to the gentlemen; the works in that place, though they are the proper study of an artist, make but an aukward figure painted in oil, and reduced to the size of easel pictures. The Capella Sistina is the production of the greatest genius that ever was employed in the arts; it is worth considering by what principles that stupendous greatness of style is produced; and endeavouring to produce something of your own on those principles will be a more advantageous method of study than copying the St. Cecilia in the Borghese, or the Herodias of Guido,[5] which may be copied to eternity without contributing one jot towards making a man a more able painter.

If you neglect visiting the Vatican often, and particularly the Capella Sistina, you will neglect receiving that peculiar advantage which Rome can give above all other cities in the world. In other places you will find casts from the antique, and capital pictures of the great painters, but it is *there* only that you can form an idea of the dignity of the art, as it is there only that you can see the works of Michael Angelo and Raffael. If you should not relish them at first, which may probably be the case, as they have none of those qualities which are captivating at first sight,[6] never cease looking till you feel something like inspiration come over you, till you think every other painter insipid in comparison, and to be admired only for petty excellencies.

I suppose you have heard of the establishment of a royal academy here; the first opportunity I have I will send you the discourse I delivered at its opening, which was the first of January. As I hope you will be hereafter be one of our body,[7] I wish you would, as opportunity offers, make memorandums of the regulations of the academies that you may visit in your travels, to be engrafted on our own, if they should be found to be useful.

I am, with the greatest esteem, yours,

J. Reynolds

On reading my letter over, I feel it requires some apology for the blunt appearance of a dictatorial style in which I have obtruded my advice. I am forced to write in a great hurry, and have little time for polishing my style.

1 Barry was studying in Rome from 1766–70.

2 Barry acknowledged this letter from JR in a reply dated Rome, 17 May 1769, and in another letter to 'The Burkes' from Rome, 8 July 1769, he mentioned a 'most obliging friendly letter which I received from Sir Joshua Reynolds'(Barry, *Works*, I, 103–08, 173–74).

3 Presumably the undated letter from Barry to 'Mr Burke' of January/February 1769: 'I am happy to find Mr Reynolds is at the head of this academy: from his known public

spirit and warm desire of raising up art amongst us ... he will, I have no doubt, contrive this institution to be productive of all the advantages that could possibly be derived from it, and ... we shall have nothing to fear from those shallows and quicksands upon which the Italian and French academies have lost themselves' (Barry, *Works*, 1809, I, 117). In his letter of 8 July 1769 (see n2), Barry repeated how happy he was at JR's Presidency, a 'mark of distinction which is bestowed upon his unquestionably superior talents' (Barry, *Works*, 1809, I, 174).

4 See Letter 6n5.

5 Domenichino's *S.Cecilia* (Borghese) and Reni's *Herodias* (Salome) in the Galleria Nazionale d'Arte Antica, Rome. Both were engraved by Robert Strange c.1761. In 1772 JR criticised the Reni as 'having little more expression than his Venus attired by the Graces' (*Fifth Discourse*, 40–44).

6 A sentiment Reynolds later repeated: 'I remember very well my own disappointment, when I first visited the Vatican; but on confessing my feelings to a brother-student ... he acknowledged that the works of Raffaelle had the same effect on him, or rather that they did not produce the effect which he expected' ('Some Account of Sir Joshua Reynolds', Malone 1819, I, xiv).

7 Barry was elected ARA 1772 and RA 1773.

23

TO [WALTER] RADCLIFFE[1] 23 APRIL 1769[2]

Source: Private Collection

Sir Joshua Reynolds presents his Compliments to Mr. Radcliffe and desires the honour of his Company to <dinner to> meet Mr. Parker &c ~~next~~ on Tuesday the 2d of May

Leicester fields April 23d
To Radcliffe Esq

1 Of Duke Street, St James's, see Letter 248.

2 See Letter 24; the date (two days after JR's knighthood) confirmed by JR's pocket book: 9 May 1769 'Parker Dinner', presumably JR's close friend John Parker (1734–88) of Saltram, Devon, who was to marry Theresa (1745–75), dau. of the 1st Baron Grantham, on 18 May 1769. Parker became Baron Boringdon in 1784. There were two children: John (1772–1840, cr. Earl of Morley 1815) and Theresa (1775–1856, who m. George Villiers in 1798). Parker was a considerable patron of JR and at Saltram (now National Trust) there remain portraits of Parker (kit cat; 1768), his wife (whole length; 1773), his wife and son (three-quarter length; 1773) and their son and daughter together (three-quarter length; 1781), see Mannings 1394, 1396–98; another half length of their daughter of 1787 is in the Huntington Library, San Marino (Mannings 1401); see Letters 30, 35 and 65.

24

TO [WALTER] RADCLIFFE 29 APRIL 1769[1]

Source: Private Collection

Sir Joshua Reynolds presents his Compliments to Mr. Radcliffe. The Party that ~~who~~ was to have met next Tuesday is put off to Tuesday sevenight May 9th: he hopes that day will be equally agreable to Mr. Radcliffe

Leicester fields April 29th
Mr. Radcliffe

1 See Letter 23.

25

TO THE HON. WILLIAM HAMILTON 17 JUNE 1770

Source: Beinecke Library (Hilles Collection)

London June 17th 1770.

Dear Sir

I delayed answering your Letter 'till we had receiv'd the Casts which you have been so obliging to give to the Royal Academy, they have been so long on their passage that we have but just now receiv'd them.[1] The Bas-relievo of Fiamingo I never saw before it is certainly a very fine group and the only thing of the kind that we have which makes it a very acceptable present, that, and the Apollo are both ordered by his Majesty to be placed in Somerset House where our Academy will remove this summer,[2] the Royal Apartments are to be converted into a Royal Academy.

I beg leave to thank you as President, you will receive with this an Official Letter of thanks from the Academy; I must acquaint you that in speaking to his Majesty some time ago of the Present you had made and mentioning some other particulars in the Letter He asked If I had the Letter about me and if he might see it I had it in my pocket and put it in his hands you have no reason to be displeased on any account but there was one circumstance rather fortunate, your having mentiond His Majesty in it with great affection and certainly without any expectation of his seeing it. I wonder he was not tempted by your lively description of the Corregio,[3] was I King of England I certainly would have it at all events, there is no Master than one wishes so much to see. Mr. Aufrere[4] has brought to England a Marriage of St Catherine by

Corregio and an undoubted true one, full of faults and full of Beauties.

I hear that you had your Choice of Lady Betty Germains Pictures[5] I have no doubt of your chusing the best. I sent no commission for any concluding they would all be sold above their value but the Julio Romano to my great vexation was sold for fifty Guineas, it is some alleviation that a person possesses it that knows the value of it Lord Ossory[6] and I have the pleasure of seeing it very often.

I beg leave to congratulate you on the honour you have acquired by the account you have given to the Royal Society of Vesuvius and AEtna[7] I hear every [*body*] speak of it with the highest encomiums as the [best?] account that has hitherto appeared. I find you are not contented with the reputation of being at the head of the Virtuosi but are extending your views to all kinds of knowledge

I dare say you have heard of the report of the alarm that has been given by our News Papers of your being cast away in some of your excursions in hunting for Burning Mountains perhaps the death of the Elder Pliny put it into somebodys head to invent the story[8] however I hope you will never suffer for your eagerness after knowledge but that you will live and return and be the Mecaenas to the rising generation of Artists which is the sincere wish and desire of Sir

Your most humble and obedient servant

Joshua Reynolds

1 Fiammingo, i.e. François Duquesnoy (1597–1643); the bas-relief was evidently that of the *Concert of Angels* from SS. Apostoli, Naples, visible over the fireplace in E.F. Burney's *Antique School at Old Somerset House* c.1780 which also shows a cast of the *Apollo Belvedere* (illus. S.C. Hutchison, *History of the Royal Academy*, 1968, fig.14, f.p. 96). Hamilton made further gifts in 1771, 1775 and 1803.

2 The Academy schools moved to Old Somerset House in 1771, while the Academy stayed in Pall Mall.

3 *Venus disarming Cupid*, now attributed to Luca Cambiaso, which Hamilton brought with him to England in 1771–72 and wished to sell for £3000 ('it is divine', wrote Horace Walpole, 'and so is the price, for nothing but a demi-god or a demi-devil, that is, a nabob, can purchase it'; 18 November 1771, *Wal. Corr.*, XXIII, 350); he left it unsold with Charles Greville; it is now in a private collection (*Vases and Volcanoes*, no. 176).

4 George René Aufrère (1715–1801), merchant and collector.

5 Lady Elizabeth Germain (1680–1769), dau. of 2nd Earl of Berkeley and 2nd wife of Sir John Germain (d. 1718); a widow for fifty years, the large collection of pictures and antiquities she had at Drayton was sold at Langford's, London, 7–10 March 1770.

6 See Appendix II; Lord Ossory's posthumous sale, Christie's, 8 April 1819, included a *Rape of a Nymph by a Sea God* by Giulio Romano.

7 'A letter, concerning further particulars on Mount Vesuvius and other volcanoes in the neighbourhood', *Philosophical Trans. of the Royal Soc.*, LIX, 1770, 21, which Hamilton wrote following a visit to Mount Etna in October 1769; six such letters from Hamilton were published in 1772 as *Observations on Mount Vesuvius, Mount Etna, and other Volcanos.*

8 Hamilton 'continued to make ascents of the volcano in all its moods, and often at some peril, until he was well over sixty years of age' (B. Fothergill, *Sir William Hamilton*, 1969, 94). JR refers to the account given by Pliny the younger, *Letters*, VI, 16, of the death of his uncle at Pompeii during the eruption of Vesuvius in 79 AD.

26

TO SIR THOMAS CHARLES BUNBURY 7 SEPTEMBER 1770

Source: Hilles 1929, XVII

Sep. 1770

Dear Sir,

I have finished the face very much to my own satisfaction;[1] it has more grace and dignity than anything I have ever done and it is the best coloured. As to the dress, I should be glad it might be left undetermined till I return from my fortnight's tour, when I return I will try different dresses. The Eastern dresses are very rich and have one sort of dignity, but it is a mock dignity in comparison of the simplicity of the antique. The impatience I have to finish it will shorten my stay in the country. I shall set out in an hour's time.[2]

I am, with the greatest respect,
Your most obliged servant,
J. Reynolds

1 According to Hilles this was the portrait of Miss Kennedy (private collection; Mannings 1033) either Polly [Jones] (d. 1781) or Kitty, a sister of two murderers, Matthew and Patrick (H. Bleackley, *Notes & Queries*, 10s., VII, 344, IX, 97; and *id.*, *Ladies Fair and Frail*, 1909, 149-88, 304–05, 316–18). Bunbury had separated from his wife, Lady Sarah Lennox, in 1769.

2 JR sitter-book, Friday, 7 September 1770: '5 o'clock, Sat out for Devonshire'. JR did not return to London until 14 October.

27

TO GEORGE, VISCOUNT NUNEHAM 26 FEBRUARY 1771

Source: Buckinghamshire Record Office (D/LE/E4/22)

Sir Joshua Reynolds presents his Compts. to Lord Lord Nuneham, He thinks the Landskip tolerably well painted but it is much disgraced by the figures if those were defaced it would be a good furniture picture.[1]

he does not know by what hand it was painted.

Leicester fields Feb 26th 1771

1 Subsequent letters in the same archive show that the figures were removed and the (unidentified) painting hung as a chimney-piece (information from Dr Kim Sloan, who kindly reported this letter); E.W. Harcourt, *Harcourt Papers,* n.d., VIII, 270, mentioned JR's assistance with the restoration of pictures at Nuneham.

28

TO THE REVD THOMAS MORRISON 2 MARCH 1771

Source: Beinecke Library (Osborn Collection)

Dear Sir

Nothing would give me greater uneasiness if you should suspect that my not answering your Letter proceeded from neglect, it would be a shamefull return for the kindness I have allways experienced from you, the truth is Mr. Coleman[1] as well as myself is allways so full of business that I have not been able to meet with him so often as I could wish, however when we do meet I have endeavourd to press him to complete the negociation by Letter as I found it impossible to persuade you to come to Town. The last time I saw him he told me he would write to you in a few days, as by this time you have probably receiv'd his Letter, you have a more explicit account than any I can give. In regard to the hundred Pounds for which I told him you would let <him> have the Tragedy,[2] he said he feard that you suspected that he wanted to decline receiving ~~the~~ it, which was not the case, that he wish'd to <receive it> and certainly would when those alterations were made, that if he gave this sum for the Tragedy, he should probably receive more profit from it than he had any right to, that he never would receive any profit but as Manager.

I beg my Compliments to Miss Morrison[3] and am with the greatest respect

Your most humble and

obedient servant

Joshua Reynolds

London

March 2d 1771

1 Manager of the Covent Garden theatre, see Appendix II.
2 Apparently a *Clytemnestra* which Colman rejected in a letter to Morrison of 23 July 1771 (*Augustan Reprint Soc.*, no. 37, 1953, xv–xvi).
3 See Letter 14n5.

The following Letter contains the first mention of the celebrated 'Club'. Reynolds had first proposed it to Samuel Johnson, probably early in 1764. Seven further members were chosen, Johnson considering nine 'a clubbable number'. They met at the Turk's Head, Gerrard Street, Soho, one evening a week and generally continued their conversation till late. Membership grew: there were twelve by 1768 and thirty-five by 1792, when Reynolds died. In 1779 at Garrick's funeral it became known as The Literary Club. By then the Club was dining once a fortnight during the meeting of Parliament. It moved to Prince's in Sackville Street in 1783, then Le Telier's in Dover Street, and in 1792 to Parsloe's, St James's Street (Boswell, I, 477–80).

29

TO THE REVD THOMAS PERCY 3 MARCH 1771[1]

Source: Hilles 1929, XVIII

Leicesterfields, 3d March

Dear Sir
I am very sorry I engaged myself for to morrow, not an hour ago, I have seen Sigr. Philippo[2] and admire him very much; I wishd then to take a sketch of him but he went abroad before I had an opportunity.

We shall see you at the Club tomorrow[3] when I hope you will fix a day when we shall have the pleasure of seeing your family in Leicesterfields

Yours sincerely
Joshua Reynolds

1 See note 3.
2 His identity remains uncertain; possibly Francois-André Danican, *dit* Philidor (1726–95), musician and chess player, who came to England in 1771, or 'an Asiatic named Phillipo' who in 1768 received an award from the RSA for mastering the art of dyeing leather (Hilles 1929, 30n3).
3 The Club met on 4 March 1771, the only year in which JR's pocket-books indicate a meeting on that date.

30

TO THOMAS, 2ND BARON GRANTHAM 3 APRIL 1772

Source: Bedfordshire and Luton Archives and Record Services (L30/14/326/1)

London ~~March~~ April 3d 1772

My Lord

I have often had it in my mind to avail myself of the leave your Lordship gave me of writing,[1] but was as often deterred from not having matter enough that appear'd worth sending so many miles, I have (at least I hope your Lordship will think so) supplied this deficiency by sending my annual Discourse,[2] which my friends tell me is the best I have yet given. I think the next will be better, for I intend to begin it immediatly and have the whole year before me. I have a great deal to say and hope to live to say it all tho' I speak but once a year.[3]

I had the honour of dining to day with Lord Ossory[4] who is but just come to town, he blames himself for not haveng wrote to your Lordship but intends it soon, Mr. Fox[5] was one of the company, he is the subject of the conversation as well as of the admiration of the whole town; Tho he is one of the busiest men in the House of Commons and appears well informed on every subject that comes before them, yet out of the House he is a mere man of pleasure, he is at present deep in the Turf, He stays up all night gaming and went this Evening from Lord Ossorys <with Mr. Fitzpatrick[6]> to reherse a play which they are preparing to act, within a day or two he is to make his motion in the House for a repeal of the marriage act.[7]

The Dilettanti Society seems to be in a declining state since your Lordship left it, I was there at the first meeting this year, and did not find a single person not even the secretary, the second meeting I was not there but I was told there were but three, the third time only five, next Sunday is the general call of the society we shall see what that will produce.[8]

Lord Carlile[9] is grown a furious Dilettanti tho he never comes to the society he buys every thing that he thinks excellent and indeed has bought some very fine ones. He is now in Paris and gone it is said purposely to buy the Duc d'Choiseul's collection of Pictures[10] which are entirely of the Flemish school.

Last Summer I went to Paris for a month in order to buy some of the Crozat collection but the Empress of Russia has bought the whole together for 18000£ which I think is not above half of what they would have sold for by auction.[11]

Our Academy goes on extremely well, and I think this year we shall have a very fine Exhibition, to which the French Painters will in some measure contribute,[12] there is at least a dozen of their most able Academicians come over to try their fortune among us and we hear of more coming; there is no employment for them in France ~~partly~~ either from the Poverty of the nation or from the declining of all Arts amongst them except that of furnishing Europe with bauble, The Arts of Painting and Sculpture are practiced only at the Gobelins and at Seve, as I have often said they seem to me to be returning to barbarism. they have gone round the circle and are pretty near at present to where they sat out.[13]

Mrs Parker who I know writes by this Packet will acquaint your Lordship with many things but she leaves it for me to say that she is as handsome as ever tho' she is at a point of time when Ladies dont look at the best.[14]

I wish I could procure Lord Chathams verses to Mr Garrick[15] but they are not worth anything but as they are Ld. Chathams however Garrick as indeed he has reason is very proud upon it.

We have a Book just published the life of Frere Gerundio a translation from the Spanish[16] from which we were taught to expect by Baretti[17] great entertainment but whatever it may be in the original, it is a very dull thing in English.

I have mentioned everything that at present occurs but for the future I intend to keep a little memorandum of every occurrence that I think your Lordship will like to hear.

I am My Lord with the greatest respect your Lordships most humble servant

Joshua Reynolds

I beg my most respectfull compliments to Mr. Robinson[18]

1 At this time Lord Grantham was British Ambassador at Madrid.

2 His *Fourth Discourse*, delivered in 1771 and published in April 1772; the source of all quotations from JR used in Dr Johnson's *Dictionary*.

3 The *Fifth Discourse*, delivered in 1772, began: 'I purpose to carry on . . . the subject which I began in my last. It was my wish upon that occasion to invite you to pursue the higher excellencies of the art. But I fear that in this particular I have been misunderstood'.

4 See Appendix II.

5 Charles James Fox (1749–1806), the whig politician and distinguished parliamentarian; son of Henry Fox, later Lord Holland.

6 Richard Fitzpatrick (1748–1813), Lord Ossory's brother, distinguished army officer, wit and politician; chief secretary of Ireland 1782; a close friend of Fox from their schooldays at Westminster. See also Letter 212n3.
7 The Royal Marriage Act of 1771 directed that all descendants of George II should acquire the King's consent before marrying; the principle of this Act would have prevented the marriage of Fox's father with Georgiana Lennox, dau. of the 1st Duke of Richmond who was descended from Charles II. When, however, Charles Fox's counter-proposals came before the House he was enjoying himself at Newmarket (L.G. Mitchell, *Charles James Fox*, 1997 ed., 20)
8 Proposed by Lord Charlemont, JR had been elected to the Dilettanti in May 1766; his pocket-book indicates engagements at the Society on 19 January, 2 February, the first and third meetings.
9 Frederick, 5th Earl of Carlisle, see Appendix II.
10 Etienne-François, duc de Choiseul (1719–85), diplomat and collector; his sale, Paris, 6–10 April 1772.
11 Between 15 August and early September 1771, see Hilles 1967 and Hilles 1969.
12 French exhibitors included P.J. de Loutherbourg, Olivier, Pasquier, and Charles Clerisseau.
13 Views repeated by JR in a note written in a copy of his *Fifteenth Discourse* (published in 1791), see Hilles 1936, 188–89.
14 Mrs Parker, Lord Grantham's sister, gave birth to her son John Parker on 3 May; see Letter 23n2.
15 William Pitt, 1st Earl of Chatham (1708–78), had written a 'poetical invitation' to Garrick to visit his home at Burton Pynsent (*Wal. Corr.*, XXIII, 387n11); the verses appear in *Chatham Corr.*, 1838–40, IV, 197n1.
16 *History of the Famous Preacher Friar Gerund*, 1772; translated from J.F. de Isla, *Historia del famoso predicador Fray Gerundio*, 1768–70.
17 See Letter 18n5.
18 Lord Grantham's brother, Frederick Robinson (1746–92), secretary at the Madrid embassy 1772–79.

31

TO AN UNKNOWN CORRESPONDENT 16 AUGUST 1772

Source: Hilles 1929, XIX

Leicesterfields, 16 Augst 1772

Sir

I forgot to ask you when I had the honour of seeing you last about Nancy Reynolds's Picture it is at present in the Possession of Sir Wm Boothby[1] who would be very glad to keep it. He had it on condition to return it to you if it was demanded if you will please by a line to signify your consent he may then have full possession of the lady. I take this opportunity of mentioning that I have a small bill on you for your own Picture and the Pieta of Palma Giovane[2] the first was twelve Guineas the other twenty.

I am, Sir with the greatest respect / your most obedient servant
Joshua Reynolds

1 Nancy Reynolds, courtesan (d. 1774); her portrait by JR is in a private collection (Mannings 1518). She was one time mistress of Sir William Boothby 1721–87), 4th Bt., army officer, Master of Horse to the Duke of York. On 20 May 1765 JR listed two payments of 25 gns from Sir William Boothby, for himself (Mannings 207) and 'for Nancy Reynolds' (Cormack, 111).

2 Unidentified.

32

TO PAUL HENRY OURRY[1] 26 SEPTEMBER 1772

Source: Plymouth Museum and Art Gallery (Cottonian Collection)

Dear Sir

Yesterday I was informed by a Letter from Lord Edgcumbe[2] that I have had the honour of being elected an Alderman of Plympton[3] for which I beg leave to return, to you in particular, my most hearty thanks, and must likewise beg the favour of troubling you to make my acknowledgments to the rest of the Bench. I am sorry it was not in my power to pay my respects to you this year and return my thanks in person however next year I hope to do myself that honour.

I beg my compliments to Mrs. Ourray,[4] Miss and all your family and am with the greatest respect Sir

Your most humble
and obliged servant
Joshua Reynolds

London Sep 26th 1772.

1 This letter has been inaccurately described as addressed to 'Mr Purvey' (e.g. Plymouth, Cottonian Collection cat., n.d., 64; exh. Plymouth 1953 and 1973, no. 87); but see Cotton 1856, 117, 124 (facsimile f.p. 116).

2 George, 3rd Baron Edgcumbe of Mount Edgcumbe (1720–95), cr. Earl of Mount Edgcumbe 1789, grandson of Richard, Letter 6.

3 JR was elected an Alderman of Plympton 1772 and in 1773 Mayor, being sworn in on 4 October 1773; he appointed a deputy to perform the civic functions and sent a self-portrait to the Mayoralty House to represent himself (Mannings 11). Following the disfranchisement of the Corporation this portrait was sold in 1838 to the 4th Earl of Egremont.

4 Charity Treby m. Paul Ourry in 1749; there were three sons and two daughters (*Commons* II, III, 240).

33

TO MRS ELIZABETH MONTAGU [MARCH–APRIL 1773]

Source: Huntington Library

Madam

Mr. Burk[1] spoke of Mr. Vesey[2] when he proposed him last Friday[3] in the same manner as you have done, and I think in the very words, that he was good humoured sensible, well bred, and had all the social virtues; it was left for you to say that he was a man of Tast without pretensions and so without jealousy and envy. I have too good an opinion of our club to entertain the least suspicion that such a man will not be unanimously elected.

I have every reason to wish Mr. Vesey success but for none more than your interesting yourself in his favour. and tho' I am very much flattered by your applying to me in this affair, you may depend on my religiously observing your injunction[4]

I am with the greatest respect
Madam
your most humble
and obliged servant
Joshua Reynolds

P.S. Mr. Cumberland[5] is not a member of the Club.

1 Edmund Burke proposed Vesey for membership of the Club as a man of gentle manners (Boswell, IV, 28).

2 Agmondesham Vesey (d. 1785), Irish MP and accountant-general in Ireland 1767, m. before 1746 the bluestocking Elizabeth Vesey; elected to the Club on 2 April 1773; he was then said to have had 'couriers stationed to bring him the quickest intelligence of his success' (*HMC Charlemont*, I, 1891, 344).

3 26 March 1773.

4 Hilles suggested she had probably requested JR not to mention her name in conjunction with Vesey's candidature, lest she be accused of meddling in what was not her business.

5 Richard Cumberland (1732–1811), dramatist; 'damn his dish-clout face!', said Garrick to JR: 'He hates you ... because you do not admire his 'Correggio' ... Romney the painter' (Gwynn, 88–89).

34

TO THE RT. HON. LUKE GARDINER [14 JULY 1773]

Source: Hilles 1929, XXII

Sir,

I intended long ago to have returned you thanks for the agreeable employment in which you have engaged me,[1] and likewise for the very obliging manner in which this favour was conferred; but immediately after the heads were finished, I was enticed away to Portsmouth, and from thence to Oxford,[2] from whence I am but just returned;[3] so that this is the first quiet minute I have had for this month past; though it is a little delayed by these holidays, it will not, upon the whole, fare the worse for it, as I am returned with a very keen appetite to the work. This picture is the great object of my mind at present. You have been already informed, I have no doubt, of the subject which we have chosen; the adorning a Term of Hymen with festoons of flowers. This affords sufficient employment to the figures, and gives an opportunity of introducing a variety of graceful historical attitudes. I have every inducement to exert myself on this occasion, both from the confidence you have placed in me, and from the subjects you have presented to me, which are such as I am never likely to meet with again as long as I live, and I flatter myself that, however inferior the picture may be to what I wish it, or what it ought, it will be the best picture I ever painted. I beg leave to congratulate you and Mrs. G—,[4] and express my sincere wishes for that perfect happiness to which you are both so well intitled.

I am, with great respect, &c.

Joshua Reynolds

I shall send away your picture (the best of the two) immediately;[5] the other I know is to remain here. I have forgot to what place it is to be sent.

1 Writing from Dublin on 27 May 1773 Gardiner had commissioned JR to paint his fiancée Elizabeth Montgomery with her two sisters 'at full length, representing some emblematical or historical subject; the idea of which, and the attitudes which will best suit their forms' to be determined by JR (Northcote 1813, 185–86; Northcote 1818, I, 290–91); the picture is now in the Tate Gallery (Mannings 1282). The sisters, daughters of Sir William Montgomery, 1st Bt., 'were reckoned the most beautiful women in Europe, and were called the Irish Graces' (*CP*); they were: Elizabeth (1751–83), who m. 3 July 1773 as his 1st wife, Luke Gardiner; Anne (c.1752–1819), m. 19 May 1773 George, 4th Viscount Townshend (cr. Marquess of Townshend 1787) and Barbara (c.1757–88), m. June 1774 as his 2nd wife, John Beresford (1738–1805), 2nd s. of the 1st Marquess of Tyrone.

2 See Letter 35.
3 JR returned to London from Oxford on 14 July, hence the dating of this letter.
4 They were married on 3 July.
5 Luke Gardiner sat to JR in February and March 1773.

35

TO THOMAS, 2ND BARON GRANTHAM 20 JULY 1773

Source: Bedfordshire and Luton Archives and Records Services (L30/14/326/2)

My Lord

I know of nothing that I have so much to accuse myself of as deferring so long to answer the most kind and obliging Letter that I ever receiv'd, I heartily thank you My Lord for it,[1] beg your pardon, and will take up no more of this letter in apologies about it.

I was very glad to hear from your Lordship the state of the Arts in Spain, Minks[2] undoubtedly ought to hold a high rank, perhaps the highest comparing him with his cotempories, but comparing him with his predecessors I fear his rank will be but low, yet perhaps I have not seen enough of his work to form a just opinion of his merit I have seen but two Historical Pictures, and some Portraits, one of the former Lord Cowper has,[3] the other I saw a few days ago at Oxford,[4] both of them have, if I may use the expression a plausible appearance but I think discover no great vigour of mind, on the contrary I think great feebleness both in the conception of the picture, which is common place, and in the execution.

I am but just returned from two great shews that have been exhibited lately the review at Portsmouth[5] and the encenia at Oxford. The King is exceeding delighted with his reception at Portsmouth, he said to a person about that he was convinced he was not so unpopular as the news papers would represent him to be, the Acclamations of the people were indeed prodigeous, On his return all the country assembled in the Towns where he changed horses. At Godalmin everyman had a branch of a tree in his hand and every woman a nosegay which they presented to the King (the horses moving as slow as possible) till he was up to the knees in Flowers, and they all singing in a tumultuous manner, God save the King, The King was so affected that he could not refrain shedding abundance of tears, and even joined in the Chorus. I told the King what I had heard at Godalmin as I pass'd through the day after He sayd he could bare abuse, he had been used to it, but he could not stand that, what I have been saying I think is no treason and yet if it were publickly known, it would go hard if they did not pick out some cause for abuse. When he came to Kew he was so impatient to see the Queen that he opend the chase himself and jumped out before any of his attendants could come to his assistance he seized the Queen whom he met at the door, round the wast and carried her in his arms in to the room; I trouble with these particulars as every thing relating to Kings is worth hearing. An instance happen'd today which shews to what an amazing degree of minuteness the Kings knowledge extends in regard to the connections of men, One Echard a Dutchman[6] was showing the King his inventions for draining land, and sayd he was in hopes of being employed to drain the Flats in Bedfordshire but that the Duke of Bedfords steward gave him but little hopes. The King turned to Sir Willm. Chambers, you say he are going to Blenheim, the Duke of Marlboroughs steward (calling him by his name) is nephew to Palmer the Duke of Bedfords steward,[7] perhaps if you will use your Interest with him, he will persuade his uncle to employ Mr Echard; This is only one instance in a Thousand, which I mention now as it happend but to day, his knowledge of this kind is incredible he knows the connections of everyman that he has anything to do with and every circumstance about them. He asked me whether Plimpton was not one of the finest Towns in the world and whether I was not very proud ~~at being~~ to be elected Mayor next year.[8]

What I am going to say of myself is not perhaps quite so interesting as speaking of the King but it is with no less pleasure to my self. I beg leave therefore to acquaint your Lordship that I receivd at the Encenia at Oxford[9] every mark of distinction possible. my name was hitched in the Verses spoken by the young Gentlemen, I was presented with a Doctors degree amidst the acclamations of the whole Theatre. Mr Vansittart[10] who presented us all, made me some very handsome compliments besides the general common place ones, I must mention the last as it is the only one that dwells on my mind – quem, cum Pictura suas habeat leges, not judicem sed legis latorem vobis inquam presento ut admittatur &c – [11]

I supped one night at Oxford with the Bishop of Chester,[12] who shewed me two Letters he had receivd one from the Prince of Wales[13] and the other from the Bishop of Osnaburgh.[14] The Princes Letter was rather in form, but the ~~other~~ Bishop of Osnaburgs I think was entirely his own. Amongst other things he said he had been walking with the King in Richmond Gardens, that he recommended him to mind his studies – & said that every man must work, those labourers work with their hands but Princes must equally work with their heads, the King gave him he said a great deal of such good advice which he never would forget as long as he lived, in short it appeard to me a very pretty boys letter and such as I think nobody wuld think of dictating to him, by what I find the little bishop is rather the favorite of those that are about them. The Prince is thought to have too much hauteur and I hear it is by order of the King they endeavour to break him of it. I did not believe till I had much higher authority than Newspapers that this was the reason why the Principality of Wales were not suffered to present their address last year. I heard an anecdote the other day that corroberates this Character and which I know to be true, The Princes shoe was unbuckled and pointing to it with his finger seemed to imply that he expected the Gentleman who was about him would buckle it up, but as this person thought it not quite right so to do, asked his R.H. if he did not know how to buckle a shoe, and immediatly unbuckled his own shoe and buckled it up again, on which the Prince very sulkily buckled up his own shoe.

We are upon a scheme at present to adorn St. Pauls Church with Pictures, five of us,[15] and I fear there is not more qualified for this purpose, have agreed each to give a large Picture, they are so poor that we must give the Pictures for they have but the Interest of 30000£ to keep that great building in repair which is not near sufficient for the purpose. All those whose consent is necessary have freely given it. We think this will be a means of introducing a general fashon for Churches to have Altar Pieces, and that St. Pauls will lead the fashon in Pictures, as St. Jamess does for dress, It will certainly be in vain to make Historical Painters if there is no means found out for employing them. After we have done this we propose to extend our scheme to have the future Monuments erected there insteed of Westminster Abby, the size of the Figures and places for them, so as to be an ornament to the building to be under the Inspection of the Academy I have had a long conversation with the Bishop of Bristol[16] who is Dean of St Pauls and who has the entire direction of the Church, and he favours the scheme extremely.

The Picture which I begun I believe before your Lordship left England of Count Hugolino[17] was at the last Exhibition and got me more credit than any I ever did before it is at present at the Engravers to make a Mezzotinto Print from it[18] which when finish'd I will do myself the honour of sending one to your Lordship.

I cannot finish this Letter without having Mr & Mrs Parker and Miss Robinsons[19] name in it, tho I have nothing to say about them and as I know you Lordship hears from them every post. The little Boy[20] which was allways a fine healthy Child is growing prodigiously handsome which I own I did not expect when he was but a month old. I shall see them all in September when I am engaged to be at Plimpton at the Election.[21]

I beg my most respectfull Compliments to Mr. Robinson[22] and am with the greatest respect

My Lord

Your Lordships most humble

and most obedient servant

Joshua Reynolds

London July 20th 1773

1 Untraced; evidently written from Madrid, where Lord Grantham was the British Ambassador.

2 Anton Raphael Mengs (1728–79), the German portrait and history painter who worked in Italy from 1752, save for two periods with the Spanish Court at Madrid 1761–69 and 1774–77. His arrival in Madrid was evidently imminent when JR wrote this letter; Lord Grantham had previously admired his work in Rome in 1760. JR was always conscious of Mengs' reputation, see Letters 54n7 and 176, but Northcote remembered that there was nothing JR 'hated so much as a distinct outline, as you see it in Mengs and the French school' (Northcote, *Conversations*, 1949 ed., 21); see also Letters 65 and 161n1.

3 George Nassau, 3rd Earl Cowper (1738–89), resided in Florence 1759–89. It is not clear which painting JR referred to; Mengs twice painted Lord Cowper (private collections) who also apparently owned three history pieces by him, see Hugh Belsey, *Burl. Mag.*, CXXIX, 1987, 733–34n20.

4 The *Noli me tangere* altarpiece commissioned for the chapel of All Souls College, Oxford, delivered in 1772.

5 Between 22–26 June the King reviewed a naval force assembled at Spithead; JR witnessed part of it from Lord Edgcumbe's flag ship, the *Ocean*; he was away from London from 17–29 June (LT, II, 27).

6 Echard, probably A.G. Eckhardt, inventor of the inclined scoop wheel used for Fenland drainage in the eighteenth century, see H. C. Darby, *The Draining of the Fens*, 1956, 220.

7 Robert Palmer (1715–87) the Duke of Bedford's London agent (identified by Hugh Belsey).

8 See Letter 32; since he was not elected until September 1773, and not sworn in until 4 October 1773, this statement shows his election was but a formality.

9 JR was made DCL in the Sheldonian Theatre, Oxford, on 9 July 1773; the ceremony was described by James Beattie (R.S. Walker ed., *James Beattie's London Diary*, 1946, 67–68).
10 Dr Robert Vansittart (1728–89) of Shottesbrook, Regius professor of Civil Law at Oxford 1767–89; he delivered *encomia* on two of the fifteen graduates, JR and James Beattie (Northcote 1818, I, 294; LT, II, 27).
11 'since a picture has its own laws, I present to you as a legislator not a judge, for admission [as Doctor of Law]'
12 William Markham (1719–1807), later Archibishop of York, preceptor to the Prince of Wales and Prince Frederick 1771–76.
13 George, Prince of Wales (1763–1830), from 1820 George IV.
14 Frederick, Duke of York (1763–1827), 2nd s. of George III, Bishop of Osnaburgh 1764, at the age of one.
15 In fact there were, six, see Letter 36: the other artists being Benjamin West, James Barry, Angelica Kauffman, Nathaniel Dance and G.B. Cipriani.
16 Thomas Newton (1704–82), Bishop of Bristol 1761–82, Dean of St Pauls 1768–82; JR showed his portrait at the RA 1774 (Lambeth Palace; Mannings 1338).
17 *Count Ugolino* (Knole), exh. RA 1774 (Mannings 2172); the subject taken from Dante, *Inferno*, canto xxxiii.
18 Engraved by John Dixon, the plate finally published on 4 February 1774.
19 Mr and Mrs Parker, see Letter 23n2. Miss Robinson, presumably Anne, the sister of Mrs Parker and of Lord Grantham.
20 John Parker, see Letter 30n14.
21 Election day was 10 October 1774.
22 Frederick Robinson, see Letter 30n18.

36

TO PHILIP, 2ND EARL OF HARDWICKE 16 OCTOBER 1773

Source: British Library (Add MSS 35350, ff.46–47)

London Oct. 16 1773

My Lord

I was out of Town when your Lordships note arrived or I should have answered it immediatly. Mr Pars says the Picture of the Lake of Como will be quite finished in a weeks time when he will send it as directed to St. James, Square, The price will be the same as that which was in the Exhibition which was eight Guineas.[1]

I fear our scheme of ornamenting St. Pauls with Pictures is at an end,[2] I have heard that it is disaproved off by the Archbishop of Canterbury[3] and by the Bishop of London.[4] For the sake of the advantage which would accrue to the Arts by establishing a fashon of having Pictures in Churches, six Painters agreed to give each of them a Picture to St Pauls[5] which were to be placed in that part of the Building which supports the Cupola & which was intended by Sir Christoph. Wren to be ornamented either with Pictures or Bas reliefs as appears from his Drawings. The Dean of St. Paul[6] and all the Chapter are very desirous of this scheme being carried in to execution but it is uncertain whether they will be able to prevail on those two great Prelates to comply with their wishes.

I am with the greatest respect

Your Lordships most humble

and obedient servant

Joshua Reynolds

1 William Pars (1742–82) exh. RA 1774 (222) *A view of Lake Como.*
2 See Letter 35.
3 Frederick Cornwallis (1713–83), Archbishop of Canterbury 1763–83.
4 Richard Terrick (1710–77) Bishop of London 1764–77.
5 See Letter 35.
6 Thomas Newton, see Letter 35n16.

37

TO BENJAMIN WEST [1773]

Source: Pierpont Morgan Library

Sir Joshua Reynolds presents his Compliment and begs to know if Mr. West can inform him where Mr. G. Hamiltons Prints[1] are to be sold.

1 Gavin Hamilton, see Letter 9n9, published in Rome in 1773 *Schola Italica Picturae, sive selectae quaedam summorum e schola Italica pictorum tabulae aere incisae cura et impensis Gavini Hamilton pictoris.*, forty engravings by Cunego and Volpato, representing an ideal collection of Italian paintings, from Raphael to Guido Reni.

38

TO ETIENNE MARIE FALCONET[1] [1773?]

Source: Private collection (draft of pp. 4 and 5)

. . . is not the power of art to execute.

It has been observed by Polybius that ~~none~~ those only are capable of writing History who have themselves been engaged in great affairs.[2] I am confident myself that none ~~are capable of~~ but great Artists, are capable of writing on their Art; the observations of such a man come home to his bosom whilst the other covers <if prudently indeed> his ignorance under general observations and florid declamation which ~~never~~ gives no rest ~~to~~ or satisfaction to an inquisitive mind.

As I have the honour of having our Academy very much at heart I am much mortified that it cannot have the honour of having the nam of Falconet ~~among the~~ <in our> list of ~~Honorary~~ Academicians; all our Academicians must ~~be settled here~~ <live> in England at least when they are chosen if you should ever come and live among us we would <most certainly> receive you with open arms, ~~but we have no honora~~ The King himself is our ~~immediate~~ Patron, and all the regulations of the Academy is under his immediate <care &> inspection he has been spoke to upon this subject ~~at present his opinion is~~/~~but~~ he then expressed himself <against> ~~the measure~~/having any honorary accademicians, if he should ever change his opinion, I think I can <venture> undertake to say that you will be one of the very first that is made.

Since I have the honour to send this Letter by your Son[3] I cannot ~~avoid mentioning~~ help expressing the pleasure I feel in the reconciliation which is likely to take place, ~~as I have/had/heard that some thing in his conduct has displeased you, since he has been whatever it may be~~ whatever cause he has given you to be displeased his ~~conduct has~~ <behavior> ~~conduct~~ since he has been in England has been certainly such as has gaind him the esteem and good will ~~of~~ from all sorts of people, ~~as I~~ and I should hope what ever his offence might be[4]

Annotated: A Copy to Falconet

1 Falconet had sent JR a plaster model of his statue *L'Hiver* (original shown at the Paris salon in 1765); it appeared in the background of JR's portrait of the Countess of Derby (RA 1777; now destroyed; Mannings 813). In 1773 JR sent him, in gratitude, a print of his *Hugolino*, see Letter 35n17 (discussed in Falconet, *Oeuvres*, II, 1781, 271–72); for the date of this print, see also Letter 40.

2 Polybius, *Rise of the Roman Empire*, XII: 'It is in fact equally impossible for a man who has had no experience of action in the field to write well about military affairs' (trans. I. Scott-Moncrieff, 1979, p.444).

3 Pierre Falconet (1741–91), painter, the sculptor's son, studied under JR in 1766; he left London in 1773 to join his father in St Petersburg, presumably the occasion of this letter. See A.B. Weinshenker, *Falconet*, Geneva, 1966, 15; Penny 1986, 52, 54n16.

4 The nature of their disagreement is not known.

39

TO JAMES BEATTIE [22 FEBRUARY 1774]

Source: Sir William Forbes, *An Account of the Life and Writings of James Beattie*, 1806, I, 331-32

London, 22nd February, 1774.

I sit down to relieve my mind from great anxiety and uneasiness, and I am very serious when I say, that this proceeds from not answering your letter sooner. This seems very strange, you will say, since the cause may be so easily removed; but the truth of the matter is, I waited to be able to inform you that your picture[1] was finished, which, however, I cannot now do. I must confess to you, that when I sat down, I did intend to tell a sort of a white lie, that it was finished: but on recollecting that I was writing to the author of truth, about a picture of truth,[2] I felt that I ought to say nothing but truth. The truth then is, that the picture probably will be finished, before you receive this letter; for there is not above a day's work remaining to be done. Mr Hume[3] has heard from somebody, that he is introduced in the picture, not much to his credit; there is only a figure covering his face with his hands, which they may call Hume, or any body else; it is true it has a tolerable broad back. As for Voltaire, I intended he should be one of the group.

I intended to write more, but I hear the postman's bell. Dr. Johnson, who is with me now, desires his compliments.

1 *Dr James Beattie: The Triumph of Truth*, exh. RA 1774 (University of Aberdeen; Mannings 138), wearing the DCL gown he had just been awarded, see Letter 35n10; it was popularly alleged that, in the lower left area of the picture, the figure of Truth drove to perdition three demons resembling Voltaire, Hume and Gibbon (LT II, 30; Gwynn 93–94).

2 JR showed Beattie's *Essay on the Immutability of Truth* (1770) in his hands.

3 David Hume (1711–76), the Scottish philosopher, whose scepticism Beattie opposed.

40

TO THOMAS, 2ND BARON GRANTHAM 2 MAY 1774

Source: Bedfordshire and Luton Archives and Record Services (L30/14/326/3)

London May 2d 1774

My Lord

Tho I had sufficient warning from Mr. Waddilove[1] to prepare a Letter for your Lordship yet my time has been so much taken up with preparation for the Exhibition that I have delayed it to the last minute, I have been forced to supply the deficiencies of others and have sent this year thirteen Pictures to the Exhibition.[2] I must leave Mr. Waddilove to give an account of them. The Pictures of Dance Cipriani and Penny are superior to any they have done before Mr. Wests is rather inferior, however he himself thinks different, and speaks of it as the very best Picture he ever painted but nobody else is of that opinion.[3]

There are many good Landskips of Lutherbourg,[4] but they are very much ~~mannered~~ manierata & they seem to be the works of a man who has taken his Ideas at second hand, from other Pictures instead of Nature I yesterday dined at the Dilettanti and staid till twelve o'clock in order to eat broiled Bones which Lord Despencer[5] says was th custom when the Society was in its perfection

There is one resolution that has been made which has given new spirit to the Society They have determined to find abroad two students and allow each sixty Pounds a year which is just the Interest of the four thousand pounds stock. These students are to be recommended to them by the Royal Academy A Print is making after Count Hugolino but it is not yet finishd. I am very sorry I can only send ~~you~~ a Proof.[6]

I have added two other Prints which I think have a great deal of merit in respect to the exectution of the Engraver. I hope your Lordship will excuse this hasty Letter.

I am with the greatest respect
Your Lordships most humble
and obedient servant
Joshua Reynolds

I beg my most respectfull compliments to Mr. Robinson[7]

Annotated: 1774 Sr Jos: Reynolds London 2d May Rcd. 15th June by M. Waddilove

1 Rev. Robert Darley Waddilove (1736–1828), chaplain to the Madrid Embassy; Dean of Ripon 1791–1828.

2 Besides the Montgomery sisters, see Letter 34, JR exhibited whole-lengths of the Duchess of Gloucester and her daughter Princess Sophia (Royal collection; Mannings 1904), Mrs Tollemache (Kenwood; Mannings 1753), Mrs Pelham (private collection; Mannings 1414) and Lord Bellomont (National Gallery of Ireland; Mannings 417); his other exhibits were: Lady Cockburn with her three children (National Gallery; Mannings 382), *Triumph of Truth* (University of Aberdeen; Mannings 138, see Letter 39), Giuseppe Baretti (private collection; Mannings 107), Edmund Burke (Scottish NPG; Mannings 285), Thomas

Newton (Lambeth Palace; Mannings 1338), Richard Edgcumbe (destroyed; Mannings 564) and the *Infant Jupiter* (destroyed; Mannings 2098).

3 Nathaniel Dance (1735–1811): *Orpheus lamenting the loss of Eurydice*; G.B. Cipriani (1727–85): *Perseus unchaining Andromeda, Vertumnus and Pomona, Death of Cleopatra (a small sketch)*; Edward Penny (1714–91): *A Profligate punished* (which Horace Walpole thought 'ridiculous') and *The Virtuous comforted*; Benjamin West (1738–1820): *Moses receiving the Tables* designed for St Paul's (untraced; a later version is now in the Palace of Westminster), *The Angels appearing to the Shepherds* and *Devout Men taking up the body of St Stephen* (St Stephen's, Walbrook).

4 P.J. de Loutherbourg (1740–1812) showed three landscapes besides two portraits of Garrick and one of the actor Thomas Weston.

5 Sir Francis Dashwood, 2nd Bt. (1708–81) who suc. as 11th Baron Le Despencer in 1763; a founder member of the Dilettanti in 1736.

6 See Letter 35n17 and Letter 38n1.

7 See Letter 30n18.

41

TO DAVID GARRICK 2 AUGUST 1774

Source: Hyde Collection

Dear Sir

The connection which I have with the Author of the Tragedy which accompany's this,[1] makes it impossible for me to refuse him the favour of presenting it to you; I shall take it as a great [*favour*] if you will take the trouble of reading it and give your opinion of it, if it will do.

I should not take this liberty if I was not in some measure authorised by the approbation of Edd Burk and Johnson The latter contrary to his custom read it quite through.

The Author will very readily make any alterations that may be suggested to him

I am Dear Sir

with the greatest respect

Yours

Joshua Reynolds

Leicesterfields Augst 2d 1774

1 Joseph Palmer, JR's nephew, had written a tragedy, *Zaphira*; Garrick thought it 'not likely to succeed, as it wants a great and interesting scene in the last act' (J. Boaden ed., *Priv. Corr. of David Garrick*, 1831, I, 646); apropos, Garrick told George Colman, 15 April 1775, that he 'hated this traffick wth friends' (*Garrick Corr.*, 1963, III, no.1002).

42

TO DAVID GARRICK 4 SEPTEMBER 1774

Source: Hilles 1929, XXVII

Leicester-fields, Sept. 4th 1774.

Dear Sir

I thought of delaying to answer your note till I should hear from the author, who is in the country;[1] but on second thoughts it must needs be altogether unnecessary to give you the trouble of reading the play, as you say it cannot be acted even if you should approve of it, for these two years to come.[2] He will undoubtedly understand your answer to be an absolute refusal to take it at any rate; I must, therefore, beg that it may be returned.[3]

I am, with great respect,

your most humble and obedient servant,

Joshua Reynolds

1 At Torrington (LT, II, 88); see Letter 41.

2 Garrick wrote on 5 September that he had 'seven plays, each of five acts, and two smaller pieces for representation' which, 'with our revised plays, will be as much as any manager can thrust with all his might in two seasons' (*Garrick Corr.*, 1963, III, no. 859).

3 But see Letter 43.

43

TO DAVID GARRICK 9 SEPTEMBER 1774

Source: Folger Shakespeare Library

Sep 9th 1774 Licesterfields

Dear Sir

I confess to you I could not conceive that you could possibly be engaged for two years to come,[1] and that I ought to understand it as a refusal, but I am now perfectly satisfied that I was mistaken, at any rate, to make use of the same expression, any appearance of sollicitude from Mr. Garrick that there should be no misunderstand<ing> [deletion] is very flattering to his sincere friend & admirer

Joshua Reynolds

David Garrick Esq

1 See Letter 42.

44

TO CHARLOTTE LENNOX 18 JANUARY 1775

Source: Houghton Library

Leicesterfields Jan 18 1775

Madam

I am very glad to find you have changed your design of publishing an edition of the Female Quixote alone, to that of publishing a complete edition of your works.[1] I am ready to contribute the ornamental part which lyes within my province whenever you are at leasure to sit.[2] I am with the greatest respect

Your most humble

and Obedient Servant

Joshua Reynolds

1 The complete edition of her works, which had been supported by Dr Johnson, did not materialise. *The Female Quixote* was first published in 1752; later editions included one of 1783 dedicated to Samuel Johnson and another of 1799 with illustrations.

2 She appears to have sat to JR only in January 1761 (LT, I, 200) for a sketch which was engraved by Bartolozzi in 1793; but see Letter 57.

45

TO CHARLES BURNEY [25 JANUARY 1775]

Source: Fitzwilliam Museum

Sir Joshua Reynolds is very sorry he was going to the Play yesterday when Dr. Burney was so kind as to send to him. Mrs. Sheridan[1] is going to sit for her Picture today and stays dinner. if Dr. Burney is unengaged would be glad of his Company.

Wednesday

He thanks him for the Musick

1 Elizabeth Linley (1754–92), the celebrated singer, m. R.B. Sheridan in 1773; she sat to JR in 1775 for her portrait as St Cecilia (Waddesdon Manor; Mannings 1614), see Letter 191. On 25 January 1775 JR's nephew, Samuel Johnson, described having dinner with his uncle when Mrs Sheridan was present and in February he wrote that the portrait was 'going forwards, and I assure you 'tis a sight quite worth coming from Devonshire to see' (*Joshua's Nephew*, 39, 60). The portrait was exh. RA from 24 April 1775. JR also painted her as the Virgin in the *Nativity* for the New College window, see Letter 70n5.

46

TO SIR WILLIAM CHAMBERS [28 JANUARY 1775]

Source: British Library (copy; Add MSS 41135, f.58v)

Dear Sir

At the last general Meeting they wished very much that the dress of the President and the Academicians might be shewn to the King, for many reasons, first, to have his majesty's opinion of it, and in the next place, that it would fix the dress so that no future President or Academician will presume to Change from any whim or fancy of [his] own, and above all that his majesty having seen and approved of them, it would come to them as an order, and be a real honour to the wearer, which they think it would not be without such Sanction and Authority.

I have an Academicians gown finished and the presidents finished on one Side, which I will send to you if you approve of this proposal[1]

I am with the greatest respect

Yours

J Reynolds

Leicester fields / Jany 28th 1775

1 Chambers replied on 30 January that 'I am inclined to believe, we are in the wrong box with respect to the Academy dresses' (Hudson 1958, 126) and the scheme was laid aside.

47

TO THE REVD THOMAS PERCY 1 MARCH [1775][1]

Source: Hilles 1929, XXIX

Leicesterfields 1st March

Sir Joshua Reynolds presents his Compliments to Dr. Percy

That Her Grace may be sure of having the very best Impression he has sent the print[2] which the Engraver gave him and will get another for himself

he finds by looking in his Book that he is engaged next Wednesday, any day after that that you will appoint

1 Written before the death of Elizabeth, Duchess of Northumberland, on 5 December 1776 and presumably concerning W. Dickinson's engraving of Percy's half-length portrait by JR, published on 2 February 1775; it shows Percy holding the MS source of his *Reliques*, which remained a closely guarded secret (A.C.C. Gaussen, *Percy, Prelate and Poet*, 1908, 53); his portrait is now destroyed, see Mannings 1437.

2 Presumably Dickinson's plate, see note 1. The Duchess took a particular interest in her collection of prints (cf. Gaussen, at n1, 131).

48

TO CALEB WHITEFOORD 15 APRIL 1775

Source: British Library (Add MSS 36595, f.206)

Sir Joshua Reynolds presents his Compliments to Mr Whitford If he has no objection should be glad ~~of his agr~~ to send his Picture to the Exhibition[1]

Leicester fields April 15th / Mr Whitford

1 JR's portrait of Whitefoord was exh. RA from 24 April 1775 (private collection; Mannings 1876).

49

TO CALEB WHITEFOORD [?23 APRIL 1775]

Source: British Library (Add MSS 36595, ff.204–05)

The scheme of hanging the Pictures Numerically[1] is frustrated from the Information the Printer[2] has given us that – after he has receiv'd the Copy of the Catalogue it will take a whole week in Printing, this is more <time> time than we can afford – for the Catalogue cannot be written till all the Pictures are hung up and number'd – when the Council adopted the scheme they thought ~~a day~~ two days were sufficient for the Printing – Pray ask Mr Woodfall[3] if he could undertake to deliver us half a dozen Impression within eight & forty hours after he has receiv'd the ~~Imp~~ Copy – I have sent an old Catalogue for him to see about what quantity of Printing is required,

Yours sincerely

JReynolds

Sunday

1 So that pictures in the RA exhibition should be numbered consecutively in the order in which they were hung. An anonymous letter (possibly from Whitefoord) on the same subject had appeared in the *Public Advertiser*, 19 April 1775. The suggestion was adopted in 1780.

2 William Griffin was printer to the RA from November 1769 to June 1775.

3 Henry Sampson Woodfall (1739–1805), printer of the *Public Advertiser* and the letters of Junius; a close friend of Whitefoord (*The Whitefoord Papers*, ed. W.A.S. Hewins, 1898, 155, 161).

50

TO HENRY THRALE 9 AUGUST 1775

Source: Beinecke Library (Hilles Collection)

Leicester fields Aug.9th 1775

Dear Sir

We shall wait on you on Saturday but we want to engage you and Mrs Thrale for the Monday following to meet Mr and Mrs Garrick, I have sent likewise to Mrs Robinson[1] and we have the chance of Dr Johnsons being returned which will add to the chance of our having a very good day

I am with the greatest respect

Yours

Joshua Reynolds

My sister desires her Compliments to you & Mrs Thrale

1 Unidentified; possibly Mrs Mary Robinson, wife of the politican John Robinson, see Letter 299.

51

TO SIR JOHN PRINGLE 4 OCTOBER 1775

Source: Hilles 1929, XXXII

Leicester-fields, Oct. 4, 1775.

Sir Joshua Reynolds presents his compliments to Sir John Pringle: he has been searching for prints of his uncle,[1] but can find but one, which he has sent him. The plate, he has been informed, is in the hands of Mr. Sayer, print-seller, in Fleet-street, who bought, after McArdell's death, most of his plates.[2] He is very glad to find that his uncle's name will be perpetuated in Mr. Granger's History,[3] and is sorry he cannot furnish him with more of his prints.

1 He had evidently asked JR for an engraving of his portrait of his uncle, the Revd John Reynolds (for whom, see Appendix I).

2 Robert Sayer (c.1724–94); JR's portrait (Eton) had been engraved by James McArdell (Mannings 1517).

3 In 1769 James Granger (1723–76) had published his *Biographical History of England*, containing engraved portraits. John Reynolds was not included in later editions of this work due to Granger's death within a year of this letter.

52

TO FREDERICK, 5TH EARL OF CARLISLE 2 NOVEMBER 1775

Source: Castle Howard Archives (J14/29/2)

London Nov 2d 1775

My Lord

I am extremely sorry for the accident which has happened to the Whole-length Picture.[1] The circumstance of the Bar getting loose never happened to me before The damage that is done can only be reme[died] by lining the Picture; for which it must be sent back again to Town, lining the Picture is pasting it on another strong canvass, and if it were full of Holes they will not be perceiv'd. The Painter being luckily still living he can restore it to its original –

I am only sorry of the disapointment which it occasions. The best way I think will be to send it rolled up. Tho it cannot be returned in that manner when it is lined

I beg leave to return my thanks for Your Lordship kind hint of wishing to see me in the North, a journey which I do not despair of being able to accomplish once more before I dye

I am with the greatest respect

Your Lordships

most humble

and obedient servant

Joshua Reynolds

Annotated: 1775 Sir Joshua Reynolds The full length portrait of Lord Carlisle

1 JR's portrait of Lord Carlisle wearing the robes of the Thistle, exh. RA 1769 (Castle Howard; Mannings 946).

53

TO DR. SAMUEL FARR 23 NOVEMBER 1775

Source: Society of Antiquaries of London (Cely-Trevilian Collection)

Dear Sir

I beg leave to recommend to your protection Mr. Waldre,[1] a very ingenious Artist who intends to succeed Mr. Poggi,[2] and I hope under yours and Mr. Mudges[3] Patronage he will meet with equal success both in the

School of Drawing, and in the School of Love and carry off triumphantly a fine young Lady with a good Fortune

I beg my Compliments [to] Mrs. Farr and my little sweetheart[4]

I am with the greatest respect

your most humble

and obedient servant

Joshua Reynolds

Leicester fields / Nov 23 1775

1 Vincent Waldré, or Vincenzo Valdré (c.1742–1814), decorative painter, b. Faenza, exh. with the FSA in London in 1774; he was patronised by the Marquess of Buckingham at Stowe and in Dublin, where he had settled by 1792 (E. Croft-Murray, *Decorative Painting in England 1537–1837*, II, 1970, 288). Waldré was presumably about to set up in the West country, Dr Farr being resident in Bristol, see Appendix II.

2 Antonio Poggi (fl. c.1769–1803), portrait painter, son of a Corsican, 'of distinguished talents, but little application' (G. Scott and F.A. Pottle ed., *Private Papers of James Boswell from Malahide Castle* ..., 1928–37, IX, 30), exh. RA 1776–81; he had been painting in Plymouth and married a lady whose family lived near Plympton (Whitley 1928, II, 300).

3 Thomas Mudge (1717–94), horologist, an old friend of JR, who had moved to Plymouth in 1771.

4 His daughter Susannah Farr (c.1763–1839), see Appendix II.

54

TO GIUSEPPE PELLI[1] 26 JANUARY 1776

Source: Beinecke Library (Hilles Collection), copy by Baretti of the original in the Uffizi Gallery, Florence

Di Londra 26 Gennaio 1776

Signior Pelli mio

Non che in Italiano, io non saprei nè tampoco esprimervi in Inglese il piacere cagionatomi dalla vostra pulitissima Lettera; che mi dice come il mio Ritratto[2] s'ha ottenuto il compatimento del Signor Arciduca Granduca,[3] che hà pur nome d'intendersi tanto d'opere di pennello, quanto d'ogn'altra bella cosa. Io sono infinitamente obligato alla sua generosità tutta reale, non solo per essersi degnato d'ammettermi in quella sua unica maravigliosissima stanza, quanto anche per avermi in quella segnato l'onerevole luogo da voi mentovatomi. Quanto averei ragione di pavoneggiarmi, se posessi ritornare a veder l'Italia, e a riconoshcermi un tratto in mezzo a quegl'illustri Eroi dell'arte che professo? Se quoque principibus permixtum agnovit Achivis.[4] Comechè, a dir vero, l'età del viaggiare mi sia oggimai passata, pure non posso impedirmi dal rallegrare frequenti volte la mia mente col pensiero di trovarmi costà. E il mio desiderio di rivedere la vostra bella Firenze, ben potete credere, Signor Pelli, che sia ora cresciuto a molti doppi, essendo ora in certo modo legato e connesso con voi, e divenuto in qualche foggia come un vostro concittadino. Ora sì, che mi chiamo pienamente pagato del mio vigoroso raccomandare negli annuali miei Ragionamenti alla nostra Accademia il merito altissimo del divino vostro Michelagnolo,[5] sempre offrendolo non solo come principale, ma come unico modello a tutti coloro che in essa coltivano l'arti del Disegno; e questa fù una delle ragioni che mi fecero accennare nel Ritratto,[6] quello che ho tante volte inculcato colle parole. Nè con questo ho io, mai inteso di accrescere onore a quel sublime uomo, ma sibbene mostrare nella mia patria che ho almeno discernimento uguale all obbligo appoggiatomi di consigliare de' discipoli, e che sometterli sulla vera strada della perfezione.

Non mi rimane ora che a ringaziare voi pure del molto sconcio da voi preso per favorirmi senz' alcuno mio previo merito, e pregarvi di qualche vostro comando, onde posse mostrarvi, che la mia riconoscenza non è minore di quel rispetto, con cui mi farò sempre mai onore di sottoscrivermi

Signor mio stimatissimo / Vostro vero e leale servidore

Joshua Reynolds

All'Illustrissimo Signore, Il Signore Giuseppe Pelli
Direttore della Reale Galleria, Firenze.
A Monsieur,
Monsieur Louis Siries,[7] à Florence, Italy

Translation: I could not express in English, let alone Italian, the great pleasure afforded by your most polite letter, telling me that my Portrait has met with the approval of the Grand Duke, who is such a respected judge of pictures and virtu. I am most deeply obliged by such Royal generosity, not simply because I am admitted to that unique and most wonderful room, but also because I have been so honourably placed within it as you describe. How proud I would be, if I came back to Italy, to see myself among the most celebrated of my profession. *Se quoque principibus permixtum agnovit Archivis.* But, to tell the truth, my time for travel is now over, though that does not prevent me from often imagining myself in Italy. You must believe, Signor Pelli, that my loss at not seeing your beautiful Florence is increased many times over now that I am so closely connected with you and, as it were, a fellow citizen. Now I may consider myself fully repaid for the vigorous recommendation I make each year to the Royal Academy of the sublime merits of your divine Michelangelo, not simply as the principal, but the only model for those who would follow the art of design. This was one of the reasons why in my portrait I alluded to what I have so many times declared in words. Not that in so doing I could in any way increase the reputation of that sublime man, but I wanted to show my country that I have at least the understanding necessary to fulfill my obligations towards my pupils, whom I place on the true path to perfection.

It only remains for me to thank you for all the trouble you have taken on my behalf, it is quite undeserved, and to ask that if there is anything I can do for you I would most willingly show that my gratitude equals the respect with which I shall always have the honour to sign myself, Dear Sir, Your loyal and true servant ...

1 This and the following letter to the Director of the Royal Gallery [Uffizi] at Florence were evidently drafted by Giuseppe Baretti, see Letter 18n5.

2 JR had been elected a member of the Accademia di Belle Arte on 3 September 1752 (M. Wynne, *Burl. Mag.*, CXXXII, 1990, 538). In 1774 Zoffany, in Florence, proposed that the Ducal Galleries should invite JR to present his self-portrait; JR painted himself in his DCL gown, the canvas proudly inscribed in the verso: *Joshua Reynolds, Eques Auratus/Academiae Regiae Londini Proeses, / Juris Civicilis, apud Oxoniensis Doctoer; / Regiae Societatis, Antiquariae, Londini Socius, / Honorarius Florentinas apud Acamdemiae Imperialis socius, / nec non oppidi natalis, dicti Plimpton Comitatu Devon, / Praefectus, Iusticiarius Morumque Censor. / Seipse Pinxit anno 1775*; the portrait was received in November 1775 (Mannings 16). It was fulsomely acknowledged by Pelli in a letter of 21 November 1775 (Hilles 1929, D), as representing 'all the beauties of Rembrands manner carried to perfection' and 'among the Portraits of the most illustrious Painters' reflected 'fresh glory' on JR.

3 Leopold (1747–92), Grand Duke of Tuscany 1765–90; he became Leopold I of Austria in 1790; younger brother of Joseph II of Austria, see Letter 94.

4 *Aeneid*, I, 488 ('And he recognised himself among the Grecian chiefs').

5 Michelangelo had been mentioned in every Discourse but the third.

6 JR holds in his right hand a scroll inscribed: *Disegni del Divino Michelagnolo Bon*[arroti].

7 For this form of address, see Letter 9n24. Luigi Siries (1743–1811), Keeper of the Uffizi Gallery. He subsequently (27 January 1776) wrote to Angelica Kauffman with extravagant praise of JR's portrait which, he said, had quite eclipsed that of Mengs – 'who boasted of standing the first'; a translation of his letter appeared in the *Public Advertiser* and a verse translation in the *Morning Chronicle* (Whitley 1928, I, 313–14, and see Letter 176).

55

TO GIUSEPPE PELLI 13 JULY 1776

Source: Beinecke Library (Hilles Collection), copy by Baretti of the original in the Uffizi Gallery, Florence

Di Londra 13. Luglio 1776

Ornatissimo Signor Pelli

Avrei prima d'ora risposto alla vostra non meno elegante che gentile de' 25 Marzo passato, se non avessi aspettato le Medaglie un dì dopo l'altro.[1] Finalmente le sono venute, ed Io non posso far altro che ringraziare colla più essequiosa riconoscenza il Real donatore, che ha così degnato di contribuire allo accrescimento del mio buon nome fra I Professori delle bell'arti. Compiacetevi, Signor mio stimatissimo, di esprimere la mia forma gratitudine all'Altezza sua tanto magnanima, e colle più vive parole che potrete, assicurandola che farò quanto potrò perchè questo pegno della sua somma bontà e condissendenza venga un pezzo conservato nella mia famiglia ande possa pure lungamente conservarsi in essa la divozione verso il mio munificente benefattore.

Vossignoria poi, Signor Pelli mio, si compiaccia di pensare a darmi qualche modo di poterle mostrare quanto la sono obbligato pel lungo incomodo che s'ha preso in favorirmi, e non voglia che la nostra ben cominciata corrispondenza ed amicizia finisca sì tosto, protestandole con tutta la sincerità e con tutto il respetto possibile, che desidero molto addentamente di mostrarmi a tutte prove

Di Vossignoria stimatissimo
Umilissimo ed affezionatisso
servidore
Joshua Reynolds

Translation: I would have replied before now to your polite and friendly letter of 25 March had I not waited for the medals to arrive. They finally came and I can do no more than offer my profoundest thanks to the Royal donor who thereby adds my name to the lists of Professors of Fine Art. Permit me, My Dear Sir, to express my heartfelt gratitude to His Royal Highness for such magnanimity, and to assure him that, I will do my utmost to ensure that this expression of his generosity and goodness will keep the name of my most liberal benefactor long revered in my family.

And you, My Dear Signor Pelli, would you please suggest some way in which I might fulfil the obligations I feel towards you for all the trouble you have taken on my behalf, and I don't want our friendly correspondence to close, without saying, with the greatest sincerity and respect, how much I desire to show myself, most distinguished Sir, your most humble and affectionate servant …

1 As with Letter 54, this is written by Baretti. Pelli had written to JR on 25 March 1776 (MS English translation, in JR's hand; private collection): 'His Royal Highness wishing to give you some mark of his esteem has ordered me to transmit to you two Medals one of Gold and the other of Silver, on which is impressed the Portrait of His R.H. and on the reverse this word merentibus, these Medals are coined expressly to be presented to those who have acquired great reputation by their Talents and more especially demand his Royal attention.' See M. Webster, *Firenze e l'Inghilterra*, exh. cat., Florence, 1971, no. 63. JR later lent the medal to Josiah Wedgwood, see Letter 203.

56

TO JAMES NORTHCOTE 3 SEPTEMBER 1776

Source: Northcote 1818, II, f.p. 1 (facsimile)

London 3 Sep. 1776

Dear Sir

I am very much obliged to you for your kind remembrance of me[1] and am very glad to hear of your great success, which you very well deserve, and I have no doubt but you will meet with the same encouragement when you come to settle in London which I hope you do not forget. Here is the place where you must think of setting up yourself[2] after you have made a short trip (at least) to Italy[3] which your success at Portsmouth and Plimouth will enable you to accomplish If I can ever be of any service to you you know you may command me.

I am dear Sir

Yours sincerely

Joshua Reynolds

I beg when you write to Mrs Northcote[4] you would thank her for her present

1 Northcote, JR's pupil, had left him on 12 May after five years and gone to Portsmouth, whence he had written to JR 'acquainting him with my success' as a portrait painter (Gwynn 1898, 115).

2 Reading ambiguous: 'Yourself', 'Your stuff'.

3 He left for Italy in March 1777 and returned in May 1780.

4 Northcote's mother in Plymouth; the present remains unidentified.

57

TO CHARLOTTE LENNOX 9 OCTOBER 1776

Source: Houghton Library

Leicesterfields Oct 9th 1776

Madam

I did not answer your Letter, waiting till I should be able to fix a time for your Sitting,[1] If next Monday will be convenient I shall be then at leasure, I will expect you at half an hour after one o'clock unless I hear to the contrary

I am with the greatest respect
Your most humble
and obedient Servant
Joshua Reynolds

1 See Letter 44n2.

58

TO GEORGE, 1ST BARON MACARTNEY 25 DECEMBER 1776

Source: Beinecke Library (Osborn Collection)

My Lord

The love your Lordship has for the Arts as well as every kind of Science has made me with the more readiness comply with the request of my friend Mr. Smith[1] of introducing him to your Lordship, He is a very ingenious young Painter belonging to our Academy and intends residing some time under your Government.[2] Tho' I am far from renouncing my obligation for any favour bestowed on the bearer of this letter, or that some apology may not be necessary for the ~~apology~~ <liberty> I have taken Yet I cannot help flattering myself that I have done your State some Service[3] and have given your Lordship an opportunity of adding, to the more solid and substantial good, which I have no doubt attends your administration, one, at least of the ornaments of life, and which without doubt will contribute not a little to civilize your barbarous subjects

I am My Lord with the greatest respect Your Lordships most humble and obedient servant Joshua Reynolds

London / 25 Dec. 1776

1 See Letter 59.
2 Macartney was Governor of the Caribbean Islands 1775–79.
3 *Othello*, V, II, 338.

59

TO CHARLES SMITH [DECEMBER 1776]

Source: Boston Public Library, Boston, Mass.

Sir Joshua Reynolds presents his Compliments to Mr. Smith[1] and has sent a letter of introduction to Lord Macartney.[2] if the direction is not right he may ~~wir~~write another himself and seal it before it is deliverd

1 An Orcadian painter, nephew of JR's friend Caleb Whitefoord, see Appendix II; he had evidently asked JR for a recommendation before setting out for the Caribbean Islands, although there is no surviving evidence of his visit. See also Letter 130.
2 See Letter 58.

60

TO [THE REVD THOMAS PERCY] 5 MARCH 1777

Source: Yale Center for British Art

March 5th 1777

Dear Sir

I have receiv'd the inclosed from Mrs. Burk[1] I need not say how much & much I wish to oblige Mrs. Burk and as I know you have the same wishes towards that family I have no doubt you will use your interest to procure what she desires

Yours sincerely

JReynolds

1 Mrs Jane Burke, wife of Edmund Burke, letter of 4 March 1777 (*Burke Corr.*, III, 331), asking JR if he could obtain, through Thomas Percy's connection with the Duke of Northumberland, a recommendation from Lord Percy (later 2nd Duke of Northumberland, serving in America 1774–77) for her brother, John Nugent (1737–1813), who was about to go to America.

61

TO HARRY VERELST 1 JULY 1777

Source: Fitzwilliam Museum

Sir Joshua Reynolds presents his Compliments to Mr. Vareilst and returns him many thanks for having indulged him with a sight of the Indian Drawings, many of which he thinks admirabl~~y~~e particularly the half dozen which he placed in the beginning of the book.[1]

He begs leave to make his apology for not knowing that it was from Mr. Vereilst himself he receivd it.

Leicester fields July 1st 1777

Address: Mr. Vareilst

1 Verelst had been governor of Bengal 1767–69. JR added below the letter the identifying numbers 28 40 30 27 20 21. The drawings were probably those of American Indians by John Verelst, Harry's ancestor, mentioned (but without an artist's name) by William Mason to Horace Walpole on 23 February 1773 ('the Indian paintings ... I found ... in a book of Mr Varelst's'; *Wal. Corr.*, XXVIII, 63).

62

TO THE REVD JOSEPH WARTON 5 JULY 1777

Source: New College, Oxford

London. July 5th 1777

Dear Sir

I shall very gladly undertake the making Cartoons for the Windows you mentioned of New College.[1] I shall have an opportunity of seeing the ~~place~~ Chapel where they are to be placed the latter end of this month, and shall then be able to form a better judgment of the expence than I can at present, tho' I think it cannot be less than twenty Guineas each figure.[2] If I find your Brother at Oxford he will be able to inform me in regard to what Figures are done, and what are to be done and every thing about it. If he should not be there I must beg you to recommend me to the Warden or some of the fellows of the College.

Tomorrow morning I set out for Mr. Rigbys[3] Garrick went yesterday we shall stay about a week, soon after which I shall set out <for> Blenheim

The West Window of the Chapel at New College, Oxford, designed by Joshua Reynolds and painted on glass by Thomas Jervais, 1779–83; engraving by Richard Earlom 1783

to Paint the whole Marlborough Family in one Picture.[4] I fear my visit to Winchester must be deferred to the next year when I certainly will make it my way to Devonshire.

I beg my Compliments to the Ladies My Sister begs me to add hers

I am with the greatest respect

your most obliged servant

Joshua Reynolds

The Revd Dr. Warton, Winchester, Hants

1 He had proposed to JR, on behalf of Dr John Oglander, Warden of New College, that he prepare designs for the large west window of the College Chapel, to be painted on glass by Thomas Jervais (d. 1799). JR made finished paintings for the twelve panels, seven of which, including the large central *Nativity*, were exh. RA between 1779 and 1781 (Mannings 2106–21). The installation of the window was completed in March 1785 and JR received final payment in May (see Woodforde 1951, 39–55; Postle 1995, 179–84).

2 JR received 20 gns. for each of the eleven smaller panels; his design for the *Nativity* was given to the College. JR recorded in his account-book, under May 1780: 'Mr Oglander [see Letters 69 and 70] has paid all the designs of the window at New College, except the Great picture of the Nativity'; see Letters 138 and 273.

3 Richard Rigby (1722–88) of Mistley Hall, Essex, MP and paymaster general 1768–82; a close friend of Garrick.

4 JR completed this huge family portrait in 1779; it remains at Blenheim (Mannings 1674).

63

TO THEOPHILA PALMER 12 AUGUST 1777

Source: Private Collection

Leicesterfields Aug 12 1777

My Dear Offee

I sett out tomorrow for Blenheim,[1] I had some thoughts of bringing you to town, as it coincided with a very pressing invitation which I had from Lord Granby to pass some days at Chively,[2] but, receiving at the same time a Letter that I was expected at Blenheim, that scheme is at an end, and how you will come to town the Lord knows. In regard to our seperation, I feel exactly as you have expressed yourself, You say you are ~~very~~ <perfectly> happy where you are, from the kindness and civility of your hostess and Miss Horneck[3] and only wish to see us, We wish likewise to see you, at the same time that we are perfectly well contented with your absence, when it is in a family which will so much contribute to confirm

<by habit> those principles in which you have been educated, which habits I have allways thought are infinitely beyond all precepts, they go into one ear and out of the other I never was a great friend to the efficacy of precept, nor a great professor of love and affection, and therefore I never told you how much I loved you [deletion] <for fear you should> grow saucy upon it. I have got a Ring and a Bracelet of my own Picture,[4] dont you tell your sister[5] that I have given you your choice

My Compliments to all the Family
and remain Dear Offee
Your affectionate Uncle,
JReynolds
Miss Palmer / at Mrs Bunbury's / Barton / near Bury / Suffolk

1 See Letter 62.
2 Charles, Lord Granby, later 4th Duke of Rutland, see Appendix II; one of his principal residences was Chevely Park, near Newmarket, see also Letter 106.
3 Her hostess was Catherine Horneck (c.1750–99) who m. in 1771 Henry William Bunbury, the artist; 'Miss Horneck' was her sister Mary Horneck (1753–1840) who m. Francis Edward Gwynn (d. 1821), equerry to the King.
4 Probably from the self-portrait he had recently sent to the Archduke at Florence, see Letter 54, which had been engraved in 1777.
5 Mary Palmer, see Appendix I.

64

TO DANIEL DAULBY 9 SEPTEMBER 1777

Source: Fitzwilliam Museum

I am just returnd from Blenheim[1] consequently did not see your Letter till yesterday as they neglected sending it to me – My prizes – for a head is thirty five Guineas – As far as the Knees seventy – and for a whole-length one hundred and fifty.

It requires in general three sittings about an hour and half each time but if the sitter chooses it ~~it~~ <the face> could be begun and finished in one day[2] it is divided into seperate times for the eass[3] convenience and ease of the person who sits, when the face is finished the rest is done without troubling the sitter

I have no picture of the kind you mention by me, when I paint any picture of invention it is allways engaged before it is half finished.

I beg leave to return my thanks for the favourable opinion you entertain of me and am with the greatest respect

Your most obedient

humble servant

Joshua Reynolds

London / Sep 9th 1777

To Mr. Daulby / to the care of / Mr. Wm. Roscoe[4] / Lord Street / Liverpool

1 See Letter 62.
2 Daulby appears not to have sat to JR.
3 This word [written with a final long 's'] appears alone as the start of a new line at the bottom of the page.
4 See Appendix II.

65

TO THOMAS, 2ND BARON GRANTHAM 1 OCTOBER 1777

Source: Bedfordshire and Luton Archives and Record Services (L30/14/326/4)

My Lord

I beg leave to assure your Lordship that the reason of my not answering your Letter sooner did not proceed from any want of attention and respect to your orders but that I might be able to give an account of those orders being executed. The second Volume of the Prints after the Duke of Devonshires drawings of Claude Lorrain[1] was finishd about a month since, It was immediatly sent to Mr. Minx[2] with the first Volume and the Ionian Antiquities,[3] he has by this time I imagine received them. The Ionian Antiquities Mr. Crowle[4] gave me for this purpose, he succeded your Lordship as Secretary, There has been a great encrease of members lately, a new room has been built for their meeting. I am now drawing two Pictures for the two ends of the room[5]

In one of them are the Portraits of Sir Wm Hamilton Sir Watkin Williams – Mr Smith Mr Taylor Mr Thomson & Mr Gallway.[6] In the other is Lord Carmarthen Lord Seaforth Lord Mulgrave Mr Greville Mr Dundass ~~Mr Greville~~ Mr Banks & Mr Crowle.[7] They are employed according to the intent of the Society in drinking and Virtù. The new Room and these Pictures have given something of a reviving spirit to the Society.

I have the pleasure to inform your Lordship that your nephew and niece[8] are two of the finest children that ever were seen the boy seems to have an understanding much above his years and very pleasing manners, and the girl promises to be very handsome I receiv'd a letter from Mr Parker[9] yesterday with a side of Venison, he still continues his kindness to me, and I hope that this appearance of neglect will not make me forfeit the kindness which I have allways experienced from your Lordship, but that I may hope to be honourd with your commands when anything offers in which I can be of the least service.

I beg my most respectfull Compliments to Mr Robinson[10]

and am with the greatest regard

Your Lordships

most obedient humble servant

Joshua Reynolds

London. Oct. 1st 1777

Annotated: 1777 / Sr J. Reynolds / London. . 1 Octr / Rcd. 21:do

1 The *Liber Veritatis*, then at Chatsworth now BMPL, engraved in mezzotint by Richard Earlom, published in two volumes by Boydell in 1776 (M. Kitson, *Liber Veritatis*, 1978, 37n59). An undated entry in JR's Ledgers reads: 'Lord Grantham for two volumes of Claude Lorrains Landskips [cancelled] paid 10 10' (Cormack, 152).

2 See Letter 35n2. Mengs, *primer pintor de cámara* at Madrid, had in fact left in February 1777 to return to Italy.

3 Compiled by Richard Chandler, Nicholas Revett and William Pars, dated 1769 but probably published in 1770 (a second volume followed in 1797 and a third in 1816). Sponsored by the Society of Dilettanti.

4 Charles John Crowle (1738–1811), MP, secretary of the Dilettanti 1774–78. There was apparently a gap between Lord Grantham's departure for Spain in the summer of 1771 and Crowle's election in 1774.

5 The pictures were completed in 1779 and remain with the Society of Dilettanti (Mannings 510–11); the new room was leased from the Star and Garter tavern (*Burl. Mag.*, CXXIX, 1987, 734n37). On his election to the Society (see letter 30n8) JR had presented the Society with his self portrait (Mannings 8), and in March 1769 he was appointed the Society's Painter, in succession to James 'Athenian' Stuart.

6 For Sir William Hamilton, see Appendix II; Sir Watkin Williams Wynn (1748–89), 4th Bt. of Wynnstay; John Smyth (1748–1811) of Heath Hall, Yorks, MP; John Taylor (d. 1786) of Lyssons Hall, Jamaica, cr. Bt. 1778, MP; Richard Thomson (1745–1820) of Escrick, York; Stephen Payne-Gallway (b. 1750) of Toft's Hall, Norfolk. The picture also includes Walter Spencer-Stanhope (1749–1822) of Cannon Hall, Barnsley, MP.

7 For Lord Carmarthen, Joseph Banks and Charles Greville see Appendix II; Kenneth Mackenzie, 1st Earl of Seaforth (1744–81); Constantine Phipps, 2nd Baron Mulgrave [I] (1744–92), Baron Mulgrave [GB] 1790, MP; Thomas Dundas (1741–1820), 2nd Bt. 1781, 2nd Baron Dundas 1794; Mr Crowle, see note 4.

8 See Letter 23n2.

9 See Letter 23n2.

10 See Letter 30n18.

66

TO POTTER 10 NOVEMBER 1777

Source: New College, Oxford

Dear Sir
I wish you would be so good as to tell the Gentleman that was with you to day at my house that tho I cannot part with the Picture, I intend they shall have a Cartoon properly finished <with> which they may do what they please[1]

I am with the
greatest respect
Yours
JReynolds

Leicesterfields / Nov.10th 1777 / Potter Esq.[2]

Annotated: Let this Letter be kept. H.P.[3]

1 Presumably this is referring to the designs for the window at New College, Oxford, see Letter 62.
2 Tentatively identified as Robert Pitters (d. 1801), fellow of New College in 1756 (Woodforde 1951, 43–44).
3 Probably Harry Peckham of New College, see Letter 273.

67

TO HANNAH MORE [10 DECEMBER 1777]

Source: Beinecke Library (Hilles Collection)

Sir Joshua Reynolds presents his compliments to Miss More[1] and begs leave to return his thanks to her and Mr. Harris[2] ~~which he sho~~ for admittance into the Orchestra, of which he should very gladly avail himself but he is obliged to attend at the Academy this Evening to distribute Praemiums he hopes to be indulged with that favour on Friday,[3]

Leicester fields Wednesd

1 Hannah More's tragedy *Percy*, with prologue and epilogue by Garrick, opened at Covent Garden on Wednesday, 10 December 1777, and ran for twenty-one nights (including Friday the 12th) see C.B. Hogan, *The London Stage 1660–1800*, V, 1968, 133.
2 Presumably Thomas Harris (fl. 1769, d. 1820), manager of the Covent Garden theatre.
3 JR distributed premiums at the RA on 12 December 1777, but did not deliver a Discourse that year.

68

TO SAMUEL JOHNSON [17 DECEMBER 1777]

Source: Freeman Fine Arts, Philadelphia, 16 December 1993, lot 67

Dec. 17th

Dear Sir

I am making additions and should wish you ~~shoul~~ to see it all together[1] If I sent it to you now, I must send it again when those additions are finished, I have not courage enough to appear in public without your imprimatur.

I am very much obliged to you for thinking about it, on Friday next I hope to send to Southwark[2] Yours most affectionately

JReynolds

1 Referring to JR's *Seven Discourses*, published in May 1778. JR was revising them for the first collected edition, in which the dedication to the King was written by Johnson (Boswell, II, 2n; III, 529; see A.T. Hazen, *Samuel Johnson's Prefaces & Dedications*, 1937, 195–97; Hilles 1936, 285–86. JR was also helped in editing by Edmond Malone, see Letter 166.

2 Johnson had an apartment in Thrale's house at Southwark from c.1765 to 1780.

69

TO THE REVD JOHN OGLANDER 27 DECEMBER 1777

Source: New College, Oxford

Leicesterfields Dec 27 1777

Sir

I am extremely glad to hear the Society have determined to place all our works together in the West window to make one complete whole, insteed of being distributed in different parts of the Chapel.[1] In my conversation with Mr Jervais[2] about it he thought it might be possible to change the Stone-work of the window so as to make a principal predominant space in the Centre without which it will be difficult to produce a great effect, as Mr. Jervais is now at Oxford

I need add no more, I have allready expressd to him how much I wishd this alteration might be practicable.

I am with the greatest respect your most obedient servant

Joshua Reynolds

1 The windows for New College, Oxford, see Letter 62.

2 The glass painter, see Letter 62n1.

70

TO THE REVD JOHN OGLANDER 9 JANUARY 1778

Source: Beinecke Library (Hilles Collection)

London Jan. 9th 1778

Dear Sir

I have inclosed a drawing[1] copied from that which was sent to Mr. Jervais,[2] leaving out what I wish to be removed, by this you will see that I have changed the first intention which regarded the lower tier of ~~the desig~~ <the divisions of> windows to that of making the large space, in the centre ~~of the window~~; The advantage the window receives from this change is so apparent at first sight that I need not add the authority and approbation of Sir Wm. Chambers to perswade you to adopt it, indeed not only Sir Willm. but every person to whom I have shewn it approve of the alteration Mr. T. Warton[3] amongst the rest thinks the beauty of the window will be much improved supposing the Pictures which are occupy[ing] the space out of the question. This change by no means weakens the window, the stone pillars which are removed, suppoting only the ornament above which are removed with it.

Supposing this scheme <to> tak<e>~~ing~~ place my Idea is to paint in the great Space in the centre Christ in the Manger, on the Principle that Corregio has done it in the famous Picture calld the Notte, making all the light proceed from Christ,[4] these tricks of the art, as they may be called, seem to be more properly adapted to Glass painting than any other kind. The middle space will be filled with the Virgin, Christ, Joseph, and Angels, ~~an~~ the two smaller spaces on each side I shall fill with the shepherds coming to worship,[5] and the seven divisions below filld with the figures of Faith Hope and Charity and the four Cardinal Virtues, which will make a proper Rustic Base or foundation for the support of the Christian Religion upon the whole it appears to me that chance has presented to us materials so well adapted to our purpose, that <if> we had the whole window of our own invention and contrivance ~~it would~~ <we should> not probably have succeeded better

Mr. Jervais is happy in the thought of having so large a field for the display of his Art, and I verily believe it will be the first work of this species of Art, that the world has yet exhibited

I am with the greatest respect
Your most humble
and obedient servant
JReynolds

1 Diagram formerly with O.R. Barrett who owned this letter. See Letter 62n2.
2 See Letter 62n2.
3 Thomas Warton, brother of Joseph Warton (see Letter 62), see Appendix II.
4 William Mason at first thought the head 'too close an imitation' of Correggio's *La Notte* (*Holy Night*; Gemäldegalerie, Dresden) and JR subsequently altered it (Cotton 1859, 58).
5 The models for two of the shepherds were Jervais and JR himself; Mrs Elizabeth Sheridan sat for the Virgin and Charity, see Letter 45n1.

71

TO SIR WILLIAM FORBES 21 APRIL 1778

Source: Private Collection

London April 21 1778

Dear Sir

My neglect in answering your Letter and your great kindness and good-nature in forgiving me covers me with confusion. Your last letter gave me the greatest comfort to find I had not lost a Friend that I so much esteem, by this seeming neglect; tho I am a bad correspondent I should be sorry to be thought to forget my friends as soon as their back is turned, I promise you I have often enquired after you from and from whatever person I enquire I have allways the pleasure of hearing some epithet added to your name – which would look too much like flattery for me to repeat to you and which contributes to add to the regret I feel for our separation, I am sorry to hear you have no thoughts of coming amongst us again, Boswell makes nothing of the journey, he seems to set out for England as a man would go a few miles in the Country to dine with a friend, He made a visit last year to Dr. Johnson when he was in Darbyshire,[1] in this easy ~~mann~~ <manner,> and when he had seen him he was satisfied and returned to Scotland, he is come now a second time[2] to the great pleasure and satisfaction of his friends and he has a great many, it is to be hoped that the next time he comes he will have ~~the~~ eloquence enough to perswade you to come with him. In regard to the young Artist[3] whom you did me the honour to introduce to me you may depend on my doing everything in my power to assist him. Dr. Johnson Mr. Langton[4] and Mr. Boswell particularly desire their Compliments. I beg to add mine likewise to Lady Forbes[5] and am with the greatest

respect your most humble

and obedient servant

Joshua Reynolds

1 Boswell, see Appendix II, stayed at Ashbourne 15–24 September 1777, during Johnson's visit there.
2 Boswell was in London 17 March–19 May 1778.
3 Conceivably Alexander Skirving (1749–1819) of Haddington who exhibited at the RA in 1778.
4 Bennet Langton, see Appendix II.
5 Elizabeth Hay (d.1802), whom he m. in 1770.

72

TO MRS. HESTER THRALE 15 SEPTEMBER 1778

Source: Hyde Collection

London Sep 15 1778

Dear Madam

I would (to use Dr. Goldsmiths mode) give five pounds to dine with you tomorrow, and I would as Mr. Thrale very justly thinks, put off a common dinner engagement, but I have unluckily above a dozen people dine with me tomorrow on Venison which Lord Granby[1] has sent me.

If Mrs. Montagu[2] has read Evelina she will tomorrow receive the same satisfaction that we have received in seeing the Author of which pleasure anxious as I was I begun to despair, and little expected to find the Author correspond to our romantic imaginations.[3] She seems to be herself the great sublime she draws.[4]

I am with the greatest respect

Your most humble

& obedient servant

Joshua Reynolds

1 Charles Manners, later 4th Duke of Rutland, see Appendix II.
2 Mrs Elizabeth Montagu, see Appendix II.
3 *Evelina* by Fanny Burney (1752–1840), daughter of Charles Burney (see Letter 45) was

published anonymously early in 1778; Burke and JR had sat up all night in order to finish it, the latter vowing he would make love to the author if she were a woman. The day before this letter was written JR and his two nieces had been the guests of Mrs Thrale at Streatham, where the young author was visiting, and in the course of the day he was let into the secret. Though Mrs Montagu had not read the novel, she was nevertheless properly impressed with its author (*Diary and Letters of Madame d'Arblay*, ed. Dobson, 1904, I, 103ff.).

4 Pope, *Essay on Criticism*, line 680; also used as the epigraph for an edition of Longinus, *On the Sublime*, pub. by W. Smith in 1739, a copy of which was in JR's library (Hilles, *Notes*).

73

TO GEORGE, 2ND EARL HARCOURT 18 SEPTEMBER 1778

Source: Hilles 1929, XLV, corrected from the original MS at Nuneham in 1931 (Hilles, *Notes*)

London Sep 18 1778

My Lord

I am endeavouring to settle my affairs working hard and postponing as much business as will enable me to take three more days of pleasure, tho I thought my holydays were over for this Summer, but Newnham is so pleasant both indoors and outdoors that it is irresistble.

My nieces[1] desire their most respectfull compliments, are extremely happy with the thoughts of seeing Newnham, and extremely proud of the honour of waiting on Lady Harcourt. We propose setting out on Tuesday next unless I hear to the contrary and hope to get to Nuneham by dinner time. I mention Tuesday only for the sake of fixing some day any other would be equally convenient

I am with the greatest respect
your Lordships most humble and
obedient servant
Joshua Reynolds

1 Mary and Theophila Palmer, see Appendix I.

74

TO THE RT REVD ROBERT LOWTH 4 NOVEMBER 1778

Source: Library of Congress, Washington

Sir Joshua Reynolds presents his most respectfull Compliments to the Bishop of London and begs leave to return his thanks for the very flattering present[1] which he has had the honour of reciving from His Lordship

Leicesterfields Nov 4th 1778

To / The Rt Revd / The Bishop of London.

1 *Isaiah, a New Translation*, in verse, published in 1778 (11th ed. 1835), see Letter 75.

75

TO THE RT REVD ROBERT LOWTH 7 NOVEMBER 1778

Source: Princeton University Library

My Lord

To the thanks which I took the liberty to transmit to your Lordship for the valuable present which I had the honour so early of receiving; I beg leave now to add my further acknowledgments for the pleasure and improvement which I have receiv'd in its perusal.[1]

The easy and intelligible manner in which your Lordship has condescended to give us the result of your enquiries into the nature of Hebrew Poetry[2] has even embolden'd me, ignorant, and illiterate to form a sort of Hypothesis on the subject; but for which I ought to make many apologies for troubling your Lordship with it.

I am inclined to believe it possible that the Version of Isaiah such as your Lordship has given us, may be as much Poetry as the Original Hebrew; I do not mean that the original is not Poetry, but that the Translation, preserving the same equality, proportion, and system of lines, but above all the same Parallelisms as the original; it would be Poetry to a Hebrew ear without requiring any other sort of metre,

I will venture to risque a question, whether the presiding principle of all metre does not consist in repetition; in a certain measure uniformly repeated, or in a repetition of the same sounds, and whether the Hebrew has not the spirit & substance of this rule tho the mode be different.

Repetition of what kind soever it may be is naturally pleasing to us, it makes a stronger impression, and is for that reason much easier retained in the memory, which is one of the peculiar effects of Poetry, and this effect the paralelisms of Hebrew has in common with other Poetry, it, at least has allways had that effect upon me – Isaiah was allways my favorite Book of the old Testament,[3] from having often read it, I had retained a great part of it by heart without any such intention at the time, but remembered it in the same manner and for the same reason I did Miltons Paradise lost, which I never should have done if either of them had been in Prose.

To show how much paralelism operates in Sister Arts, it may be observed that Harmony of Colouring, which is in Painting what Metre is in Poetry, is produced entirely by repetition, that is, what ever Colour or Colours are predominant, that same Colour must be often repeated in various parts of the Picture[4] – The beauty of repetition, in Architecture, of Pillars and other ornaments I should imagine proceeds from the same principle and I believe the result of an inquiry into the rationale of our passions and affections would be That similar impulses whether made on the Eye or the Ear affect us more powerfully than any one impulse, unless that one be of a prodigious magnitude indeed such as a view of the Ocean – or God's commanding the creation of Light.

It really upon the whole appears to me a question, whether if we were early used to this mode or fashion of Poetry, it would not be thought as agreable and becoming a dress as Rhime, or any other kind of metre whether an artfull varied repetition of sense is not fully equivalent to a repetition of sound or a repetition of the same measure as in the Greek or Latin Poetry or in our blank Verse.

My Lord

I hesitated a great while whether I should take the liberty of troubling your Lordship with my crudities, but the consideration that it would at least shew your Lordship that I had not immediatly placed the book on its shelve, but had considerd it with all the attention I was capable, and that I was interested very much in the subject has determined me.[5]

I am with the greatest respect
Your Lordships
most humble
and most obliged servant
Joshua Reynolds
Leicesterfields / Nov. 7th 1778

1 *Isaiah, a New Translation*, see Letter 74.

2 In a 'preliminary dissertation' Lowth stated that although it had previously been accepted that Isaiah was written in prose, it nevertheless had all the qualities of Hebrew verse: 'the Poetical and the Prophetical character of style and composition, though generally supposed to be different, yet are really one and the same' (1778 ed., iii).

3 As a boy JR had apparently been more impressed with *Ecclesiasticus* (LT, I, 467).

4 Elsewhere JR wrote: 'the same colour which makes the largest mass, [must] be diffused and [must] appear to revive in different parts of the picture; for a single colour will make a spot or blot' (Malone 1819, III, 156); 'I have allways observ'd in my Discourses to place the principls of our art parellel with other arts' (Hilles 1936, 236).

5 Lowth replied to JR, 9 November 1778 (copy Bodleian Library, MS Eng. lit. c. 574 f. 49), saying 'You do me and my Book great honour ... you carry my Theory further than I have done'.

76

TO JOSEPH BANKS 11 DECEMBER 1778

Source: Hyde Collection

Sir Joshua Reynolds present his Compliments to Mr. Banks and has the pleasure to acquaint him that he was this Evening elected a member of the Club at the Turks head Gerard street, he need not add unanimously, as one black ball would have excluded him they hope to have the honour of his Company next Friday.[1]

Leicesterfields Dec 11th 1778

1 Banks had been elected President of the Royal Society eleven days before this letter. On 31 October Johnson had written to Bennett Langton: 'Mr Banks desires to be admitted; he will be a very honourable accession', and on 21 November he told Boswell that Banks would make 'a reputable member'(Boswell, III, 365, 368).

77

TO ADMIRAL AUGUSTUS KEPPEL 12 FEBRUARY 1779

Source: Hilles 1929, XLVIII

London, February 12th, 1779

Sir, –

Amidst the rejoicing of your friends, I cannot resist offering my congratulations for the complete victory you have gained over your enemies. We talk of nothing but your heroic conduct in voluntarily submitting to suspicions against yourself, in order to screen Sir Hugh Palliser[1] and preserve unanimity in the navy, and the kindness of Sir Hugh in publishing to the world what would otherwise have never been known.

Lord North[2] said of himself, that he was kicked up stairs; I will not use so harsh an expression, but it is the universal opinion that your Court-martial is unique of its kind. It would have been thought sufficient if you had had no honour taken from you, – nobody expected that you could have had more heaped on a measure already full.

My opinion in these matters can be of very little value; but it may be some satisfaction to know that this is the opinion of all parties and men of every denomination. Whatever fatigue and expense this business has occasioned is amply repaid you in additional honour and glory; and I hope you begin to think yourself that you have had a bargain.

The illumination yesterday was universal, I believe, without the exception of a single house; we are continuing this night in the same manner.

Poor Sir Hugh's house in Pall Mall was entirely gutted,[3] and its contents burnt in St. James's-square, in spite of a large body of horse and foot, who came to protect it.

Lord North and Lord Bute[4] had their windows broke. The Admiralty gates were unhinged, and the windows of Lord Sandwich and Lord Lisburne broke. Lord Mulgrave's[5] house, I am told, has likewise suffered, as well as Captain Hood's.[6] Tonight, I hear, Sir Hugh is to be burnt in effigy before your door.

I have taken the liberty, without waiting for leave, to lend your picture to an engraver,[7] to make a large print from it.

I am, with the greatest respect, your most humble and most obedient servant,

Joshua Reynolds

1 Keppel had unsuccessfully attacked the French fleet in the Channel in July 1778, his failure generally perceived as due to the disobedience of Sir Hugh Palliser (1723–96, vice-admiral 1778), who held the third post in the command of the Channel fleet under Keppel. Palliser demanded an apology from Keppel, but not receiving it, had him court-martialled at Portsmouth. This letter was written the day after Keppel's honourable acquittal. Palliser himself was subsequently acquitted after a court-martial.

2 Frederick, Lord North (1732–92), Prime Minister 1770–82.

3 'The fury of the populace became so ungovernable that it was necessary to read the riot act' (Keppel, *Life of Augustus Viscount Keppel*, 1842, II, 191).

4 John Stuart, 3rd Earl of Bute (1713–92), former tutor and favourite of George III, Prime Minister 1762–63.

5 John Montagu, 4th Earl of Sandwich (1718–92), first lord of the Admiralty 1771–82; Wilmot Vaughan, 1st Earl of Lisburne (c.1730–1800), lord of the Admiralty 1770–82; Baron Mulgrave, see Letter 65n7, lord of the Admiralty 1777–82.

6 Alexander Hood (1727–1814), later Admiral, had been in Palliser's division and given evidence against Keppel.

7 The engraver was JR's former pupil William Doughty, see Letter 90n4.

78

TO GEORGE MICHAEL MOSER 24 FEBRUARY [1779]

Source: Beinecke Library (in Frances Reynolds's hand)

Sir Joshua Reynolds presents his compliments to Mr Moser and desires the honor of his company to dinner on Monday next the 1st of March – at 4 o'clock – The favour of an answer is desired.

Feb. 24[1]

1 Between 1769, when JR was knighted, and 1783, when Moser died, March 1 fell on a Monday in 1773 and 1779: on 1 March 1779 JR's sitter-book shows he was 'at home' at four. On the verso of this invitation is a pen and ink sketch of a peasant in a straw hat.

79

TO THOMAS CADELL 29 MARCH 1779

Source: Beinecke Library

Sir Joshua Reynolds's Compts to Mr. Cadell and begs he would get bound in marble Paper one hundred and fifty Discourses and six in Gold Paper with the Edges gilt[1] – He cannot fix the time when he shall be able to present them to the King, before which they cannot be published but will let Mr. Cadell know in time

Leicesterfields / March 29th 1779

1 The *Eighth Discourse*, delivered 10 December 1778.

80

TO THOMAS CADELL 2 APRIL [1779]

Source: National Art Library, Victoria and Albert Museum

Sir Joshua Reynold's Compliments to Mr. Cadell and begs he would send him fifty more Discourses bound in Marble Paper <in> the same manner as those already sent to him

Leicesterfields April 2nd[1]

1 This letter appears to follow Letter 79.

81

TO SIR ROBERT CHAMBERS[1] 18 MAY 1779

Source: Private Collection

London May 18 1779

Dear Sir

I have often resolved to write to you tho I had nothing to say that seemed worth sending so many miles, it was therefore put off from time to time, till it seemed too late to write at all. The motive of my writing at present is at the request of a fair Lady[2] who desires the honour of being introduced to Lady Chambers I beg you would believe I was very glad of this opportunity of endeavouring to recover what I hope I never totally lost, your kind remembrance of me. The neglect of not answering your obliging letter <wrote> soon after your arrival at Calcutta,[3] I confess makes very bad against me, but the truth is I could give no other answer to what you mentioned concerning my Nephew[4] than that it was not in my power to serve him, The place which he sollicited and which was represented so easy to be procurd, I was inform'd many would gladly purchase for four thousand pounds, it was therefore a much greater thing than I had interest to procure besides all my friends are in opposition, if they ever come into place I shall certainly be very glad to exert all my interest in his favour.

The thanks and gratitude of all his family are due to you for your great kindness to him, you have made the fortune of a young man that I believe will in no respect disgrace your patronage. I am sorry that the hurry with which I am obliged now to write prevents me from endeavouring to entertain you by any circumstances or adventures relating to our friends. It is something however to know that things remain much as you left them, The Death of Garrick[5] indeed is such a loss, as the public have not had ~~before~~ for these many years.

But to return to the original cause of this letter. The bearer of this is Miss Forbes. She is on a visit to her brother Capt Forbes of Artillery at Bengal, and Cousin to Major Drummond <aid de con to General Clinton>[6] whom I happend to dine with last week at Lord Townsends[7] just before he sat out for America.

I beg my most respectfull Compliments to lady Chambers Mrs Chambers[8] and my nephew

I am Dear Sir

Yours most sincerely

Joshua Reynolds

My nieces[9] likewise desire their Compts.

PS. I have sent by the same fair messenger my Discourses, with the last Discourse:[10] She presents herself to you in the Eastern manner not empty handed.

Annotated: Sir Joshua Reynolds, May 18th 1779, Recd March 1780

1 Chambers had gone to India in 1774 as judge of the Supreme Court in Bengal under Elijah Impey.
2 Anne Forbes (1745–1840), Scottish painter, who had already been in Italy 1767–71.
3 Chambers sailed for Calcutta in April 1774.
4 William Johnson went to India in 1774, see Appendix I.
5 20 January 1779.
6 Captain John Forbes, brother of Anne Forbes (see note 2) with whom he had been in Italy. General Sir Henry Clinton (c.1738–95), c.-in-c. America 1778–81; Major Drummond unidentified.
7 Lord Townshend, see Letter 34n1.
8 Chambers's mother had accompanied him and his wife to India.
9 Theophila and Mary Palmer, see Appendix I.
10 The *Seven Discourses*, published in May 1778 (see Letter 68), and the *Eighth Discourse*, delivered on 10 December 1778, which had just been printed, see Letters 79 and 80 (Hilles 1936, 285–87). See also Letter 236.

82

TO SIR WILLIAM FORBES 6 AUGUST 1779

Source: Private Collection

Dear Sir

Tho you very kindly insinuate an apology for the fading of the Colour of Lord Errol's Picture,[1] by its hanging in a Castle near the sea, yet I cannot in conscience avail myself of this excuse as I know it would have equally changed wherever it had been placed, the truth is for many years I was extremely fond of a very treacherous colour called Carmine, very beautifull to look at, but of no substance; however I have now supplied its place with a colour that defy's all climates.[2]

In regard to the Print,[3] the Engravers are very ready to undertake it on condition that forty prints be taken, I could engage them I have not do~~b~~ubt in lower conditions but I should imagine that the family will want that number of the best impressions, which will be difficult afterwards to procure.

The Picture frame as well as the Picture was packed up, which was a needless encrease of the bulk of the case.

Will you give me leave my Dear sir to trouble you with a business relating to this Picture – which is that it has not been paid for as well as some other pictures of which I sent Lord Errol a Bill many years since but never receiv'd an Answer. I desired Dr. Beati[4] to speak to my Lord but I neve heard whether he did or not. I hope you will excuse this liberty – if you have any scruple about the propriety of your speaking to Lady Errol I beg you would decline it, and I will resend the Bill to Her Ladyship myself.

The Bill[5] which I sent to my Lord and which probably may be found amongst his papers the following is a Copy.

For Lord Errol –	£105-0
For Lady Errol –	026-5
For a Copy –	026-5
For Mending a Picture –	005-5
For a packing case –	5
	163-0

I beg my most respectfull Complim[ents] to Lady Forbes I remain Dear Si[r]

Your most humble

and obliged serva[nt]

Joshua Reynolds

London August 6 1779 / Sir Willm. Forbes, Bart., Edinburgh.

1 James, 15th Earl of Erroll, had died on 3 July. JR had painted his full-length portrait in 1763–64.
2 For JR's fugitive reds, see Kirby Talley jr. in Penny 1986, 65.
3 Plate engraved by Thomas Watson, see Letter 89.
4 James Beattie, see Appendix II.
5 See Letters 272 and 277.

83

TO MISS P. MORE 30 AUGUST 1779

Source: Sotheby's, 19 July 1993

Sir Joshua Reynolds by this act and deed conveys to Miss P. More[1] a specimen of his hand writing – but begs leave to observe that he does not value himself very much upon his writing in any sense. It would, as Hamlet says, be more germain to the matter[2] if Miss More had desired a sketch or a Drawing, ars illi census erat[3] art gives him his estimation.

London Aug. 30th 1779

1 Presumably one of the four sisters of Hannah More, see Letter 67: Mary (c.1738–1813), Elizabeth (c. 1740–1816), Martha (c.1750–1819) or Sarah (c.1753–1817), see W. Derry ed., *Journals and Letters of Fanny Burney*, IX, 1982, 154n17. When sold at Sotheby's, 19 July 1993 (187) identified as Martha.

2 Hamlet, v, ii, 165.

3 Ovid, *Metamorphoses*, iii, 588.

84

TO JOHN, 2ND EARL OF UPPER OSSORY 21 SEPTEMBER 1779

Source: Hilles 1929, L

London, Sept. 21, 1779

My Lord, –

I return your Lordship many thanks for the present of venison which I had the honour of receiving to-day, safe, and in perfect good order: it is remarkably fine, and worthy for its beauty to sit for its picture.

I have been as busy this summer in my little way as the rest of the world have been in preparing against the invasion:[1] from the emptiness of the town I have been able to do more work than I think I ever did in any summer before. My mind has been so much occupied with my business that I have escaped feeling those terrors that seem to have possessed all the rest of mankind. It is to be hoped that it is now all over, at least for this year.

I beg my most respectful compliments to Lady Ossory.

I am, with the greatest respect,

Your Lordship's most humble

and obedient servant,

Joshua Reynolds

1 The French had attacked Jersey in May and threatened to invade England or Ireland throughout the summer. See Letter 77.

85

TO THOMAS EVANS 13 OCTOBER 1779

Source: Houghton Library

Leicester fields Oct. 13 1770

Sir

I am very glad to hear that a compleat edition of Dr. Goldsmith's works is intended to be published. I have nothing myself but what has been already printed in some of the public papers Two young ladies of my acquaintance[1] have a very humorous letter half prose and half ~~poe~~ verse which If I can procure from them I will put into your hands. I can have no objection to the dedication,[2] on the contrary consider it as a great honour

I am with great respect

Your most obedient servant

Joshua Reynolds

1 The Horneck sisters, see Letter 63n3. Their letter was not printed by Evans (see *Letters of Oliver Goldsmith*, 1928, 80ff.).

2 Evans had asked whether he might dedicate his edition of Goldsmith's plays and poems to Reynolds; it was published in 1780 and his fulsome dedication was printed in Northcote 1818, I, 335–36.

86

TO NICHOLAS POCOCK 4 MAY 1780

Source: Hilles 1929, LI

Leicester Fields, May 4th, 1780.

Dear Sir,

Your picture came too late for the exhibition.[1] It is much beyond what I had expected from a first essay in oil colours: all the parts separately are extremely well painted; but there wants a harmony in the whole together; there is no union between the clouds, the sea, and the sails. Though the sea appears sometimes as green as you have painted it, yet it is a choice very unfavourable to the art; it seems to me absolutely necessary in order to produce harmony, and that the picture should appear to be painted, as the phrase is, from one palette, that those three great objects of ship-painting should be very much of the same colour as was the practice of Vandevelde, and he seems to be driven to this conduct by necessity.[2] Whatever colour predominates in a picture, that colour must be introduced in other parts; but no green colour, such as you have given to the sea, can make a part of a sky. I believe the truth is, that, however the sea may appear green, when you are looking down on it, and it is very near – at such a distance as your ships are supposed to be, it assumes the colour of the sky.

I would recommend to you, above all things, to paint from nature instead of drawing; to carry your palette and pencils to the water side. This was the practice of Vernet, whom I knew at Rome;[3] he then showed me his studies in colours, which struck me very much, for that truth which those works only have which are produced while the impression is warm from nature: at that time he was a perfect master of the character of water, if I may use the expression, he is now reduced to a mere mannerist, and no longer to be recommended for imitation, except you would imitate him by uniting landscape to ship-painting, which certainly makes a more pleasing composition than either alone.

I am, with great respect,

Your most humble and obedient servant,

Joshua Reynolds

1 At the annual RA exhibition. Pocock, the marine painter, had first exhibited at the RA in 1782.

2 Willem van de Velde (1633–1707) or his father Willem van de Velde (c.1611–93), Dutch marine painters, working in England between 1673 and 1707. JR described Van de Velde as the 'Raphael of Ship Painters' (*Farington Diary*, 27 July 1805).

3 C.-J. [Joseph] Vernet (1714–89), French marine painter, who worked in Rome 1734–51.

87

TO SAMUEL JOHNSON [10 MAY 1780]

Source: Hyde Collection

Dear Sir

I have receivd the enclosed from Miss Monckton[1] I have answerd it that I am myself engaged <as I really am to Mrs Walsingham>[2] What answer do you give

I shall meet you on Thursday at ~~Mrs Thral~~ Lady Lucans[3] or ~~It~~ if you will give me leave to send my coach for you, we will go together

I have <a> sitter waiting so you must excuse the Blots

Your

JR

Dr. Johnson

1 The Hon. Mary Monckton (1746–1840), dau. of the 1st Viscount Galway; an eccentric bluestocking who enchanted Dr Johnson; she m. 1786 the 7th Earl of Cork and Orrery as his second wife. She sat to JR in 1779 (Tate Gallery; Mannings 1268). Her invitation to JR and Johnson (also Hyde Collection) was for 'Sunday evening' and asked JR to contact Johnson accordingly.

2 Charlotte Williams Walsingham (1738–90), whose husband, the Hon. Robert Boyle Walsingham, went down with his ship, the *Thunderer*, in October 1779. JR recorded three engagements with her on a Sunday: 25 April 1779 (when Johnson and JR dined together on 24 April and visited Boswell together on the 26th; 10 February 1782 (Johnson was then ill) and 14 May 1780, which therefore seems most likely.

3 Margaret Smyth Bingham (d. 1814), m. 1760 Charles Bingham (later Lord Lucan, see Letter 135n2); she was an amateur painter.

88

TO WARREN HASTINGS 6 JULY 1780

Source: British Library (Add MSS 39871, ff.6–7)

London July 6th 1780

Sir

At the distance of so many years,[1] and the very small pretensions I have of claiming the honour of being known to you, tho it might prevent me from troubling you on other subjects, yet in the present instance I should hope you would think me excusable.

Mr. Hickey[2] who is the bearer of this, is a very ingenious young Painter who from seeing the success that has attended others who, with certainly not higher pretensions, have made fortunes by their profession in India; wishes to make a trial of his own abilities. It was natural [illegible] to have recourse to the President of the Academy for recommendation and it would have been as unnatural in him to refuse giving every assistance to a brother Artist.

I only mean this as an apology for the liberty I have now taken of recommending any person, however deserving they may be of your excellencys protection.

I am with the greatest respect your most humble and obedient Servant

Joshua Reynolds

1 Hastings had sat to JR in 1766 and 1767 (National Portrait Gallery; Mannings 861).

2 Thomas Hickey (1741–1824), Irish painter, sailed for India on 27 July 1780 (possibly with William Doughty, see Letter 90n4); his ship was captured on 9 August by French and Spanish fleet and he was then in Spain until 1784; he finally arrived at Calcutta on March 1784. He stayed in India 1784–91 and 1798–1824 (M. Archer, *India and British Portraiture 1770–1825*, 1979, 205–33).

89

TO SIR WILLIAM FORBES 29 JULY 1780

Source: Private Collection

London July 29th 1780

Dear Sir
I deferred answering your Letter till I should be able to give you an account of the whole business of the Picture and Print being compleated,[1] which as you see by the inclosed bill of lading I have sent by sea, <but> under convoy of two men of war, so that in the opinion of those who have experience in such matters there is less risque than by land, for if it had been sent by land it must have been packed up in the same manner as it came, as the frame could not be taken to pieces without being absolutely spoilt, frames which are to be put together afterwards, are made in a particular manner for that purpose.

In regard to <the> prints ~~which~~ <they> are in a separate case with the Plate, I thought as the expence of the Prints would be be [*sic*] nearly equal to that of the purchace of the whole plate, it would be more agreable to Lady Errol to have the plate her self; as nobody can now have them but as a present from Lady Errol herself the compliment is <therefore> enhanced; and this is frequently done by many persons whose pictures I have drawn <who> have had prints made, taken off a certain number of Impressions which when they give to their friends <and> consider it as giving a miniature picture, it certainly falls under the definition which Swift[2] gives of a present that it should be something of no great value, but which cannot be bought.

The frame was very much damaged in the carriage the expence of mending that and the case is charged by Vials the frame maker 3-4-0.

Mr. Watson's bill is 52-10 for the Plate and 3-3-0 for paper and printing 100 prints and [deletion] three shillings for packing case,[3] In regard to my bill <on Lady Errol> I am very well contented to wait your convenience. I am ashamed to send you so blotted a letter but I write in company who are waiting for me.

I hope you have seen Dr. Johnsons lives of the Poets as far as he is advanced. he is still at work – he has given me a sight of Addison Prior and Rowe[4] which are admirable ~~ther~~ It is very lucky this opportunity of bringing out his critical knowledge which I take to be his chief excellence.

I am extremely sorry for the bad account you give me of poor Dr. Beattie[5] I am much flatterd by his kind remembrance. I beg my most respectfull Compliments

I am Dear Sir / Your most humble / and obedient servant
Joshua Reynolds

1 See Letter 82.
2 '[Stella] used to define a present That it was a gift to a friend of something he wanted or was fond of, and which could not easily be gotten for money' ('On the Death of Mrs Johnson' [first pub.1765], *Prose Works*, ed. H. Davis, v, 1962, 233).
3 See Letter 82.
4 These appeared in 1781 in volumes v and vi of his *Prefaces . . . to the Works of the English Poets.* The first four volumes were published in 1779.
5 Dr. Beattie was staying with Forbes in Edinburgh 10–21 June, 28 June–8 July, 11–13 and 24–26 July, with trips to Durham etc.; he was then much concerned over the mental instability of his wife.

90

TO JOHN HELY HUTCHINSON [1780?][1]

Source: Yale Center for British Art

Dear Sir

I take the opportunity of a young Painter who is going to Ireland,[2] to thank you for the honour you have done me in introducing me to the acquaintance of your Son,[3] which I hope to cultivate with all the attention which he so well deserves, indeed he appears to me the most pleasing young man I ever saw and in every respect such a son as a father has good reason to be proud off

I do assure you I am very much flatter'd by your wishing we should be acquainted as it implies the good estimation in which I have the honour to stand in your opinion which I need not say how much I value

The young Painters name is Doughty[4] he intends residing in Ireland a few months he wishes to have it known that I recommend him as he fancies it will be of service to him, when his portraits are seen they will speak for themselves and will stand in no need of recommendation I have myself a very high opinion of his abilities in his art, and have no doubt that he will be one of the first Painters of the Age.

I beg my most respectfull Compliments to Mrs. Hutchinson and am with the most sincere regard

Your most humble & obedient

servant

Joshua Reynolds

Annotated: Sir J. Reynolds 1780.

1 Written in 1780 according to the annotation, but see notes 2, 4 and 5 below.

2 Where Hutchinson was secretary of state (1777–94) and provost of Trinity College, Dublin (1774–94). A three-quarter length portrait of him by JR, dateable c.1778, is in the NG of Ireland (Mannings 981), but this letter could imply that JR had not then met him.

3 Probably Richard Hely Hutchinson (1756–1825), called to the Irish bar in 1777; subsequently Viscount Donoughmore (1797), Earl of Donoughmore (1800) and Viscount Hutchinson (1821).

4 William Doughty (1757–1782), painter and engraver, JR's pupil from 1775; he is said to have left London in 1778 to practise in York and Ireland, which might suggest a date of 1778–79 for this letter; between March and December 1779 he scraped five mezzotints after JR; in 1780 (probably July, cf. Letter 88n2) he sailed for India, but died en route. His widow sailed on to India where she was living in 1782 (letter from William Johnson to JR, 25 October 1782; William Johnson Letterbook, Beinecke Library).

91

TO WILLIAM JOHNSON 17 JANUARY 1781

Source: Yale Center for British Art

London Jan 17th 1781

Dear Nephew

You are totally mistaken in regard to the cause of my silence,[1] it is no more nor less than a dislike to writing. I work hard all day and require rest in the evening from all kind of business. Mr. Palmer[2] complains in the same manner that he has receiv'd but one letter from me ever since he has been in Ireland, but I should not be so easy if I did not hear about you from my nieces or my sister;[3] I have considerd writing as a matter of ceremony which might be dispensed with by near relation, but I should be sorry that it should be interpreted as neglect or want of affection, but to speak to you now with the same open<n>ess and sincerity which you have wrote to me, it was impossible for me to get rid of a suspicion that the children of a father and mother who professedly hate me, have been set against me, your mother has given it under her own hand that she thinks me the greatest villain upon the earth, is it possible for children that hear such opinions from such an authority as ~~the~~ a mother, not to be prejuded by them, and is it possible for me with such <a> suspicion to act with that openess that so near relations might expect: this is my apology for not having had so much attention to the family of one sister as to another, – when I perceive that those prejudices are eradicated my suspicions shall be likewise thrown away.

I sincerely rejoice at your success and whatever is in my power to promote it you may allways command. I am now drawing a wholelength of Mr. Barwell[4] and his son for Mr. Hastings,[5] when the Picture goes to India I shall write at the same time in your favour. Mr. Macpherson[6] who is appointed one of the Supreme Council has promised me ~~to~~ in a very emphatic manner to serve you, in whatever you want his assistance, I have given him your name in writing, you will wait on him of course as soon as he arrives which will be at the same time with this letter.

Tho I have been some years acquainted with Mr. Macpherson yet I have lately cemented that acquaintance on your account. I have dined twice this week in company with him and Mr. Devaines[7] whose acquaintance I am likewise cultivating ~~on your~~ for the same reason.

I return you many thanks for the Pipe of Madeira. ~~which~~ I have not receivd <it>; the Swallow[8] is at Limerick in Ireland and will return to the East Indies without coming at all to England. I have sent therefore orders to Ireland to have it sent to me from thence.

Let me recommend one thing to you – to make your[*self*] master of the Politicks of India of every kind. With superior knowledge, things fall into your hands, and but little interest is required; I would learn at my leasure hours the Persian language which would certainly facilitate your progress, and contribute to make you a usefull man. To make it peoples interest to advance you, that their business will be better done by you than any other person, is the only solid foundation of hope, the rest is accident.

I am your most affectionate Uncle

Joshua Reynolds

My Compliments to Sir Robert & Lady Chambers.[9]

1 William had apparently written some years before, perhaps c.1777. In acknowledging this letter on 25 October 1782 William mentioned an 'Altercation between you and my Father' and his mother's strictures on Reynolds's character, which derived from 'her

ideas of Religion'; he had first written to JR from India, he said, when his family were 'in want of common necessaries' and when he was anxious to remove 'that Resentment, which appeared from the letters of my own family and your seeming inattention to me, to have taken strong hold of your mind' (William Johnson Letterbook, Beinecke Library); see also *Joshua's Nephew*, 105, 123–25.

2 JR's nephew Joseph Palmer, see Appendix I.

3 Mrs Mary Palmer and her daughters Mary, Theophila and Elizabeth, see Appendix I.

4 Richard Barwell (1741–1804), Anglo-Indian, b. Calcutta; served on the council in Bengal under Hastings; retired to England 1780 with an immense fortune; MP 1781–96. Two versions of JR's portrait of him with his son are in private collections (Mannings 128–29).

5 Warren Hastings, see Letter 88.

6 John Macpherson (1745–1821); served with the East India Co. 1770–76; MP 1779–82; returned to India in 1782 as a member of the supreme council at Calcutta; governor general 1785–86; cr. Bt. 1786; MP 1796–1802.

7 William Devaynes (c.1730–1809), banker; a director of the East India Company between 1770–1805; MP 1774–80, 1784–1806.

8 The ship which had sailed from Calcutta.

9 See Letter 81.

92

TO JAMES BOSWELL 12 APRIL [1781]

Source: Beinecke Library

Dear Sir

When I came home last night I found a Card to remind me of my engagement to dine with Mrs. Garrick[1] next Munday to meet Dr. Johnson this engagement was made at The Bishop of St. Asaphs[2] on Tuesday, but neglecting to put it down in my book I thought myself unengaged and gladly accepted the invitation of General Paoli[3] I must beg therefore you would make my apology to him

Yours sincerely

JReynolds

12 April

1 Eva Maria Veigel (1724–1822) m. David Garrick in 1749.

2 John Shipley, Bishop of St Asaph 1769–88, with whom JR and Johnson dined on Tuesday, 10 April 1781; Boswell accompanied them, but did not stay to dinner (see Hilles 1952, 147–48).

3 Pasquali Paoli (1725–1807), Corsican general and patriot, led an uprising against the Genoese 1755, but was defeated by Genoese and French forces 1768–69; lived in England 1769–89 and 1795–1807. He said of JR that he 'paints so very naturally that his colours fade as fast as those in the natural face' (2 April 1783; Boswell Papers, *The Applause of the Jury*, ed. I. Lustig and F.A. Pottle, 1982, 92).

93

TO MRS THEOPHILA GWATKIN 3 JUNE 1781

Source: Private Collection

My Dear Offy

I intended to have answer'd your Letter immediatly and to have wrote at the same time to Mr. Gwatkin but was prevented and have been prevented every evening since however I proposed doing it this Evening and disengaged myself from Mrs Elliots[1] (where Polly[2] is gone) on purpose but this moment Mr. E. Burke[3] has calld on me and proposes a party, but ~~insists~~ desires I would write while he waits at my elbow for that he will add something himself, you must suppose therefore that I have wished and expressed every thing that my affection to you and friendship to Mr. Gwatkin would dictate that you may be as happy as you both deserve is my wish and you will be the happiest couple in England. So God bless you, I will leave the rest for Mr. Burke

Your most affectionate

Uncle

JReynolds

June 3d 1781

Annotated: July 3d 1781. My Uncle Sir J. R. & Mr. Burke. Answered/ Letter of Congratulation on my marriage/ T. G.

1 Mrs Elliot, assumed by Hilles to be Catherine Elliston who m. 1756 Edward Eliot (1727–1804), cr. 1784 Baron Eliot of Port Eliot; MP 1748–84, lord of trade 1760–76, one of JR's 'most familiar and valued friends' (LT, II, 431); elected to the Club in 1782.

2 Mary Palmer, Theophila's sister, see Appendix I.

3 For Edmund Burke's postcript to this letter ('we who hoped a great deal from Offy Palmer, should see a great deal performed by Mrs. Gwatkin'), see *Burke Corr.*, IV, 353.

94

TO EDMUND BURKE 2 AUGUST 1781

Source: Hilles 1929, LVII (the original exhibited at the Yale Center for British Art, Reynolds, 1973, no. 28)

Brusseles, Aug 2d, 1781

Dear Sir

We arrived at Brussels the thirtieth,[1] and shall probably set out this Evening for Antwerp. Nothing hitherto has happend worth mentioning, nor have we seen any pictures better than we have at home, Ghent and Alost have two or three pictures of Rubens and Brussels perhaps a dozen, the people seem to make so much of his works that it requires some circumspection not to run on the other side; The Pictures hitherto have not answered our expectation, we have been very well amused, and pass out time very agreably Yesterday we dined at Mr. Fitzherberts[2] with the Duke of Richmond,[3] and Mr. Lenox,[4] and we all behaved very well. I don't know whether I might expect too much, but I thought Mr. Fitz would have laid himself out more for our amusement, he has returned our visit, and given us a dinner, or rather, let us dine with him at the same time with the Duke of Richmond and thats all.–

The Emperor[5] will probably not return to Brussels, he has left an impression on every rank of people very much to his honour.

The Dutchess of Chandos[6] recommended to him in a very absurd manner the Princess Royal[7] for a wife. The Emperor said he was too old for her, but she would not accept the excuse, and added that her Duke was as much older than she was and yet they lived very happily together; Mr. Fitzherbert said the Emperor told this to every person he saw that day we propose going to Dusseldorp. consequently shall take the Spa in our way.

I write with continual interruption, having so little to say and so little time to say that little, that I believe I should not have ventured to have wrote, if I had not had an opportunity of enclosing my letter in a cover to Mr. Fraser.[8]

The chase is at the door for Antwerp, where if anything occurs you will hear from me again.[9] we shall stay there as we do at every other place, just as long as we can amuse ourselves and hitherto we have been exactly of the same opinion Yours,[10]

Joshua Reynolds

Edmund Burke Esq., Charles Street, St James's Square.

1 JR travelled with Philip Metcalfe (1735–1818), a distiller and MP, later treasurer 1794–1808 and secretary 1797–1808 of the Society of Dilettanti. They left London on 24 July and sailed to Ostend from Margate; they returned to London on 16 September (Journey 1996, 1). JR's revisions of the notes he made on this journey were first published posthumously as 'A Journey to Flanders and Holland in the Year 1781' by Malone, Works, 1797; the most authoritative edition is that edited by Harry Mount, 1996 (*Journey* 1996).

2 Alleyne Fitzherbert, later Baron St Helens (1753–1839), British minister at Brussels.

3 Charles Lennox, 3rd Duke of Richmond (1735–1806).

Joshua Reynolds, *Edmund Burke*, 1767–69; engraving by James Watson 1770

4 Lenox, probably Charles Lennox (1764–1819), the 3rd Duke's nephew who succeeded him in 1806.
5 Joseph II (1741–90), Emperor of Austria 1765–90, older brother of Leopold of Tuscany (see Letters 54, 55), had visited Brussels from the end of May until the second week of July; the following year he suppressed the monasteries, see Letters 139 and 140.
6 In 1777 the James Brydges, 3rd and last Duke of Chandos (1731–89) m. 2ndly Anne Eliza Gamon (d. 1813), widow of John Elletson.
7 Charlotte, the Princess Royal (1766–1828) who m. 1797 Frederick William, prince of Würtemberg.
8 Hilles supposed this may have been William Fraser (c.1727–1802), under-secretary of state 1765–89.
9 See Letter 95.
10 Cotton 1856, 160, stated the end of the letter had been torn off.

95

TO EDMUND BURKE 10 AUGUST 1781

Source: Yale Center for British Art

Roterdam Aug 10. 1781

Dear Sir

I wrote from Brussels in a great hurry[1] and now that I have more leasure have nothing that appears to me worth writing about except the Pictures and that is too long an affair to begin upon, it has raised my Idea of Rubens upon the whole. I ~~have~~ shall have materials to form a more correct judment of the rank he ought to hold when I have seen Dusseldorp where we intend going.

Roterdam has a more extraordinary appearance, is more striking than any thing we have hitherto seen, in many parts it has the appearance of Venice.

But the Keys are magnificent, rows of fine houses, high at least and fine in their half a mole long perfectly in a strait line with a Row of Elms between the houses and the ships which lye close to the ~~K~~Quey so that the branches touch the masts whilst on the other side the Canal the shipping have for their background the rows of Trees with houses appearing between them this uncommon mixture of Trees <houses> and ships you may imagine has an extraordinary effect.

The Country is not calculated for a Landskip painter, tho I am no great Enemy to strait lines yet here is a little too much of it, their dykes a miles long without the least curviture but it is still very striking, and their patience and perseverance to throw up such a quantity of earth, or cut such canals must raise the admiration of every traveller.

I observe allmost all the houses which have not been lately built are out of the perpendicular and lean forward I think full as much as the tower at Pisa and would be as much remarked if they were as high.

The horses here as well as in Flanders a nobler animal than ours, they have more substance the Cows and oxen are of a much neater make they are all spotted black and white among many hundreds which we saw comeing hither we ~~did not~~ saw but one red cow –

Here is nothing to be seen in the Picture way so we shall leave it tomorrow for the Hague – I wish I had had the precaution to have made memorandums of whatever occurred but sitting down to write and not mentioning any <thing> of pictures where I have made very copious observations, I dont know where to begin for every thing is to a certain degree particular, the women here seem better than those we left at Antwerp, what the Gentlewomen are there we had no means of knowing they being all in the country, but the ordinary people are the most ordinary I ever say I think without one exception they were all ugly.

We have had a very pleasant tour hitherto and are very well pleased with each other as much leasure as I thought I had I find the messenger is come for my letter so am obliged to conclude

Yours most affectionately

JReynolds

This letter belongs to Antwerp according to promise but we travellers cannot do everything just as they choose

1 See Letter 94.

96

TO EDMUND BURKE 14, 24, 30 AUGUST 1781

Source: Sheffield Archives (WWM Bk P1/1459)

Hague Aug 14 1781

We have been here three days, and propose staying here three days <longer> to enjoy ourselves after our fatigue, I promise you we have not been idle, hitherto, every minute of the day has been employed in travelling or staring. The Prince of Oranges Gallery[1] is the only magazine of pictures that we have seen here, and the only we are likely to see, The possessor of another collection, Mr. Van Uteren[2] is not in town, he is at Amsterdam, The Greffier[3] has sent to him, but it is suspected <it will be> without effect, as he has the keys with him, and will never suffer his pictures to be seen but when he his present. The Greffier has shewn us every civility possible; he returned our visit immediatly, and we dined with him the next day. He is a most amiable character, of the greatest simplicity of manners, and has not the least tincture of that insolence of office, or, I should say (thinking of [deletion] <a person at Brussels>) that indolence of office who think his [*deletion*] whole business is to appear negligent and at their ease. By the attention which has been paid us by the Greffier, his nephew, and the rest of his family, the attention of the town upon us has been much excited, this is but a small place, and in many respects like Bath, where the people have nothing to do but to talk of each other, and it may be compared to Bath likewise for its beauty, It abounds in squares which you would be charmed with as they <are> full of Trees; ~~that are more like than~~ not disposed in a meagre scanty row [deletion] <but> are more like woods with walks in the middle

The Prince of Orange whom we saw two or three times is very like King George but not so handsome, he has a heavy look, short person, with somewhat a round belly;[4] The Greffier frequently expressed his concern that he was not able to do for us all he wished such as introducing us to the Prince &c on account of the situation of affairs. we have seen the collection I mentiond in the beginning, <which was> – scarce worth the trouble of sending so far for the Keys. Dutch Pictures are a representation of nature, just as it is seen in a Camera Obscura ~~when~~ after having seen the best of each master one has no violent desire of seeing any more. They are certainly to be admired, but do not shine much in description, a figure asleep with another figure tickling his or her nose, which is a common subject with the Painters of this School, however admirable [deletion] <their effect> would have no effect in writing

Amsterdam Aug. 24.

The above letter was wrote as you see at the Hague, tomorrow we leave Amsterdam for Dusseldorp. The face of this country is very striking from its being unlike everything else. The length and straitness of their artificial roads, often with double rows of trees which in the perspective finish in a point the perseverance of their industry and labour to form those dykes, and preserve them in such perfect repair, is an idea that must occur to every mind, and is truly sublime. this country is, I should imagine the most artificial country in the world [deletion] <This City> is more like Venice than any other place I ever saw, in many places, it is an exact likeness where the water reaches to the houses, but this is not common, in the middle of every street are canals and on each side those canals, keys and rows of trees, another idea of their industry and perseverance which amounts I think to the sublime is that the foundation, of their ~~houses whiand Churches~~ buildings <which is piles> costs as much as much as what appears above ground both in labour and expence, the Stadhouse is founded on 13659 piles. I have often thought the habit they have acquired of fighting against nature has given them a disposition never to leave nature as they find her, [deletion] but in order to see the Dutch Tast in its highest degree we spent a day in North Holland, we went to a Village called Brock,[5] which appeard so different from any thing we had seen before that it appeared rather like an enchanted village, such as we read off in the Arabian tales;[6] – not a person to be seen, except a servant here and there; the houses are very low, with a door towards the street, which is not used nor ever has been used except when they go out of it to be married, after which it is again shut up, the streets, if they may be so called, for carriages cannot enter them, are sanded with fine inksand; the houses painted from top to bottom, green, red, and all sorts of Colours. The little gardens with little fountains and flower-knots as neat as possible and trees cut into all kinds of shapes. Indeed, I much doubt if you can find a tree in its natural shape all over Holland, and we may add, nor water neither, which is everywhere kept within bounds, we have been extraordinary well receivd by Mr. Hope[7] we are every day dining or supping with him, and one great dinner seem'd to be made on purpose for us,

Aug 30th 1781 Dusseldorp

On the 25th we sat out from Amsterdam, and to-morrow we propose going from hence to Aix d'Chapell, and then after staying a day or two there turn our faces directly for England. If I do not send away this

<Letter> now I shall bring it with me to England. I really did intend writing to you from ~~ever~~ the Hague & from Amsterdam, but the difficulty of finding time to finish my letter has been the reason of my carrying it about with me

We are very well contented with our visit to Dusseldorp, Rubens reigns here and revels.[8] His Pictures of the fallen Angels – and the last Judgment, give a higher idea of his genius than any other of his works, there is one Picture of Raffielle in his first manner,[9] which is the only picture of consequence of the Roman school, the collection is made up of Flemish and Dutch Pictures, but they are the best of those schools.

The ease with which this Gallery is seen, and the indulgence to the young Painters who wish to copy any of the Pictures is beyond [*deletion*] any thing I ever saw in any other place, we have had every attention possible from the Keeper of the Pictures who as soon as he knew who I was sent into the Country to his principal[10] who is likewise President of the Academy, who immediatly came to town and has been attending us ever since.

Yours sincerely
JReynolds

1 Willem V (1748–1806), Stadholder of Holland 1751–95; the majority of his pictures are now in the Mauritshuis.

2 Adriaan van Heteren (1722–1800), mentioned in JR's published journal, 15 or 16 August (*Journey* 1996, 90–91, 168n435).

3 Hendrik Fagel (1706–90), greffier (i.e. secretary) of the States General 1744–90; his pictures were sold, London, 22–23 May 1801 (*Journey* 1996, 168n425).

4 Hilles compared with *Henry IV part 2*, I, ii, 212.

5 Broek-in-Waterland, north of Amsterdam.

6 JR's copy of *The Arabian Nights*, is now in Yale University Library.

7 Henry Hope (c.1739–1811), banker of Hope & Co., one of a Scottish family who had emigrated to Amsterdam in the seventeenth century. His business partner and cousin John (1737–84) in Amsterdam appears to have owned most of the Hope pictures seen by JR, but it was Henry who entertained him (*Journey* 1996, 170n465).

8 'reigns here and revels', Milton, *Paradise Lost*, IV, 765 (Hilles, *Notes*). Rubens's *Fallen Angels* and *Last Judgment* are now in the Alkte Pinakothek, Munich (*Journey* 1996, 131, 133, 177nn693, 696).

9 *Holy Family* now in the Alte Pinakothek, Munich (*Journey* 1996, 120, 177n653).

10 Lambert Krahe (1712–90), painter and collector of drawings (*Journey* 1996, 176n624).

97

TO MRS THEOPHILA GWATKIN [29 SEPTEMBER?] 1781[1]

Source: Private Collection

London Saturday

Dear Offy

I am just come home and finding your Letter I would not neglect answering it, tho ~~Iho~~ it wants ~~by~~ but five minutes of eleven to let you know that I expect you with great impatience. I am sorry to hear of both your illness but I hope it will not prevent your coming the beginning of the week. I beg my compliments to Mr. Gwatkin and tell him how glad I shall be to see him.

Yours most affectionately

JReynolds

Mrs. Gwin[2] is come to town, not well. has an ague Lord Richard Cavendish died at Naples about a fortnight since[3]

1 JR returned to London from Holland on Sunday 16 September, and see note 3; probably either Saturday 22 or 29 September.

2 See Letter 63n3.

3 Lord Richard Cavendish (1752–81), second son of the 4th Duke of Devonshire, had died at Naples on 7 September.

98

TO FRANCES REYNOLDS [1781]

Source: Hilles 1929, LVI

Dear Sister

I am very much obliged to you for your kind and generous offer in regard to the house at Richmond[1] not only on giving me leave to use it occasionally but even as long as I live provided I will give it to you, but as I have no such thoughts at present I can only thank you for your kindness – tho I am much older than you[2] I hope I am not yet arrived to dotage as you seem to think I am, voluntarily to put myself in the situation of receiving the favour of living in my own house instead of conferring the favour of letting you live in it[3]

I am your most affectionate

Brother

J Reynolds

[1781]

I have enclosed a Bank Bill of ten Pounds[4]

Mrs. Reynolds Richmond

Annotated: (by Frances Reynolds) Sir Joshua I believe in 81

1 See endorsement; Letter 105 confirms she was living at Richmond by September 1782 in the small villa which JR had built at Richmond Hill to the designs of William Chambers for his summer recreation (cf. Northcote 1818, I, 304).
2 He was six years her senior.
3 The house was to pass to JR's niece, Mary Palmer, who once described it as 'a house stuck upon the top of a hill without a bit of garden or ground of any sort near it but what is as public as St James's Park' (LT, II, 542).
4 Frances Reynolds once described the income allowed her by JR as sufficient to keep her within the sphere of gentility (LT, I, 92n); in March 1788 JR began regular payments to her of £25 per quarter (draft on Coutts Bank; 25 March 1788; Hyde Collection).

99

TO OZIAS HUMPHRY [1 FEBRUARY 1782][1]

Source: Hilles 1929, LIX

February 1st

Sir Joshua Reynolds' compliments to Mr. Humphry, he has been informed by Bartolozzi[2] that Mr. Humphry had sent to him for the Lord Chancellor's picture,[3] begs he will be so kind as to inform Sir Joshua whether he has any such order from the Lord Chancellor, or, upon what authority he sent for it.

1 The year in which Bartolozzi engraved Thurlow's portrait; previously dated 1780 or 1781.
2 Francesco Bartolozzi (1727–1815), engraver, foundation RA 1768.
3 Edward Thurlow, 1st Baron Thurlow (1727–1815), lord chancellor 1778–83; he sat to JR in 1781, but considered him 'a great scoundrel & a bad painter', inferior to Romney (LT, II, 132n).

100

TO THOMAS COLLINGWOOD 28 FEBRUARY 1782

Source: Foundling Hospital, London

Leicesterfields Feb 28th 1782

Sir

I beg my most respectfull Compts. may be presented to the Governors,[1] I consider the nomination of myself to be one of the Stewards as a great honour conferr'd on me[2] and will certainly attend at the Hospital on the Anniversary in May next.[3]

I am with great respect / Sir / Your most obedient / humble servant

JReynolds

Annotated: Sir Joshua Reynolds 28 Feb: 1782, recd same day. Read with Commee 3 April 1782

1 Collingwood was secretary of the Foundling Hospital 1758–90.

2 JR was elected Governor and Guardian of the Hospital on 26 December 1759, after he had presented the full-length portrait of Earl of Dartmouth.

3 He visited the Hospital on 8 May 'to see Pictures' (pocket-book).

101

TO JAMES BEATTIE 30 MARCH 1782

Source: Aberdeen University Library (AUL MS 30/B24/4/1)

London 30 March 1782.

Dear Sir

I am very much flatterd by your giving me a sight of your Essay[1] which I assure you I have read over and over with the greatest attention, and I may add with the greatest pleasure and improvement. About twenty years ~~ago~~ since I thought much on this subject[2] and am now glad to find many of those Ideas which then passed in my mind put in such good order by so excellent a metaphisician My view of the question did not extend beyond my own profession, it regarded only the beauty of form, which I attributed entirely to custom or habit. You have taken a larger compass including indeed everything that gives delight every mental and corporial excellence and have adorned your Philosophy with the most happy illustrations which are both convincing and entertaining, indeed the question appears to me to be very thoroughly investigated I thought once I should have returned you an Essay as long as yours, I wrote many sheets and some long reasonings but found them at last entirely needless, that you had done all that was necessary, and in a much better manner, so threw them in the fire.

I am much obliged to you for the honourable place you have give me Cheek by Joul with Raffielle and Titian, but I seriously think these names are too great to be associated with any modern name whatever; even if that modern was equal to either of them it would oppose too strongly our prejudices. I am far from wishing to decline the honour of having my name inserted but I should think it will do better by itself. – supposing it was thus: but we do not find this affectation in the Pictures of Reynolds and in his Discourses he has particularly cautiond the student against it[3] and in the second place where I am mentiond, leaving out ~~Raffielle~~ Titian, I shall make a respectable figure;[4] Sometimes by endeavouring to do too much, the effect of the whole is lost. I fear you will think me very impertinent in taking such liberties.

Your Idea of producing the line of beauty by taking the medium of the two extremes, exactly coincides with my Idea, and its beauty I think may fairly be deduced from habit, all lines are either curved or strait, and that which partakes equally of each, is the medium or averidge of all lines and therefore more beautifull than any other line, notwithstanding this, an artist would act preposterously that should take every opportunity to introduce this line in his works as Hogarth himself did, who appears to have taken an aversion to a strait line, His pictures therefore want that firmness and stability which is produced by strait lines,[5] this conduct therefore may truly be said to be unnatural for it is not the conduct of nature.

What you have imputed to convenience and contrivanec [*sic*], I think may without any violence be put to the account of habit as we are more used to that form in Nature (and I believe in art too) which is the <u>most</u> convenient. Fitness and beauty being allways united in animals as well as men, ~~that is~~ they are fit in proportion as they are beautifull, ~~in pro~~ and beautifull in proportion as they are fit, <which> makes it difficult to determine ~~which is~~ <what is> the original cause; As I said before, I am inclined to habit, and that we determine by habit in regard to beauty without waiting for the slower determination of reason.

I am aware that this reasoning goes upon a supposition that we are more used to beauty than deformity, <and> that we are so, I think I have proved in a little essay which I wrote about twenty five year since <and> which Dr. Johnson publishd in his Idler, if you think it worth while to look into it.[6]

May not all beauty proceeding from association of Ideas be reduced to the principle of habit or experience? you see I am for bringing every into my old principle, but I will ~~hav~~ now have done for fear I should through this letter likewise in the fire, and now conclude with my sincere thanks for the pleasure you have given and indeed the compliment you have paid me in thinking me worthy of seeing this work in manuscript. I ought likewise to make some apology for keeping it so long, the truth is, when I receivd it, I was very busy in writing notes on Masons translation of Fresnoys Poem on Painting, which Mr Mason waited for and it is now printing at York[7]

I am with the greatest respect

Your most Obliged

humble servant

Joshua Reynolds

Dr Beattie.

1 Beattie's MS of his *Dissertation on Imagination*, first published in 1783 in Beattie's *Dissertations Moral and Critical*, 110–42 (Hilles).
2 In *The Idler*, no. 82, 10 November 1759; Beattie quotes from it in the *Dissertation* (120n).
3 Adapted *verbatim* (*Dissertation*, 123).
4 'Andromache smiling in tears would be as interesting an object now, as she was three thousand years ago: and the Venus, and the Lavinia, of the Mantuan poet, if copied by Reynolds, would still be the perfection of feminine grace, and feminine tenderness' (*Dissertation*, 138).
5 Beattie adapted JR's phrase (*Dissertation*, 119).
6 *The Idler*, 10 November 1759, see note 2.
7 Du Fresnoy's *De Arte Graphica* (1668) had previously been translated by Dryden in 1695. William Mason (1725–97), poet and dilettante, rector of Aston, Yorkshire, 1754, and precentor at York 1762; published plays, *Elfrida* (1752) and *Caractacus* (1759), and poetry, *The English Garden* (1772–81); greatly admired by Horace Walpole; sat to JR in 1774 (Pembroke College, Cambridge); see *A Candidate for Praise*, exh. cat., York, 1973.

102

TO THOMAS WARTON 13 MAY 1782

Source: British Library (Add MSS 33652D, f.14–14v)

London May 13th 1782

Dear Sir

This is the first minute I have had to thank you for the Verses which I had the honour and pleasure of receiving a week ago.[1] It is a bijoux, it is a beautifull little thing, and I think I should have equally admired it, if I had not been so much interested in it as I certainly am; I owe you great obligations for the Sacrifice which you have made, or pretend to have made, to modern Art,[2] I say pretend, for tho' it it allowed that you have like a true Poet feigned marvellously well, and have opposed the two different stiles with the skill of a Connoisseur, yet I may be allowed to entertain some doubts of the sincerity of your conversion, I have no great confidence in the recantation of such an old offender.[3]

It is short, but it is a complete composition; it is a whole, the struggle is I think eminently beautifull – From bliss long felt unwillingly we part

Ah spare the weakness of a lovers heart;[4]

It is not much to say that your Verse are by far the best that ever my name was concernd in. I am sorry therefore my name was not hitchd in in the body of the Poem, if the title page should be lost it will appear to be addressed to Mr. Jervais[5]

I am Dear Sir

with the greatest respect

your most humble

and obliged servant

J Reynolds

To Mr. Tho Warton

1 Warton, whose brother Joseph had first approached JR over the New College windows (see Letter 62), had sent JR his newly published *Verses on Sir Joshua Reynolds's Painted Window at New-College Oxford.*

2 'Thy powerful hand has broke the Gothic chain,/And brought my bosom back to truth again' (lines 63–64), as quoted by D. Fairer, *Thomas Warton Corr.*, 1995, 452–53.

3 i.e. Warton's classical tendencies (Hilles).

4 Lines 35–36.

5 JR is named on the first page of the poem, and in the 2nd ed. of 1783 'Reynolds' is substituted for 'Artist' in the conclusion. Thomas Jervais, the glass painter, see Letter 62n1.

103

TO THE AGENT OF THE 4TH DUKE OF RUTLAND 6 JUNE 1782

Source: Belvoir Castle MSS

June 6th 1782

Dear Sir

I shall certainly execute the Commission which His Grace[1] has orderd with the greatest care possible as soon as ever I receive the Picture, and hope it will be such a Picture as will give an opportunity of doing something that shall correspond to His Grace's idea;

I knew very little of Lord Robert,[2] but was very well acquainted with his Graces great affection to him. I therefore felt and simpathised with him I really think in losing him we have paid the full value of what we have got, it is the general opinion that we have lost the most promising Youth in the whole navy, and I am sure from ~~the~~ what I saw of him and the Letters I have seen from him I am most perfectly inclined to confirm their opinion

I beg my most respectful compliments to their Graces and am

Dear Sir

Your most humble

and obedient servant

JReynolds

1 This letter was probably directed to the Duke's agent, Joseph Hill, see Letter 28n1.

2 Lord Robert Manners (1758–82), the Duke's younger brother, died from wounds received while serving under Rodney in the West Indies; JR was commissioned to paint his posthumous portrait (Mannings 1215).

104

TO A NOBLEMAN 17 JUNE 1782

Source: Collection Frits Lugt, Fondation Custodia

Leicesterfields June 17 1782

My Lord

The Duke of Dorset[1] did me the honour to call yesterday morning to speak about the Picture which I did many years since for your Lordship, indeed so long ago that some of them possibly are not so interesting as they were when they were painted, I have therefore in the account made it as easy as possible to your Lordship, charging for them only half-price, as I consider the reason of their not being sent home before as partly my own fault in not reminding your Lordship of them.

As they are painted in the Historical stile I flatter myself they are worth what have charged even to those who have concern in them as likenesses.

The Picture of Miss Obrien which was sent home soon after it was painted[2] I shall have no objection if your Lordship thinks proper of taking it again and strike it out of the bill as I am very certain I could sell it at a higher price than what it is charged.

I am with the greatest respect

your Lordships
most humble and most obedient servant
Joshua Reynolds

1 John Sackville, 3rd Duke of Dorset (1745–99), 'a most admirable cricket-player' (*CP*) and outstanding patron of JR (see J. Coleman, *Apollo*, CXLIII, 1996, 24–30). This letter is possibly addressed to his cousin, Lord George Sackville (1716–85), youngest son of the 1st Duke of Dorset, styled Lord George Germain 1770–82, cr. Viscount Sackville 12 February 1782.

2 Nelly O'Brien (d. 1768), courtesan; JR painted her at least twice c.1762–64 (Wallace Collection and Hunterian, Glasgow; Mannings 1353–54); she was once kept by Lord Thanet (see Letter 278).

105

TO BENNETT LANGTON 12 SEPTEMBER 1782

Source: Beinecke Library (Boswell Papers)

Leicesterfields. Sep. 12 1782

Dear Sir

Tho I am but a tardy correspondent I would not neglect thanking you for your kind invitation, but it is too late in the season to think of any excu<r>sion into the country,

I have seen little of Dr. Johnson this year, he is totally absorbed by Mrs. Thrale I hear however that he is tolerably well and gone to Brightelmstone with Mrs. Thrale,[1] the papers says that they are going afterwards to Italy but of this I have heard nothing from authority, if they go I suppose Miss Burney[2] will be one of the Party as she lives in a manner entirely in that set, I hope you like her last Novel Cecilia, Mr. Burke is in raptures and has writ her a complimentary letter, Mr. Fox[3] says it is a wonderfull performance,

The mirror which you mention I never saw but I have heard a good character of it and that some of the first Scot<c>h Geniuses were engaged in it, some of the Papers are said to written by Wedderburn.[4]

I had a letter from Boswell about a fortnight ago, tho' I think it was more, for it was before his fathers death,[5] he writes in good spirits and expresses his longings after London, Mr. Burke often talks of him[6] and appears to have great affection towards him, he says he is by much the most agreable man he ever saw in all his life,

I hope we shall see you in Town early in the season and be a regular attender at the Club I find Adam Smith[7] intends publishing this winter an Essay on the reason why Imitation pleases, The last day he was there the conversation turned upon that subject. I found it was a subject he had considerd with attention, when I saw him afterwards I told him that my Notions ~~on th~~ perfectly agreed with his that I had wrote a great deal on detach'd bitts of Paper, which I would put together[8] and beg him to look over it, he said he could not for the reason above mentiond that was about finishing an Essay on that Subject

I beg my most respectfull compliments to Lady Rothes[9] My Niece[10] would join with me but she is in the West, and my sister[11] is at my house at Richmond so that I am quite a batchelor

I am with the greatest respect

Yours

JReynolds

1 Johnson did not go to Brighton with Mrs Thrale until 7 October, confirming JR was out of touch with him.
2 Frances Burney published *Evelina* in 1778, see Letter 72, and *Cecilia* in 1782.
3 Charles James Fox (1749–1806).
4 Alexander Wedderburn (1733–1805), Scottish advocate, MP 1761–80, Lord Chancellor 1793–1801; cr. Baron 1780 and Earl of Rosslyn 1801. *The Mirror*, modelled on *The Rambler*, published January 1779–May 1780.
5 Boswell's father had died on 30 August.
6 See Letter 107.
7 Adam Smith (1723–90), Scottish economist, published *The Wealth of Nations*, 1776. JR refers to his essay 'Of the nature of that imitation which takes place in what are called the imitative arts', published in *Essays on Philosophical Subjects*, 1795.
8 Printed in Hilles 1952, 156–58.
9 Mary Lloyd (c.1743–1820), m. 1stly 1763 John, 8th Earl of Rothes (d. 1767), and 2ndly 1770 Bennet Langton.
10 Mary Palmer had left for Devonshire on 14 August.
11 Frances Reynolds, see Letter 98.

106

TO CHARLES, 4TH DUKE OF RUTLAND 13 SEPTEMBER 1782

Source: Belvoir Castle MSS

London Sep 13 1782

My Lord

As the fifteenth is so near, when your Grace said you should be in Town, I have nothing to say but what may be deferrd till that time. The business of this Letter is to thank your Grace (which I forgot to do when I was at Chevely[1]) for the Letter which I receivd from the Keeper of the Park, to inform me that A Buck was ready when ever I should send for it, and I am now ready for the Buck. I have company dine with me next Thursday which I think is the nineteenth[2] and should be glad to have it by that time.

I should have wrote to the Keeper not to trouble your Grace, but I have forgot his name, tho I have not forgot his countenance, which struck me very much.

I am with the greatest respect

Yours Graces

most humble

and obedient servant

JReynolds

1 JR had been at Chevely Park, see Letter 63n2, in the last week of August.

2 JR's pocket-book, 19 September: 'Mr Gibbon &c'.

107

TO JAMES BOSWELL 1 OCTOBER 1782

Source: Beinecke Library (Boswell Papers)

London Oct. 1 1782

Dear Boswell

I take it very kindly that you are so good as to write to me tho I have been so backward in answering your Letters; if I felt the same reluctance in taking a Pencil in my hand as I do a pen I should be as bad a Painter as I am a correspondent, everybody has their tast I love the correspondence of viva voce over a bottle with a great deal of noise and a great deal of nonsence. Mr. Burke dined with me yesterday he talked much of you and with great affection, he says you are the pleasantest man he ever saw[1] and sincerely wishes you would come & live amongst us, all your friends <u>here</u> I believe will subscribe to that wish. Suppose we send you a round Robin, such as we sent to Dr. Johnson,[2] to invite you, will that be an inducement I think I have many in my Eye that would be eager to subscribe – what dye think of Lord Keppell[3] and the Franker of this letter.[4]

My dear Sir I had wrote thus far above a week since[5] but having never spent an evening at home neglected finishing it; I find by the Papers that

Joshua Reynolds, *James Boswell*, 1785; engraving by John Jones 1786

you have lost your Father[6] for which I sincerely condole with you but I hope this accident will not remove at a further distance the hope of seeing you in London.

I am Dear Sir

Yours most affectionately

JReynolds

To / James Boswell Esqre. / of Auchinleck / ~~Edinburgh~~ / By Kilmarnock.[7]
Annotated: (by Boswell) Received 17 Octr. 1782. Sir Joshua Reynolds An agreable letter of freindship.

1 See Letter 105.
2 'The Round Robin we sent [Dr Johnson] from Sir J. Reynolds's to persuade him to alter Goldsmiths epitaph' (Barnard to Boswell, 15 October 1785; Fifer 1976, 216).
3 Augustus Keppel, see Appendix II, had been cr. Viscount Keppel in March 1782.
4 Edward Eliot, see Letter 93n1.
5 This paragraph is written with a different pen.
6 Boswell's father's death was announced in the *St. James's Chronicle* for 5–7 September.
7 The address in Eliot's hand, amended by Lawrie, see Fifer 1976, 127.

108

TO WILLIAM JOHNSON 19 JANUARY 1783

Source: Yale Center for British Art

London Jan 19 1783

My Dear Nephew
I intended to have taken this opportunity of paying the debt I owe you of a long Letter, but delayed it on account of a violent inflammation in my Eyes which prevented me from writing.[1] I am not recover'd, but Mr. Meyers[2] sets out tomorrow morning which must apologise for the shortness of this letter. the whole business of which is to recommend and introduce Mr. Meyers to you. He is the son of a particular friend of mine, and I have no doubt <you> will do him, on my account, as well as his own, whatever services are in your power; Your character is such that I dont wonder every Father wishes to have his son introduced to you.

I suppose you have heard that Offe is married to Mr. Gwatkin and has got a daughter.[3]

I beg my Love to ~~all~~ your Brother – My Neeces & Mr. Young.[4] To Governour Hastings Sir Robert Chambers <& Lady Chambers> & Mr. Macpherson.[5]

I remain
Yours most affectionately
Joshua Reynolds

Polly[6] desires her love to you and all her Cousins

1 Late in the previous year JR had suffered from a 'slight paralytick affection' (Malone 1819, I, cvii).
2 George Charles Meyer (1767–91, son of the miniature painter Jeremiah Meyer (c.1735–89); he became assistant secretary to the preparer of reports in the revenue department at Calcutta (*Bengal Calendar*, 1788, 12) but, having made '18 or £20000', took his own life in Calcutta (*Farington Diary*, 8 November 1793). On 25 September 1783 Johnson wrote to JR that Meyer 'seems a very fine young man' (William Johnson Letterbook, Beinecke Library).
3 See Letter 93.
4 Richard Johnson, his two sisters Elizabeth and Jane, and Philip Yonge (c.1755–88) who married Jane, see Appendix I.
5 See Letter 91n6.
6 Mary Palmer, see Appendix I.

109

TO THE RT REVD THOMAS PERCY 12 FEBRUARY 1783

Source: Hilles 1929, LXVI

London, Feb.12, 1783.

My Lord,

I am ashamed of not answering your Lordship's letter sooner, but I will not fill this with apologies. I spoke to Sir Joseph Banks about it,[1] who says, that on the receipt of Mr. Trocke's letter he gave the bill of lading, which he received from Mr. Trocke, to his broker; that, on his leaving town, at the end of August, he had not received from his broker any account of the wine being arrived; that during his stay in the country, he having confidence in his broker and his broker in him, nothing passed between them concerning the wine; that Mr. Trocke's letter of September 30 was answered, not by return of post, as Sir Joseph thought it useless, but with his first leisure. On his return to town he found the wine lodged in Mr Colman's[2] cellar, according to his orders, and forwarded, without delay, the certificate to Mr Trocke.

The wine was tasted, at the Turk's Head, the meeting before the last, and was pronounced to be good wine, but not yet fit for drinking; we have, therefore, postponed any further progress in it till next year, when, I hope, your Lordship will have an opportunity of tasting it yourself.

I wished to have an opportunity of sending you my last Discourse,[3] though it is scarce worth sending so many miles.

The Club seems to flourish this year; we have had Mr. Fox, Burke, and Johnson very often. I mention this because they are, or have been, the greatest truants.[4] Mr Mason has at last published his translation of Fresnoy,[5] which I would send your Lordship, with the Discourse, if I knew how.

I beg my most respectful compliments to Mrs Percy, and am, with the greatest respect,

Your Lordship's most humble and most
obedient servant,
Joshua Reynolds

1 Percy had sent the Club a hogshead of claret and, not hearing of its arrival, had written to JR (A.C.C. Gaussen, *Percy: Prelate and Poet,* 1908, 194).

2 George Colman, see Appendix II.

3 The *Eleventh Discourse*, delivered on 10 December 1782.

4 Johnson and Fox attended none of the Club dinners in 1781, and in 1782 Johnson and Burke were present three times and Fox once. In each of these years the Club met sixteen times (*Annals of the Club*, 1914, 26ff.).

5 *The Art of Painting of Charles Alphonse Du Fresnoy . . . with annotations by Sir Joshua Reynolds*, York, 1783; see Letter 101.

110

TO THE REVD GEORGE CRABBE 4 MARCH 1783

Source: Hyde Collection

March 4th 1783

Dear Sir

I have ~~sen~~ returned your Poem[1] with Dr. Johnsons Letter to me[2] – if you knew how sparing Dr. Johnson deals out his praises[3] you would be very well content with what he says. I feel myself in some measure flatter'd in the success of my prognostication

Yours sincerely
JReynolds

The Revd / Mr. Crabbe

1 Crabbe's poem, *The Village*, published in May 1783.

2 Dated 4 March 1783, describing Crabbe's poem as 'original, vigorous, and elegant' and suggesting some alterations (Boswell, IV, 175n4, 510).

3 'I am very unwilling to read the manuscripts of authours, and give them by opinion' (Boswell, II, 195).

III

TO PHILIP, 2ND EARL OF HARDWICKE 5 MARCH 1783

Source: British Library (Add MSS 35350, ff.48–48v)

March 5 1783

My Lord

The subject which your Lordship mentions of the interview between the Duke of Monmouth and James the 2d[1] is certainly better calculated for a Picture, than that of the old Duke of Bedford, tho I think even this has scarce enough of intelligeable action and perhaps the expression is too delicate for our art. But the insuperable objection to subjects of that period is the dress. The first effect of such a picture will be allways mean and vulgar and to depart from ~~it~~ <the Costume> is as bad on the other side[2] It was the late Charles Townsend that recommended me the ~~sub~~ interview of The Duke of Bedford and K. James as a subject for a Picture.[3]

I wish it was in my power to answer the Postcript in regard to a subject for the accession of the present R Family What Your Lordship cannot find is very unlikely to occur to me

I am with the greatest respect

Your Lordships most humbe and

obedient servan

JReynolds

1 When Monmouth was captured he 'fell upon his knees, and begged his life in the most abject terms. He even signed a paper, offered him by the king, declaring his own illegitimacy; and then the stern tyrant assured him, that his crime was of such a nature, as could not be pardoned. The duke perceiving that he had nothing to hope from the clemency of his uncle, recollected his spirits, rose up, and retired with an air of disdain' (Goldsmith, *History of England*, 1771, IV, 9f.).

2 JR had vainly urged Benjamin West to clothe the characters in his *Death of Wolfe* in the costumes of antiquity (cf. *Seventh Discourse*, 735–38, and *Tenth Discourse*, 374–76), but later admitted that he had erred (see LT, I, 405–06; J. Galt, *Life of Benjamin West*, 1820, II, 46–50).

3 Charles Townsend (1725–67), Chancellor of the Exchequer, sat to JR in 1755 and 1764 (private collections; Mannings 1758–59). The subject he suggested was the interview in which the distracted king, asking Bedford for aid, is reminded that William Russell (Bedford's son) had been executed as a rebel.

112

TO VALENTINE GREEN 6 MAY 1783

Source: Hilles 1929, LXIX (later in Dobell's Catalogue of Autograph Letters, 1941, no.68)

Sir Joshua Reynolds presents his compliments to Mr. Green – if the choice of the engraver depends on him, he will certainly remember Mr. Green's first application.[1] Her wish, and the ladies who were with her when she sat, appears to be for an engraved print, not a mezzotinto; but the picture is but just begun, and in a state of uncertainty whether it will be a picture worth making a print from it or not.

1 Green had asked to engrave JR's *Mrs Siddons as the Tragic Muse* (exh. RA 1784; Mannings 1619). See Letter 113.

113

TO VALENTINE GREEN 1 JUNE 1783

Source: Private Collection

Leicesterfields June 1st 1783

Sir

You have the pleasure, if it is any pleasure to you of reducing me to a most mortifying situation, I must either treat your hard accusation of being a Liar with the contempt of silence, (which you and your friends may think implies guilt) or I must submit to vindicate myself like a criminal from this heavy charge.[1]

I mentioned in conversation when I had the honour of seeing you last at my house that Mrs. Siddons had wrote a note to me respecting the print;[2] when I assert anything, I have the happiness of knowing that my friends believe what I say without being put to the blush, as I am at present, by being forced to produce proofs, since you tell me in your letter that Mrs. Siddons never did write or even speak to me in favour of any artist.

But ~~Sidd~~ supposing Mrs. Siddons out of the question, my words (on which you ground your demand as right and not as a favour) I do not see can any way be interpreted as such an absolute promise, I intended it to mean only, that you having made the first application ~~should be remembered~~ as a circumstance <should be rememberd by me and> that it should

Joshua Reynolds, *Mrs Siddons*, 1782; engraving by Francis Haward 1787

turn the scale in your favour, supposing equality in other respects

You say you wait the result of my determination. what determination can you expect after such a Letter.

You have been so good as to recommend to me to give for the future unequivocal answers I shall immediatly follow your advice, and do now in the most unequivocal manner inform you that you shall not do the Print[3]

I am Sir

with all humility

and due acknowledgement

of your dignity

your most humble servant

Joshua Reynolds

To Valentine Green, Esq. Associate of the Royal Academy, Mezzotinto Engraver to his Majesty, and to the Elector Palatine[4]

1 Mrs Siddons wrote to JR, 7 May, saying that 'with all submission to his better judgment, that the Picture should be put into the hands of that person, (whose name she cannot at this moment recollect) who has executed the Print of the children from a Picture of Sir Joshua, in so masterly a manner' (Folger Library, Washington); she refers to Francis Haward, the stipple engraver, whose plate after JR's portrait was to be published in 1787 (Whitley 1928, II, 10; Penny 1986, 305–06, and see n3). The wishes of Mrs Siddons, as the sitter, were final.

2 Green wrote to JR, 31 May 1783 (private collection; Hilles 1929, 245–48) accusing him of double-dealing over an engraver's rights: 'at all events it may be Worthy your consideration in future to give unequivocal answers to plain propositions'.

3 See A. Griffiths in *Gainsborough and Reynolds in the British Museum*, 1978, 38–39.

4 Address as recorded by Hilles 1929, 103n2 (taken from the *Literary Gazette*, 1822, 86).

114

TO MRS THEOPHILA GWATKIN 18 SEPTEMBER 1783

Source: Private Collection

Saltram.[1] Thursday Sep 18 1783.

My Dear Offy

I am very much mortified that I could not stay at Port-Elliot till your arrival which I hear will be on Saturday but it would disarange all our schemes Mr. Burke wishes to get to Town as soon as possible, I have full as great a desire to be there, If I was to quit Mr. Burke I should have no excuse left for not visiting all my friends which would take up at least a fortnight longer. However I hope to <see> Mr. Gwatkin and yourself in London this next Winter with your daughter[2] whom I long much to see.

Mr. & Mrs. Burke & Mr. R. Burke[3] desire their Compliments they are more than contented with Port-Elliot and the kind and polite reception they met with from that family

This Letter will probably find you at Port Elliot, if you are gone Mr. Elliot[4] will of course send it after you, if you are there pray make my most respectfull compliments to all the Family and to Miss Munro.[5]

I intended writing to you from London when I had the pleasure of receiving your last Letter and have still a Frank for that purpose but you know what a bad correspondent I am, I hope you will never interpret my neglect to want of that affection which I shall ever have for my dearest Offy.

Yours sincerely

JReynolds

My love to Mr. Gwatkin and if he will not come to see me next year I will come to see him in Cornwall.

1 Saltram, Devonshire, home of the Parker family, see Letter 23n2.
2 Theophila Gwatkin, the original of JR's *Simplicity*.
3 Edmund and Mrs Jane Burke and their son Richard Burke (1758–94), see *Burke Corr.*, v, 113.
4 Edward Eliot, see Letter 93n1.
5 Unidentified.

115

TO SIR WILLIAM FORBES 18 OCTOBER 1783

Source: Private Collection

My Dear Sir

I would not neglect a minute acknowledging the receipt of your letter, tho I must tell you this is not very usual with me. It gave me more pleasure to hear you were in England and intend coming to Town, than even the news you give me in it concerning the payment of Lord Errols bill:[1] you dont mention the time of your being here, I hope if you stint your time to a couple of weeks that those weeks will be when the Town is full, at present it is a desert, I never knew it so empty as it is at present. the only object of entertainment I think is Mrs. Siddons[2] of whom I dare say you have heard much talk.

I have wrote by this post to Mr. Wauchope with a duplicate of Lord Errols Bill[3]

I beg my most respectfull to Lady Forbes.

I am

Dear Sir

Your most humble

and obedient servant

Joshua Reynolds

Annotated: Sir Joshua Reynolds/Londn/18 Octr/1783

1 See Letters 82, 272, 277.

2 Mrs Siddons had taken London by storm in the 1782–83 Drury Lane season, playing the lead in Garrick's *Isabella* between 10 October 1782 and 5 June 1783 and again on 8 October 1783; by the Queen's command she was made reader to the Royal princesses (C.B. Hogan ed., *The London Stage 1660–1800*, v, 1968, 541, 560, 650).

3 John Wauchope W.S., see Letter 277.

116

TO THE REVD JOSEPH PALMER 28 NOVEMBER 1783

Source: Private Collection

London Nov 28 1783

Dear Nephew

I am very glad to hear of Mr. Dicksons[1] success – In regard to yourself – Mr. Burke tells me, and I believe it is true, that ~~the~~ a recommendation from hence is not worth a farthing, that it is ridiculous to ask it.

I wonder you have not seen Mr. Pelham.[2] I know him very well, & waited on him the moment I heard he was appointed secretary he was not at home, but returned my visit the next day, when I mentiond you to him he expressd himself as very much inclined to do you service and in reality I have more hopes from him than from any <of the> other Secretaries, he is a very amiable character we used to meet often at Mr. Parkers,[3] you must make some apology for not having waited on him sooner – I hear this moment that he is arrived in ~~Tow~~ London – if true I shall have an opportunity probably of seeing him.

Miss Palmer is at Roscrow but I believe intends to leave it soon and go to Port Elliot,[4] it will be some time before she will be in Town.

Yours with the greatest
affection
JReynolds

I beg my most respectfull Compts to the Archbishop and Lord Naas.[5]

1 Probably the Revd. William Dickson (1745–1804), first chaplain to Lord Northington, lord lieutenant of Ireland 1783–84; on 12 December 1783 he was made Bishop of Down and Connor.

2 Thomas Pelham (1756–1826), 2nd Earl of Chichester 1805; chief secretary to the lord lieutenant of Ireland (Lord Northington) August 1783–January 1784.

3 At Saltram, Devonshire.

4 Roscrow, near Penryn, Cornwall, formerly the home of Alexander Pendarves; Port Elliot, home of Edward Eliot (later Lord Eliot, see Letter 93n1), at St German's, Cornwall.

5 Charles Agar (1736–1809), Archbishop of Cashel 1779–1801, later Baron Somerton (1795), Viscount Somerton (1800) and Earl of Normanton (1806); John Bourke (c.1729–92), styled Lord Naas, son of Viscount (later Earl of) Mayo; Irish MP 1763–90.

117

TO PHILIP, 2ND EARL OF HARDWICK 5 DECEMBER 1783

Source: British Library (Add MSS 35350, ff.49–49v)

Dec 5th 1783

My Lord

May I presume to ~~ha~~ <beg> a particular favour of your Lordship – I have a Nephew at Cambridge[1] who wishes to take orders, but he wants the qualification necessary, which is a curacy in the Diocese of Ely, without such qualification, or a recommendation to the Bishop, whom he has not the honour of knowing, he will probably not be so soon ordained as he wishes, he having a Living promised him immediatly on that event. – what I would request of your Lordship is a Line to your Lordships Brother[2] to desire if my Nephew – Mr. Palmer has every other requisite that he would dispense with his want of a Curacy in Cambridge-shire

I hope your Lordship will pardon the liberty which I have taken

I am with the greatest respect
Your Lordships
most humble
and most obedient servant
Joshua Reynolds

P S Mr Palmer is now in Town and if His Lordship pleases would be glad to carry a line from His Lordship to his Brother the Bishop

1 JR's nephew John Palmer, see Appendix I.
2 James Yorke (1730–1808) Bishop of Ely 1781–1808. On 7 December Lord Hardwicke forwarded to his brother JR's letter, endorsed: 'Be so good as to let me know what Answr I shall make to Sir Joshua He is one I wd willingly oblige if I could'.

118

TO JAMES BOSWELL 18 FEBRUARY 1784

Source: National Library of Scotland (Acc.4796, Box 87)

London Feb. 18 1784

My Dear Sir

I am glad to hear we shall have the pleasure of seeing you soon amongst us,[1] we find you wanting at our club, The business of the house of Commons[2] has prevented our having had much of their Company this year; we have elected two new members, good men and true Lord Palmerston and Sir Willm. Hamilton[3]

In regard to Dr. Johnson he has not been out of door for some months, I fear grows worse and worse, the Doctors however do not despair. He seldom sees any of his friends, he sleeps half the day in consequence of the quantity of Opium which he continually taking; The answer today to my enquiry was that he was but poorly, his legs are much swelled which I fear is but a bad ~~sipt~~ simptom. We still hope that he will weather it the loss would be terrible, we have been acquainted for thirty years, if it was possible to supply the place of such a man I am too old to begin new affections.

I thank you for your book, we are of the same general opinion concerning subordination, but I am not politician enough to know how or to what degree they are applicable to the subject of your pamphlet.[4]

I beg my most respectfull compliments to Sir Wm. Forbes, I thought it very unlucky that Miss Palmer[5] was not in Town to have paid her respects to Lady Forbes, I wishd very much to have had an oportunity of seeing more than I did of that very amiable Lady.

I am with the greatest respect

Yours sincerely

JReynolds

James Boswell Esq / Edinburgh

Postmark: 16 / FE[6]

1 See Letter 107.
2 The Club had supported Fox's India Bill, the rejection of which by the Lords, at the King's direction, led to the dissolution of the Fox–North coalition and the appointment of William Pitt as Prime Minister. The bitterly contested March election centred on the relationship between the King and Parliament.
3 Henry Temple, 2nd Viscount Palmerston (1739–1802), MP 1762–1802 (father of the 19th-century Prime Minister) and Sir William Hamilton (see Appendix II); JR proposed them both for the Club in 1783 and they were elected in December. Palmerston had previously been black-balled in July.
4 *A Letter to the People of Scotland*, 1783.
5 Mary Palmer, see Appendix I.
6 But the date of the letter is written as 18 February.

119

TO THOMAS ASTLE 8 MARCH 1784

Source: Pierpont Morgan Library

London March 8th 1784

Dear Sir

I am very much flattered by your kind communication of that part of your work which relates to Painting and illuminations which I have read with great pleasure and improvement.[1] I can easily perceive that it will be a learned and accurate work, my studies have been very little in that line, consequently cannot throw in even a mite of assistance

I am with the greatest respect

Your most humble

& obedient servant

JReynolds

I dont know whether it is generally known that the word Limner ~~comes~~

~~fro~~ is a corruption of Illuminator – Painters in miniature in Water Colours are still called Limners with propriety – The vulgar as improperly call us painters in Oil Limners.

1 Astle's *Origin and Progress of Writing*, 1784, in which he discussed (chapter viii) the paintings, ornaments and illuminations in old books (Hilles).

120

TO [STEPHEN FULLER][1] 8 APRIL 1784

Source: Historical Society of Pennsylvania

Leicesterfields April 8th 1784

Dear Sir

I have the pleasure to inform ~~that~~ you that the Academicians have unanimously given the preference to Mr. Bacons model for the Statue of Lord Rodney[2] – he intends waiting on you tomorrow to receive your further orders

I am with great respect

Your most obedient

humble servant

JReynolds

1 Fuller was the London agent for the Jamaica House of Assembly, to whom this letter was presumably addressed (LT, II, 442).

2 John Bacon, see Appendix II. At the RA Council meeting of 27 February, two letters were read from Jamaica requesting the Academy to choose a sculptor to design a statue of Admiral George Brydges Rodney, 1st Baron Rodney (1719–92), whose defeat of the comte de Grasse in 1782 had saved Jamaica from the French. Bacon's monument, dated 1786, remains in Spanish Town, Jamaica, and a *modello* is in the Victoria and Albert Museum.

121

TO EDMUND BURKE 24 AUGUST 1784

Source: Sheffield Archives (WWM Bk P 1/1914)

London Aug 24 1784

Dear Sir

Tho I have but a minute to spare I would not neglect letting you know, (<u>you</u> who interest yourself so very sincerely in every thing that relate to me) that I receiv'd a Letter yesterday from the Lord Chamberlain[1] appointing me the Kings principal Painter[2] – I beg my Compliments to Mrs Burk – Miss Palmer[3] sat out this Evening for Devonshire

Yours sincerely

JReynolds

1 James, 7th Earl of Salisbury, see Appendix II.

2 See Letters 123–25.

3 Mary Palmer, see Appendix I.

122

TO THE BRISTOL CORPORATION 31 AUGUST 1784

Source: Bristol Record Office

London August 31t 1784

Sir

I have the honour to inform you that Lord Ashburtons Picture[1] will be sent to morrow morning by Wiltshires Waggon, which I hope will arrive safe and meet with the approbation of the Corporation my price for that size, which is what we call half-length, is one hundred Guineas

I am with the greatest respect

your most obedient servant

Joshua Reynolds

1 John Dunning (1731–83), cr. Baron Ashburton 1782, MP 1768–82, who moved the resolution in the House of Commons, that 'the power of the Crown has increased, is increasing, and ought to be diminished', elected to the Club 1777; a remarkably ugly man, he sat to JR in 1768 and 1772–73. This portrait for the Bristol Corporation was destroyed by fire in 1831 (Mannings 541).

123

TO JAMES BOSWELL 2 SEPTEMBER 1784

Source: Beinecke Library (Boswell Papers)

London Sep 2d 1784

Dear Sir

I had no news to write you relating to our friend Dr. Johnson till today when the Lord Chancellor called on <me> to acquaint me with the consequence of his <u>pious</u> negociation,[1] He express'd himself much mortified that it was recievd not with the warmth he expected. He says he did his utmost but he fears he has not the art of begging successfully – he would take another opportunity but you know says he we must not teize people, however I would by no means have this journey put off if necessary to the establishment of his health on account of the expence, It would be scandalous & shamefull that the paltry consideration of mony should stand in the way to prevent any thing from being done that may any way contribute to the health or amusement of such a man, a man who is an honour to the country. He desired me to inform him that in the meantime he should mortgage his Pension to him (the Lord Chancellor) and should draw on him to the amount of five or six hundred Pounds.[2] The Chancellor explained the Idea of the mortgage to be only this, that he wished this business to be conducted in such a manner as that Dr. Johnson should appear to be under the least possible obligation. I would not neglect acquainting you with this negociation which can hardly be called a successfull one tho I have just wrote a long letter to Dr. Johnson, and have company with me.

Poor Ramsay is dead and your humble servant succeeds him as Kings Principal Painter[3] – if I had known what a shabby miserable place it is, I would not have asked for it; besides as things have turned out I think a certain person is not worth speaking to, nor speaking of so I shall conclude

Yours sincerely
JReynolds

James Boswell Esq / Edinburgh

1 With JR's approval, Boswell had written to the Lord Chancellor, Lord Thurlow, requesting a Royal Bounty for the dying Dr Johnson, so that he could travel in Italy; Thurlow told Boswell (letter of 28 June 1784) he would consult JR as to the necessary sum, as described in this letter (LT, II, 445). Johnson thanked JR in his letter of 9 September 1784. See Boswell, IV, 327, 336, 348.

2 Thurlow had not in fact applied to the King, but was here making an offer on his own account (LT, II, 450–51).

3 Ramsay had died on 10 August; for the office of King's Principal Painter, see Letters 124 and 125.

124

TO CHARLES, 4TH DUKE OF RUTLAND 24 SEPTEMBER 1784

Source: Belvoir Castle MSS

London Sep 24th 1784

My Lord
I beg leave to return my most sincere thanks for the kind Letter[1] which I had the honour of receiving yesterday and particularly to thank your Grace for your good intention towards my Nephew,[2] I am very sensible that even in your high situation you cannot allways serve those whom you most wish to serve, but I was so thoroughly persuaded of your Graces good inclinations, that tho I have sollicited every Lord Lieutenant that has gone to Ireland I have <not> said anything to your Grace, from a certain confidence that when an opportunity offerd my Nephew would not be forgot.

Your Graces Picture is finishd and I will immediatly make the alteration required in Lord Chathams Picture and send them both to Belvoir Castle.[3]

I dined with Lady Lucan[4] last Sunday who told me of her intention of painting a Picture for your Grace but was undetermined what it should be I shall call on her tomorrow to acquaint her with what your Grace mentions about the Protector Duke of Somersets picture[5] which I should think would be the best thing for her to do. I question her success in an Historical picture.

In regard to the Nativity[6] the falling off of the Colour must be occasioned by the shaking in the Carriage, but as it now is in a state of rest it will remain as it is for ever, what it wants I will next year go on purpose to mend it, and from Belvoir I should be glad to proceed to Ireland, but I heard yesterday from Mrs Siddons such a sad account of the liberty boys[7] that I have hardly courage to venture She came away in a terrible fright and has not yet recoverd herself.

The Place which I have the honour of holding of the Kings principal painter is a place of not so much profit and of near equal dignity with His Majestys Rat-catcher[8] The salary is £38 per annum and for every whole-length I am to paid £50 insteed of £200 which I have from every body else Your Grace sees that this new honour is not likely to elate me very much. I need not make any resolution to behave with the same familiarity as I used to with my old acquaintance.

I am with the greatest respect
Your Graces most humble and
most obedient servant
Joshua Reynolds

Miss Palmer's[9] in Devonshire but I beg my most respectfull compliments to the Duchess

1 Dated 16 September (Yale Center for British Art).
2 Joseph Palmer had been given an Irish living by Lord Townshend and wished to be advanced. On 11 February Rutland had been appointed lord lieutenant of Ireland in succession to Lord Northington.
3 'Your Graces Picture' could refer either to Lord Robert Manners (Mannings 1215; see Letter 103) or the whole length of the Duke exh. RA 1785 (destroyed; Mannings 1186). The 2nd Earl of Chatham (1756–1835) sat to JR in 1779 (Mannings 1454), but the picture was destroyed at Belvoir in 1816, see Letter 283.
4 See Letter 87.
5 Edward Seymour, 1st Earl of Hertford and Duke of Somerset (c.1506–52), Protector of the Realm 1547–49.
6 JR's painting for the New College window, see Letters 62 and 70 (see Mannings 2106).
7 As lord lieutenant of Ireland, Rutland received a petition in July demanding protection for Irish trade, freedom of the press and more equal representation; by September discontent was spreading through Ireland. For Mrs Siddons in Dublin, see Letter 125.
8 JR was sworn in as Principal Painter on 1 September (LT, II, 448); His Majesty's Rat Catcher was paid £48. 3s 4d per annum. See Letter 135.
9 Mary Palmer, see Letter 121.

125

TO THE RT REVD JONATHAN SHIPLEY 25 SEPTEMBER 1784

Source: Beinecke Library (Hilles Collection)

London Sep 25 1784

My Lord

Your Lordship congratulation on my succeeding Mr. Ramsay I take very kindly but it is a most miserable office, it is reduced from two hundred to thirty eight pounds per annum, the Kings Rat catcher I believe is a better place, and I am to be paid <for the Pictures> only a fourth part of what I have from other people, so that the Portraits of their Majesties are not likely to be better done now, then they used to be,[1] I should be ruined if I was to paint them myself.

I thank your Lordship for your kind invitation to Chilbolton,[2] but I fear it is impracticable this year. It is not impossible but next year I may have the honour of waiting on your Lordship at St. Asaph, If I go to Ireland I certainly will go that way. I have just receivd an Invitation from the Duke of Rutland either to come this year or the next, if he stays there so long, of that he seems to have some doubt, Mrs. Siddons who is just returned gives a most terrible account of the liberty boys.[3] They pelted the Duke and Dutches. All the time the Play was acting. She receivd a great many blows which were intended she believes for them, however of this she is not sure, she considers herself as having had a very narrow escape from being tarred and featherd. She receivd Letters that this would certainly be case unless she gave a certain portion of her profits to the Poor, <to> this request she was not likely to comply and was therefore privately conceild for three day in the house of the Dutchess of Leinster[4] from whence she retired to Cork in great fear, being told that <at> every avenue of Dublin a watch was set to catch her. It was impossible in the midst of her narration which she made very pathetic, to ~~mak~~ prevent smiling every now and then when the Words came tarring & feathering were repeated with such solemnity as if she thought there were no words in the English language that would excite so much horror. This is certainly very excusable in a person than has been so much frightend at it, but I cannot help smiling ~~at~~ this minute at the Idea of Mrs Siddons being tarred & featherd.

The punishment threatend to the Duke of Rutland is to cut off his Ears, and she says that two or three times he has very narrowly escaped falling into their hands, this mode of punishment has not much more heroic sound than the other, however it is seriously terrible to think even of the possibility of such a thing happening Mrs. Siddons thinks he is in real danger

I beg my most respectfull compliments to Mrs. Shipley and all the family / and am with the greatest respect

Your Lordships most humble and most obedient servant

Joshua Reynolds

1 JR's predecessor, Allan Ramsay (1713–84), had employed a studio for the production of replicas of his Royal portraits, of which over 150 pairs are recorded.

2 Shipley, Bishop of St Asaph, was also rector of Chilbolton, Hampshire, from 1761; he sat to JR in 1776 (Mannings 1616) and had entertained JR in London in the spring of 1784 (pocket-books).

3 See also Letter 124. Mrs Siddons was in Ireland from the end of June to the beginning of September. She arrived in Dublin on 24 June and she also played in Belfast, Cork

and Limerick; on 10 June she played Lady Randolph in Home's *Douglas* for the Viceroy's command performance at the Theatre Royal, Dublin, which was wholly disrupted by 'the clamour of a justly incensed people' against the Westminster government (see H.M. Burke, *Eighteenth Century Life*, 22, III, 1998, 13–18); in August she was ill; she was then accused of not performing in Dublin for the benefit of William Brereton, so that on 5 October 1784 at Drury Lane she was loudly hissed (T. Campbell, *Mrs Siddons*, 1839 ed., 143–50; C.B. Hogan ed., *The London Stage 1660–1800*, V, 1968, 742).

4 Letter 9n14. The principal Leinster seat was Carton, Maynooth.

126

TO WILLIAM ROSCOE 2 OCTOBER 1784

Source: Liverpool Record Office (Roscoe MSS 920 ROS 3112)

London Oct. 2d 1784

Sir

I ought to be ashamed to acknowledge receiving a second letter before I have answer'd the first, but I beg you to believe that I allways intended it, however I may have been prevented. I am now to return you my thanks for the present of your poetical works,[1] which I have read with the greatest pleasure, it is approaching to impertinence to say that I <was> much surprised at seeing such excellence in a work which I had never heard of before or the Authors name ever reachd my ears. However I found other people were not quite so ignorant I mentioned the Poem to Mr. Mason who dined with me a few days ago.[2] I dont recollect that he knew your name, but he was well acquainted with the Poem which he read when it was first publish'd. I had the satisfaction of hearing my opinion fully confirmed by his authority.

I am very glad to hear of the success of your Exhibition. I shall allways wish to contribute to it to the best of my power[3]

What I said in the beginning of the letter requires some apology, it dropt involuntary from me, the truth is I receive such a quantity of insipid common-place poetry that I hope you will excuse by suspecting yours to be of that class, but I do assure you very sincerely I never was more agreably disapointed

I am with the greatest respect

your most obedient servant

Joshua Reynolds

Willm. Roscoe Esq Liverpool

1 In 1777 Roscoe published *Mount Pleasant, a descriptive Poem and An Ode on the Institution of a Society of Art in Liverpool.*
2 William Mason, see Letter 101n7, had recently translated Du Fresnoy's *Art of Painting,* see Letter 109; he had dined with JR on 26 September (pocket-book).
3 Roscoe was both Treasurer and Vice-President of the Society for promoting Painting and Design in Liverpool; JR was represented at the Society's second exhibition in 1784 with Col. Banastre Tarleton (National Gallery; Mannings 1733), and *View of the Thames from Richmond* (Tate Gallery; Mannings 2189), see Letters 127 and 129, and E. Morris and E. Roberts, *The Liverpool Academy and Other Exhibitions of Contemporary Art in Liverpool 1774–1867,* 1998, 507).

127

TO WILLIAM ROSCOE 18 OCTOBER 1784

Source: Yale Center for British Art

London Oct. 18 1784

Dear Sir

I am very glad you have not sent away Coll. Tarletons Picture, it belongs to his brother who employed me,[1] and tho I am not paid for it, yet I would by no means be thought to detain the Picture for that reason, if therefore Mrs. Tarleton or any of the family wish to have it in their possession I beg they would send for it.

I think myself much obliged to you for your trouble and attention in this business

I am with the greatest respect
your most obedient
humble servant
Joshua Reynolds

Wm. Roscoe Esq Liverpool

1 Col. Banastre Tarleton (1754–1833, Bt. 1816) sat to JR for the full-length exh. RA 1782 (National Gallery; Mannings 1733) also exh. at Liverpool in 1784 (see Letter 126); the picture had been dispatched to 'his mother, near Liverpool' (Cormack, 165), and Judy Egerton has plausibly suggested that the entry 'Col. Tarleton 210.0.0' in JR's Ledgers should be dated on, or soon after, 10 July 1792 (National Gallery cat., *British School,* 1998, 227n43); in March 1791 the sitter's brother, John Tarleton (b. 1755), requested payment to JR of 250 gns. (J. Meyer, *Early Art in Liverpool,* 1876, 54; Penny 1986, 300).

128

TO THE RT REVD JONATHAN SHIPLEY 26 OCTOBER 1784

Source: Hilles 1929, LXXX

London Oct. 26 1784

My Lord

I am ashamed of the mistakes which I daily make. The accident of writing Kimbolton insteed of Chilbolton[1] was occasiond by a Gentleman present assuring me that it was spelt with a K, the I and M. followed of course, and having but a moderate opinion of my own memory, and allways in a hurry, I did not give myself the trouble of looking for your Lordship's Letter.

The publication which is consigned to Mr. Burke, is as I understand a plan of an Establishment in India for promoting all knowledge relating to the east, the government, natural history, language, &c.[2]

I remember Sir Francis Bacon advises as a refined piece of art, to mention sometimes in a postscript, as if just recollected what is in reality the chief subject of the Letter.[3] But as I dont love tricks of any kind, I confess to your Lordship that my chief reason of writing now is in consequence of meeting lately the Burkes, we were talking of the cause of the dean of St. Asaph[4] being to be argued next term in the Kings-bench, and from thence talked of the great advantage it would be if young Richard – Mr Burkes son was engaged in a cause of so great importance and public attention.

I thought afterwards that as many thing are not done, not because they were thought improper but merely from not being thought off, I would take the liberty of mentioning this to your Lordship. I confess I should be extremely happy, if by such an accident as this I should be the means, through your Lordship, of giving an opportunity of bringing into public notice a young man of whose abilities I have the highest opinion, it may be something too, that he will of course have the assistance of the abilities of that extraordinary family.

I trust your Lordship will excuse the liberty I have taken, even tho it approaches, as I fear it does, to impertinence in recommending a young advocate in a matter of so great consequence but I am confident if he has the opportunity he will acquit himself with honour to himself and to yr. Lordships satisfaction.

I am with the greatest respect
Your Lordships most obedient servant
Joshua Reynolds

1 See Letter 125, where JR alleges he wrote Kimbolton.
2 On 27 February 1784 Sir William Jones had written to Burke from India enclosing his *Discourse on the institution of a Society for inquiring into the history . . . antiquities, arts, sciences, and literature of Asia*; this became the Royal Asiatic Society of Bengal (*Burke Corr.*, v, 127–28).
3 Bacon's Essays, 'Of Cunning': 'I knew one, that when he wrote a Letter, he would put that which was most Materiall, in the Post-script, as if it had been a By-matter'. JR re-read Bacon while revising the *Discourses* for a collected edition (Hilles 1936, 190).
4 William Davies Shipley (1745–1826), Dean of St. Asaph 1774–1826, Bishop Shipley's son. He had been responsible for having reprinted a pamphlet by Sir William Jones (the Bishop's son-in-law) on the evils of representation; he was prosecuted for libel but he was acquitted after the case was heard at the King's Bench, beginning 8 November 1784 (Hilles, quoting T.B. Howell, *State Trials*, 1816, XXI, 847f.).

129

TO WILLIAM ROSCOE 19 NOVEMBER 1784

Source: Hilles 1929, LXXXI (original sold Sotheby's, 1 August 1939, lot 774)

London Nov 19. 1784

Dear Sir

I have receiv'd the Landskip perfectly safe,[1] I do not remember being told by anybody that it had receiv'd any damage on its arrival at Liverpool. Mr. Pack[2] called on me a few days since to desire I would lend him a picture to copy for his improvement; about three or four years ago I lent him many for that purpose, and he used to bring me his works from the life, in order to be told their faults, as he was only one of many that did the same, I did not recollect the name, nor am I sure I ever knew it. If all those whom I have endeavourd to help forward by lending them pictures and telling them their faults should do me the honour of calling themselves my scholars, I should have the greatest school that ever Painter had. If those young Painters think that from such an intercourse they have a right to say they are my scholars, they are very welcome, I have no kind of objection to it. There is certainly no great harm done in their endeavouring to produce a prejudice in their favour. If I may without vanity suppose this to be the reason of their wishing such an opinion to be entertained in the Country, and as you see, it is not entirely without some foundation.

I return you many thanks for your kind intention of speaking to Mr. John Tarleton ab[out] the Picture when he returns from France.[3]

I am with the greatest respect
your most faithfull and
obedient servant
J Reynolds

1 *View of the Thames from Richmond*, see Letter 126n3.
2 Faithful Christopher Packe (1750–1840), painter from Norwich, working in Liverpool 1783-86.
3 See Letter 127.

130

TO CHARLES SMITH 3 DECEMBER 1784

Source: Hilles 1929, LXXXII

London, Dec. 3, 1784

Dear Sir,

I take this opportunity of returning you my sincere thanks for the present you was so obliging as to send me of the yellow colour, which is certainly very beautiful, and I believe will do very well in oil, though perhaps better with water.[1]

I hope you meet with the success you so well deserve. I am only concerned that you are so much out of the way of making that improvement which your Genius would certainly have enabled you to make, if you had staid in England. A painter who has no rivals, and who never sees better works than his own, is but too apt to rest satisfied, and not take what appears to be a needless trouble, of exerting himself to the utmost, pressing his Genius as far as it will go.

I saw the other day, at Mr. Bromil's,[2] a picture of a child with a dog, which, after a pretty close examination, I thought my own painting; but it was a copy, it seems, that you made many years ago.

I am with great respect,
Your most obedient humble servant,
Joshua Reynolds

1 Smith had arrived in Calcutta in September 1783, see Appendix II; see also Letters 58 and 59.
2 William Brummell (d. 1794), father of Beau Brummell; private secretary to Lord North 1770–82; JR's portrait of his sons was exh. RA 1783 (Kenwood; Mannings 269).

131

TO EDMUND BURKE 18 DECEMBER 1784

Source: Sheffield Archives (WWM Bk P1/1956)

Dear Sir

If I thought this Letter was to be paid for, I really believe it would have stopt my writing, as I have not any thing to say worth twopence. We can scarce expect you would come to town on purpose to attend the Funeral.[1] If you think of doing Dr. Johnsons memory that honour, we have fixed on you as the first Pall Bearer with Mr. Fox, the Rest are Lord Palmerstone Mr. Windham Genl Paoli & Mr. Langton[2]

We meet at ten o'clock on Monday in Bolt Court, by eleven we must set out in order to be at the Abbey by twelve

I am just come from Lord Palmerstones Dinner it was composed of the Club only, except Dr. Warren who is likewise to be of the Club if it so please his Brother Doctor.[3]

I am with the greatest respect

Yours

J Reynolds

Annotated: (in Mrs Burke's hand) Sir Joshua Reynolds Wrote Decr 18th 1784

1 Dr Johnson had died on 13 December 1784.

2 Charles Fox, see Letter 30n5; 2nd Viscount Palmerston, see Letter 118n3; William Windham, see Letter 187n2; General Pasquale Paoli, see Letter 92n3, and Bennet Langton, Appendix II; each was a member of the Club.

3 Dr Richard Warren (1731–97), who attended Dr Johnson in his last illness, was elected on 14 December 1784. The only other member with a medical degree was Dr George Fordyce (1736–1802).

132

TO EDMOND MALONE [DECEMBER 1784]

Source: Folger Shakespeare Library

Dear Sir

You must be a zede signifies, you wont be again said, you will have your wicked will.

In the other instance, How a man a zed is exactly what we find in Shakespear and other old writers You have said now.[1]

[DECEMBER 1784]

The Exmoor Dialogue might be much better done if instead of making an z for an s the author had saught after the old language the old words which still exist or at least did exist when I was a boy, such as daverd,[2] applied to a faded flower or a woman past her prime derived undoubtedly from cadavorosus; a word that Milton would have seized with greediness if it had occurred to him.

I have sent by your servant my Discourse[3] which I shall take as a ~~fa~~ great favour if you not only will examine critically but will likewise add a little elegance.

Yours sincerely

J Reynolds

1 An Exmoor Scolding ... between two Sisters ... also an Exmoor Courtship, anon., 1771, contains 'a zed' three times, but without a gloss. JR refers to *Othello*, IV, ii, 204.

2 Mary Palmer wrote a *Devonshire Dialogue*, published by her grandson James F. Palmer in 1837, in which (37) the expression 'like a daver'd rose' is glossed (42) as from Daveren, teut., to tremble.

3 Apparently the *Twelfth Discourse*, delivered on 10 December 1784; Malone later stated that 'four of the latter Discourses ... the author did me the honour to submit to my perusal' (Malone, 1819, I, xliv). Hilles 1929 dated this letter 1788, but subsequently changed this to 1784 (Hilles, *Notes*).

133

TO MISS [MARY] HAMILTON [JANUARY 1785]

Source: Beinecke Library (Hilles Collection)

Sir Joshua Reynolds presents his Compliments to Miss Hamilton[1] and begs to know if any time between three and four o'clock to day would be convenient for him to wait on her.

Leicesterfields Friday

1 Doubtless Mary Hamilton (1756–1816) niece of Sir William Hamilton. Probably written early in 1785 when JR was renovating his half-length portrait of Sir William Hamilton (Mannings 822) which the sitter had just presented to Mary Hamilton; JR's fee for this work was a kiss (E.G. & F. Anson ed., *Mary Hamilton*, 1925, 269).

134

TO CHARLES, 4TH DUKE OF RUTLAND 30 MAY 1785

Source: Belvoir Castle MSS

London May 30th 1785

My Lord

I hope your Grace will never think that it was want of respect has made me so long defer answering your Letter. I waited till the Exhibition opend, in order to see the works of the Landskip painters. The person I fixed on to send to Ireland I had not till lately an opportunity of speaking to, on the subject.

Mr Webber[1] is the person who has accepted the proposal and intends setting out for Ireland in about three weeks He is much in the habit of taking views from Nature, some of which are in the Exhibition which he did from drawings he made when he was with Capt. Cook they are excellent Pictures and I am sure Your Grace will approve of his manner of Painting.

The Picture of Rubens' Wife was sold at a greater price than it <was> worth. It was not one of Rubens best works and there was a seperation of the Pannel on which it was painted from top to bottom which had been ill mended.[2]

We are going to erect a Monument to the memory of Dr. Johnson. we have all subscribed two Guineas each. I will in consequence of what Your Grace has said take the liberty of putting down your name for that sum.[3] I acquainted Lady Lucan[4] with your Graces request in your own words as they were so flattering to her Ladyship. She answerd that she should set about it immediatly as she has now found a Picture of the Protector Duke of Somerset which is in the possession of the Marquis of Buckingham,[5] but she says it is but an indifferent Picture and she fears her Copy will be no great ornament to your Cabinet.

I dont know how to give a description of my Venus[6] as it is called; it is no more than a Naked woman sitting on the ground leaning her back against a tree, and a boy peeping behind another tree, I have made the landskips as well as I could in the Manner [deletion] of Titian. Tho it meets with the approbation of my friends it is not what it ought to be, nor what I thought I should make it. The next I paint I am confident will be better.

I have begun a whole length of the Duc de Chartres for the Prince of Wales and the Prince is to sit for him.[7] I have sent a head of the Prince to the Exhibition which I hear is much approved off. He dined with the Academy at our Great dinner before the opening of the Exhibition as did likewise the Duc de Chartres, The Prince behaved with great propriety, we were all mightily pleased with him I am sorry – spatiis exclusus iniquis[8] I have only room to say that I shall take care to execute your Graces Orders respecting the Pictures of the young Lords when it comes from the Exhibition.[9] I am with the greatest & c

J Reynolds

1 A set of four Irish landscapes by Solomon Delane (1727–1812) remain at Belvoir Castle, and it was presumably the commissioning of these views which concerned JR at this time. John Webber (1752–93), landscape painter, accompanied Captain James Cook on his last expedition to the South Seas in 1779–80; he showed eight oriental landscapes at the RA in 1785.
2 From the Van Haveren collection in Antwerp, where it hung with the celebrated *Chapeau de paille* by Rubens (now National Gallery, London); in 1781 JR noted that 'though equally well painted, from not having the same advantage of dress receives no attention' (*Journey* 1996, 81, 165n340, 207; now private collection, Brussels).
3 Rutland's name does not appear on the list of subscribers as printed *GM*, LX, 1790, I, 3f.
4 See Letter 87n3.
5 See Letter 178 and Appendix II.
6 Exh. RA 1785 (private collection; Mannings 2174); the second version of 1786 (private collection; Mannings 2175), see Letter 154.
7 The duc de Chartres: Philippe 'Egalité', later duc d'Orléans (1747–93); the whole-length portrait, in hussar uniform, is in the Royal collection (Mannings 1145). JR painted a whole-length of the Prince of Wales in 1786 which was given to the Marquess of Hastings (now Arundel Castle; Mannings 721), see Letters 285–87.
8 Virgil, *Georgics*, IV, 147.
9 Rutland's three sons, Lords Charles, Robert and William Manners (Mannings 1217), see Letter 141.

135

TO CHARLES, 4TH DUKE OF RUTLAND 20 [JUNE] 1785

Source: Belvoir Castle MSS

Leicesterfields July 20 1785[1]

My Lord

Lord Lucan who is just about setting out for Ireland will present to Your Grace the Picture which Lady Lucan has made of the Protector Duke of Somerset.[2]

The Landskip Painter <Mr. Webber> which I have engagd is at least equal, I think better than Marlow.[3] In regard to <my> visiting Ireland this

Summer I am loth to abandon the Idea, at the same time it appears impossible, when I consider the quantity of work which I have before me

May I now how beg Your Graces indulgence and sollicit your interest in a matter which relates to my self. I believe I mentioned to Your Grace the reduction of the Salary of the Kings Painter from two hundred to fifty Pounds per annum.[4] As there is great difficulty of having the old salary restored as it would open the door to such numerous Sollicitations, I thought there was an opportunity of giving me a very honourable compensation in making me secretary & Register to the Order of the Bath; Upon this ground, by means of Mr. Elliot[5] I asked for it, but it was too late ~~he had~~ Mr. Pitt had already promised it to Mr. Lake[6] a Gentleman who has some office in the Treasury. Since this negociation Mr. Lake has been appointed one of the Commissioners of Accounts, a place of a thousand a year for life and is supposed to be incompatable with his holding this place of Secretary &c at the same time, this latter is only three hundred a year so that there can be no doubt if he can hold only one, which he will keep.

I have therefore to entreat Your Grace to procure from Mr. Pitt that in case Mr. Lake relinquishes it, I may be the next oars.[7]

If Your Grace had been in London when Mr. Whitehead[8] dyed I should not have despaired of having had the first promise I have very little confidence in Mr. Elliots interest and therefore have not made a second application to him

Tho as I said before, the difficult~~es~~y of my visiting Ireland are very great, yet in this case If Your Grace can procure me this honourable place I should ~~thi~~ think it an indispensible duty to make my personal appearance, to return my thanks with the Order about my neck, tho not on my shoulder

Mr. Pitt I fear has not much attention to the arts. If he had, he would think it reasonable, that a man who had given up ~~such~~ so much of his time to the establishment of an Academy, and had attended sixteen <years> without any emolument whatever and who unluckily when made the Kings Painter was the first person in that place who had their salary reduced to a ~~third~~ fourth part, that he should have some compensation. I am confident Your Grace would have seen it in this light had the place been in your Gift, but a thousand apologies are necessary for my presuming to hope for your Graces influence with Mr. Pitt in my behalf.

I am with the greatest respect
Your Graces &c &c
JReynolds

1 This date is clearly written, but it was surely mistaken. In Letter 139, written to the same correspondent on 19 July, JR clearly stated he was travelling to Brussels on 20 July.
2 See Letter 134. Charles Bingham, 1st Baron Lucan (1735–99), MP for Co. Mayo 1761–76 and for Northampton 1782–84; m. 1760 Margaret Smyth Bingham (see Letter 87n3).
3 William Marlow (1740–1813), JR's neighbour in Leicester Fields.
4 See Letter 124.
5 Edward Eliot, who had accompanied Pitt to France in 1783 and was about to marry Lady Harriot, Pitt's sister; see Letter 93n1.
6 John Martyn Leake, one of the chief clerks of the Treasury.
7 'Next oars' was a Thames boatman's cry meaning 'next'; a cartoon of 1744 is entitled Next Sculls at the Adm***ty' (F.G. Stephens, *Cat. of Political and Personal Satires*, British Museum, III, i, 1877, no. 2614). Leake's position was given to William Fauquier.
8 William Whitehead (1715–85), poet laureate, died on 14 April; he was succeeded, largely through the efforts of JR, by Thomas Warton.

136

TO CHARLES, 4TH DUKE OF RUTLAND 5 JULY 1785

Source: Belvoir Castle MSS

July 5th 1785

My Lord
I wish I could express the gratitude I feel for your Graces kindness to me in interesting yourself so much in my business which I think is likely to turn out very successfull.[1]

In regard to the subject of Mr Beyers Letter I would by all means recommend Your Grace to close with it,[2] Tho two thousand pounds is a great sum, a great object of art is procured by it, perhaps a greater than any we have at present in this nation. Poussin certainly ranks amongst the first of the first rank of Painters, and to have such a set of Pictures of such an Artist will really & truly enrich the nation. I have not the least scruple about the sending copies for originals, not only from the character of Beyers but if that trick had been intended he would not have mentiond a word about his having copies made. I dont wish to take them out of your Graces hands but I certainly would be glad to be the purchaser myself. I only mean that I recommend only what I would do myself. I really think they are very cheap.

Mr. Webber[3] has declined undertaking his intended journey to Ireland, and that partly by my advice. I found he misunderstood Your Graces intention which was, as I apprehend, to give him your protection and encouragement so far as employing for six Pictures he I find expected that his expences would be defrayed besides paying for those Pictures, in short I thought it would be a troublesome business and that it would be better to have done with it.

Madame La Comtesse Genlis[4] is just arrived I had the honour of her Company yesterday to dinner. She speaks English tolerably well and has very pleasing manners. Today she is gone to Windsor, the Queen have<ing> sent to desire to see her.

I am with the greatest respect

Your Graces

most obedient humble servant

Joshua Reynolds

I perfectly agree with Your Grace that they should be sent as they are, without being cleaned or varnishd[5]

1 Possibly the Duke's response to Letter 135, see also Letter 141.

2 The Scottish antiquary James Byres (1734–1817), long resident in Rome (see Ingamells 1997, 169–72), had written to the Duke on 10 June (*HMC Rutland*, III, 214) saying he was now able to purchase the Poussin *Sacraments* from the Boccapaduli Palace, having arranged to substitute copies for the originals so that the papal authorities would not realise their loss. When the transaction was completed (see Letters 154, 157) Byres insisted that 'it should never be mentioned through whose hands [the Duke] got [the pictures], for my name being mentioned might be attended with the worst consequences to me here, where we live under a despotic government who are more jealous than ever of fine things going out of Rome' (*HMC Rutland*, III, 310).

3 See Letter 134.

4 Stéphanie-Félicité Ducrest de Saint-Aubin, comtesse de Genlis (1746–1830), a well-known bluestocking.

5 Byres had written that 'They must all of them be lined and cleaned', see note 2.

137

TO JAMES BOSWELL [7 JULY 1785]

Source: Hyde Collection

I am obliged to you for carrying me yesterday to see the execution <at Newgate> of the five Malefactors[1] it is a vulgar error, the opinion that it is so terrible a spectacle or that it any way implies a hardness of ~~th~~ heart or cruelty of disposition, ~~I saw nothing~~ any more than ~~the~~ such a disposition is implied in <seeking> ~~being~~ delighted <from> ~~with~~ the representation of a Tragedy such an Execution as we saw where there was no torture of the body or <expression of> agony of the mind ~~expressd~~ but on the contrary appeard perfectly composed [deletion] without <the least> trembling, ready to <speak> and answer with ~~polite~~ civility & attention any question that was proposed neither in a state of torpidity <or insensibility> ~~nor aff~~ but grave and composed ~~in the most . . . manner~~ as of some great matter to begin

I am convinced from what we saw and ~~looking~~ from the report of Mr. Akerman,[2] that it is a state of suspense that is the most irksome and intolerable for the <human> mind, and that certainty, though of the worst, is a more eligible state; that the mind soon ~~makes~~ <reconciles> it self ~~up to it~~ even to the worst, when that worst is fixed as fate. Thus bankrupts

I consider it is natural to desire to see such sights and if I may venture to take delight in them ~~as~~ in order to ~~give~~ stir & interest the mind, to give it some emotion, ~~as for~~ as <moderate exercise> it is necessary for the body [deletion] this execution is not more, though I expected it to be too much. If they <criminals> had expressed great agony of mind, the spectators must infallibly sympathise; but so far was the fact from it, that you regard with admiration the serenity & composure of the countenances and <whole> deportment . . .

1 One was Peter Shaw, formerly a servant of Edmund Burke, convicted of robbery (LT, II, 588, said he was Mrs Thrale's servant). The *Public Advertiser*, 7 July 1785, reported, quoting Boswell's own words, that 'the first person who appeared upon the scaffold was Mr. Boswell. That was nothing extraordinary, but it was surprising when he was followed by Sir Joshua Reynolds … it is strange how that hard Scot should have prevailed on the amiable painter to attend so shocking a spectacle'; Shaw, 'a tall handsome fellow', bowed 'gracefully from beneath the gallows' to JR and Boswell; John Boydell (see Appendix II), then sheriff of London, would have provided then with good seats (Whitley 1928, II, 52; Fifer 1976, 199–200).

2 Richard Akerman (c.1722–99), Keeper of Newgate, Boswell's esteemed friend (Boswell, III, 431f.).

138

TO THE REVD JOHN OGLANDER 9 JULY 1785

Source: New College, Oxford

Leicesterfields July 9th 1785

Sir

Tho I have not the least remembrance of having said to Mr. Jervais that I should not charge anything for the designs for the Middle part of the Window,[1] I am very willing to abide by his declaration, especially as you say this proposal principally influenced the College to adopt the plan. Such a discourse might very prob~~ly~~<ably> pass between Mr. Jervais & myself that rather than such a scheme should not be adopted I would give the designs gratis, but I think I am confident that if I had seriously commisioned him to make such a proposal to the College, I should not have forgot it, <the> respect due to the society would have imprinted it on my memory.

Whatever shall be the determination of the College I shall acquiesce with the greatest satisfaction

I am with great respect

Your most humble

and most obedient servant

Joshua Reynolds

1 See Letter 62. JR's ledger, after May 1780 has: 'Mr Oglander has paid for all the designs of the window at New College, except the Great picture of the Nativity', no sum given (Cormack, 160); see Letter 273.

139

TO CHARLES, 4TH DUKE OF RUTLAND 19 JULY 1785

Source: Belvoir Castle MSS

London July 19 1785

My Lord

I set out tomorrow morning for Brussels and consequently take the liberty of writing to Your Grace in the midst of hurry and confusion. I have but just receiv'd a Catalogue of the Pictures which are now on View at Brussels, The Emperor has suppressd sixty-six Religious houses the Pictures of which are to be sold by Auction, Le Comte de Kageneck[1] informs me The Emperor has selected for himself some of the principal pictures However there is one Altar Piece which belonged to the Convent of the Dames Blanches at Louvain which is to be sold. The subject is the adoration of the Magi, ten feet by seven feet eight Inches, which I take to be about the [hight] size of your Picture of Rubens,[2] I do not recollect this Picture accurately and what is <u>valde diflendus</u>[3] I have no notes to refer to, they are alas in Your Graces possession,[4] This Picture [is] I suspect is the only one worth purchasing. If Your Grace has any such intention, or will honour me with discretionary orders in regard to other Pictures. I shall leave order for your Letter to be forwarded to me at Brussels. The sale does not begin till the twelveth of September during the whole month of August the Pictures are shut up but for what reason I cannot imagine The principal object of my journey is to reexamine and leave a commission for a Picture of Rubens of a St. Justus a figure with his head in his hands after it had been cut off, as I wish to have it for the exccellency of its painting, the boldness of the subject will I hope make it cheap, whether it will be a bargain or not, I am resolved to have it at any rate[5]

I have taken the liberty, to take Mr. Crabs verses[6] with me, having but just now receiv'd Your Graces Letter in which they were contained, I shall have time to examine them critically on the Road. I shall have the honour of writing to Your Grace again from Brussels. I am with the Greatest respect

Your Graces &c,

J Reynolds

1 Envoy extraordinary and minister plenipotentiary from Austria and Germany 1782–86; see Letter 285.

2 *Virgin and Child with SS Catherine, Agnes and other Saints,* bought at the Verhulst sale, Brussels, 16 August 1779; now Toledo Museum of Art (*Journey* 1996, 157n129).

3 'completely gone away'.

4 See Letter 140. JR had written of the *Adoration of the Magi*: 'a slight performance. The Virgin holds the Infant but aukwardly, appearing to pinch the thigh'; JR did not succeed in buying it (*Journey* 1996, 142, 182n764; now King's College, Cambridge).

5 'Every part of this picture is touched in such a style that it may be considered as a pattern for imitation'; JR did not succeed in buying it (*Journey* 1996, 73, 163n292; now musée des Beaux-Arts, Bordeaux).

6 George Crabbe, see Letter 110; the verses in question were doubtless *The Newspaper*, which Crabbe dated February 1785.

140

TO CHARLES, 4TH DUKE OF RUTLAND 22 AUGUST 1785

Source: Belvoir Castle MSS

London Aug. 22d 1785

My Lord

I sat out for Brussells the day after I wrote to Your Grace,[1] but left word, that if any answer arrived, to be sent after me. but my stay abroad was so short that I missed it, however I have since receivd it in London. I was much disapointed in the Pictures of the suppressed Religious houses,[2] they are the saddest trash that ever were collected together The Adoration of the Magi & St. Justus by Rubens, and a Crucifixion by Vandyck were the only tolerable Pictures,[3] ~~and~~ but these are not the best of those masters. I did not like the Justus as well I did before, but I think of sending a small commission for it. The two others I dare say will not go to above £200 each The Vandyck was in the Church of the Dominicaines at Antwerp.

I was shewn some of the Pictures which were reserved by the Emperor[4] which were not a jota better than the common run of the rest of the collection.

Tho I was disapointed in the object of my journey, I have made some very considerable purchases from private collections.[5] I have bought a very capital Picture of Rubens of Hercules and Omphale a composition of seven or eight figures perfectly preserved and as bright as colouring can be carried; The figures are rather less than life the hight of the picture I believe is not above seven feet. I have likewise a holy family, ~~by Rubens~~ a Silenus and Baccanalians, and two Portraits all by Rubens, I have a Virgin & infant Christ, and two Portraits by Vandyck: and two of the best Huntings of Wild Beasts by Snyders & De Vos that I ever saw. I begin now to be impatient for their arrival, which I expect every day.

The banker Mr. Danoot[6] was very ill when we were at Brussels supposed to be dying, if that should happen his Pictures will be sold.

There <are> no Pictures of Mieris either at Antwerp or Brussels, All the Pictures in those two Places which were worth bringing home I have bought, I mean of those which were upon sale, except indeed one – the Rape of the Sabines[7] for which they asked £3500, excepting this, I have swept the country, and for this, I would not exchange my Hercules & Omphale.

I return Mr. Crabbs Verses[8] with many thanks and many apologies I ought to make for the liberty I took in carrying them abroad with me there are very beautifull lines in it, but it is not so much finishd as some of his other works

If Your Grace should chuse to send any commisions for the Altar piece of Rubens or for the Vandyck the sale begins the twelvth of September,[9] you will please to let me know time enough before the sale for the commision to arrive at Brussels.

I am with the greatest respect
Your Graces most humble
and most obedient servant
Joshua Reynolds

1 Again travelling with Philip Metcalfe (see Letter 94), JR left London on 20 July and passed through Saint-Omer and Lille on his way to Brussels (24 July), Antwerp (29–30 July), Ghent (3 August); he was back in London by 10 August (*Journey* 1996, 202).

2 JR's main purpose was to preview this sale brought about by the suppression of monasteries belonging to the Carmelite, Capuchin and Franciscan nuns and to the nuns of the Order of St Clare in the hereditary lands of Austria by the Emperor Joseph II through an imperial rescript of 1782 (*Wal. Corr.*, xxv, 236n7; *Journey* 1996, 201; LT, II, 419, 480).

3 None bought by JR. Rubens: *Adoration* now King's College, Cambridge (*Journey* 1996, 182n764); *Justus* (musée des Beaux-Arts, Bordeaux; *Journey* 1996, 73, 163n292); Van Dyck: *Crucifixion* (Museum voor Schone Kunsten, Antwerp), see *Journey* 1996, 159n188.

4 Joseph II, see Letter 94n5.

5 Only one of the pictures listed, a portrait of a lady by Rubens bought in Antwerp for £15 (Broun 1987, II, 151–52; *Journey* 1996, 208), is identifiable today (Barber Institute, Birmingham, as after Rubens). The remainder are discussed in *Journey* 1996, 201, 206–08, and Broun 1987, II, 106, 111, 118, 139–40, 158–60, 161–62, 164; JR spent £805 in Antwerp (Rubens *Hercules and Omphale*, £500, 'Head of an Old Man' £20; Van Dyck, *Self portrait*, £200, *Isabella Clara Eugenia*, £30; 'De Vos Boar Hunt', £25; 'Snyders – Wolf Hunting', £30), and £240 in Brussels (Rubens, *Holy Family*); the cost of the Rubens *Silenus* and the Van Dyck *Virgin and Infant Christ* is not recorded.

6 A sale of Daniel Danoot's collection, probably the same, Brussels, 22–23 December 1828 (*Journey* 1996, 19–20, 154n76).

7 Rubens, now National Gallery (no. 38); *Journey* 1996, 81–82, 165n350.

8 See Letter 139.

9 Brussels, 12ff. September 1785 (270 pictures).

141

TO CHARLES, 4TH DUKE OF RUTLAND 10 SEPTEMBER 1785

Source: Belvoir Castle MSS

London Sep 10th 1785

My Lord

Tho I have not been so punctual in answering your Graces Letters as I ought, yet I took care that nothing should prevent me from writing to my correspondent in Flanders, to desire he would go so far as four hundred Guineas for the Vandyck, and three hundred for the Rubens I could not in conscience give him a higher commission;[1] Your Grace will certainly have them, I think ~~at~~ within the commission. I must beg leave to mention to Your Grace the person I have employed in this business. His name is De Gray[2] a very excellent Painter in Chiaro oscuro, in imitation of Basrelievos. He paints likewise Portraits in oil & in crayons extremely well He was very civil and attentive to me when I was at Antwerp, and was the means of my purchasing some very fine Pictures. He then told me he intended going to Ireland having been invited by Mr. Cunningham[3] and I promised to recommend him to Your Graces protection, which I can with a very safe conscience not only as a very ingenious Artist but a young man of very pleasing manners. I have no doubt but he is very happy in this opportunity of doing any thing to oblige Your Grace, and will be very zealous in the performance

I dont know how to account for the Pictures at Antwerp not appearing so striking to me this last journey as they did the first I was disapointed in many other Pictures besides those on sale. it ought at least to teach me this lesson, not to be very impatient when any one differs with me about the degree of excellence of any Pictures since I find I differ so much from my self at different times.

I have inclosed the title and that part of the Catalogue which has the Rubens & the Vandyck, which I apprehend is all that your Grace wished to see.

The Picture will be sent away on Monday by way of Liverpool.[4]

In the hurry of Pictures I have neglected thanking Your Grace for your kind sollicitations in my favour with Mr. Pitt.[5] I am as I certainly might be, as gratefull as if it had been crowned with success.

If Your Grace wishes to remain longer in Ireland I think I may congratulate you on losing the Irish Propositions.[6] If they had passed it is most certain there would have been a great commotion here by addresses from the Manufacturers and inflammatory speeches to mobbs, that would probably have gone near to shake the Administration, but now all is quiet and settled again, and that Grace may long continue in that hight station which you fill with so much honour to yourself is the sincere wish of Your Graces

most humble and most
obliged servant
Joshua Reynolds

1 See Letter 139; Rubens, *Adoration*, now King's College, Cambridge, and Van Dyck, *Crucifixion*, St Romboutskathedral, Mechelen (*Journey* 1996, 24, 142, 156n116, 182n764).
2 Pieter de Gree (1751–89) came to England and settled in Ireland (see Letter 147).
3 Probably Robert Cunningham (c.1728–1801), later (1796) 1st Baron Rossmore, lived in Ireland from 1751; army officer and Irish MP 1751–96, MP 1788–89; but see also Letter 146n1.
4 JR's portrait of the Duke's three sons ('sent to Ireland September 1785, £300'; Cormack, 162); see Letter 134; it was destroyed by fire at Belvoir Castle in 1816 (Mannings 1217).
5 See Letters 135 and 136.
6 Twenty propositions passed by Parliament respecting Ireland's right to self-government were defeated on 12 August (*GM*, LV, 1785, II, 657).

142

TO CHARLES, 4TH DUKE OF RUTLAND 22 SEPTEMBER 1785

Source: Belvoir Castle MSS

London Sep. 22d 1785

My Lord
I am sorry to acquaint Your Grace that there is nothing bought at the sale. I have inclosed Mr. De Grees[1] Letter by which it appears they went much above even the commission that you wished me to send, I cannot think either the Rubens or Vandyck were worth half the mony they sold for.[2] The Vandyck was an immense Picture and very scantily filled, it had more defects than beauties, and as to the Rubens I think Your Graces is worth a hundred of them. They are so large too that it would cost near two hundred pounds bringing them to England.

I have sent the Catalogue to Lord Sydneys[3] office to be forwarded to your Grace

I am with the greatest respect
Your Graces
most humble & most
obedient servant
J Reynolds

1 See Letter 141n2.
2 See Letter 141n1.
3 Thomas Townshend, 1st Baron Sydney (1733–1800), cr. Viscount Sydney 1789, secretary of state to the home department 1782–83 and 1783–89.

143

TO CHARLES, 4TH DUKE OF RUTLAND 26 SEPTEMBER 1785

Source: Belvoir Castle MSS

London Sep 26 1785

My Lord
Immediatly on the receipt of Your Graces Letter I wrote to De Gree[1] to make enquiries to whom the Pictures were sold, and whether they would part with them again at a certain profit, At the same time I am confident if Your Grace saw them you would not be very anxious about possessing them. The Poussins[2] are a real national object, and I rejoice to hear that <the> scheme of their coming to England is in such forwardness.

Mr. Boswell has just sent me his Johnsoniana which is one of the most entertaining books I ever read.[3] If Your Grace ~~pleases~~ I will send it by the same conveyance as the Catalogue I think you will be agriably amused for a few hours, there are Johnsons opinions upon a great variety of subjects, and Boswell has drawn his character in a very masterly manner. The Bishop of Killaloo[4] who knew Johnson very well, I think will subscribe to the justness and truth of the drawing.

I am with the greatest respect
Your Graces most humble and
most obliged servant
Joshua Reynolds

1 See Letter 141n2.
2 See Letter 136.
3 An advance copy of Boswell's *Journal of a Tour to the Hebrides*, published on 1 October 1785.
4 Thomas Barnard, see Appendix II.

144

TO ANDREW STRAHAN 23 OCTOBER 1785

Source: Houghton Library

London Oct 23 1785

Dear Sir

As without doubt you wish to make this New Edition of Johnson's Dicty,[1] as complete as possible, I take the liberty of acquainting you, that Mr. Dyer[2] a friend of Dr. Johnson's had by the Doctor's desire made notes, explanations and corrections of words to be used in a future edition; for this purpose the Dictionary was divided into four Folio Volumes, with a certain number of blank leaves at the end of each volume. Mr. Ed. Burke (who was likewise an intimate friend of Mr. Dyer) is in possession of those Volumes,[3] I mentioned to him that I believe you would be glad have the use of them for your new Edition, to which he readily consented. If you think this worth your attention I will desire Mr. Burke to send them to Town.

Mr. Dyer was a very judicious and learned Critic, and held in the highest estimation in our Club. I have heard Mr. Burke say that he never knew a man of more extensive knowledge; not having publishd any thing his name is not much known in the world. He overlooked the English Translation of Plutarch and translated some of the Lives from the Original Greek, the Old Translation being too bad to use any part of it.[4]

I am with great respect

Yours &c

J. Reynolds

Annotated: Answered in person Oct 24.

1 Strahan was about to publish the sixth edition, announced in the *London Chronicle*, 13–15 October 1785; on 25–27 October the publishers announced that JR had 'with a Liberality which distinguishes his Character, indulged the Proprietors with the use' of copy bequeathed to him by Johnson, but there was no mention, here or subsequently, of Dyer's copy. For JR's copy of the *Dictionary* (Rylands Library, Manchester), see G.J. Kolb and J.H. Sledd, 'The Reynolds copy of Johnson's Dictionary', *Bull. of the John Rylands Library Manchester*, XXXVII, 1955, 446–75.

2 Samuel Dyer (1725–72), the first additional member of the Club in 1764, sat to JR in 1770.

3 Burke's copy of the Dictionary (BL) is in 2 volumes 'with a certain number of blank leaves at the end of each volume' on which are written Dyer's additions and corrections.

4 For Tonson's new edition of Plutarch's *Lives*, published in 1758, Dyer translated the lives of Pericles and Democritus and revised the entire work.

145

TO [DANIEL] WALDRON 5 NOVEMBER 1785

Source: Yale Center for British Art

Sir Joshua Reynolds presents his Compliments to Mr. Waldron[1] and will take it as a favour if he will trust the bearer with the Picture he mention'd of Milton[2] he will take care to return it safe

Leicesterfields Nov 5 1785

1 The collection of a Daniel Waldron (c.1741–1806), shoemaker, was sold 9–23 February 1807 (*Farington Diary*, 13 February 1807).
2 JR had acquired in 1784 a miniature by Samuel Cooper, said to be of Milton, which he was to bequeath to William Mason (now private collection; LT, II, 440–41, 636); thereafter he took a particular interest in the poet's iconography (see *Candidate for Praise*, exh. cat. York, 1973, 45–46, no. III).

146

TO CUNNINGHAM[1] 25 NOVEMBER 1785

Source: Yale Center for British Art

London Nov. 25 1785

Dear Sir

I return you a thousand thanks for your kind attention to my wishes about the two pictures of Rubens at the Capuchins,[2] and you give me some hopes of a possibility of coming at them. I believe what I have offer'd, £300 for the two Pictures, is their full value, they have been much damaged and ill mended. As they are at present they appear to be worth little or nothing. I go upon speculation that I can mend them, and restore them to their original beauty, which if I can accomplish, I shall have got a prize, if they will not clean it will be so much mony thrown away. This is exactly the state of the Case. – In regard to the copies being made, I will be at that additional expence, I would send over a young Artist who formerly lived with me, for that purpose, and will give him proper directions how to give the copy an old appearance, so that few, even amongst the Connoiseurs shall distinguish the difference.

If it is represented to the family by whom the Picture was given, that they are allmost destroyed and will soon be totally lost, they may reasonably think that putting copies in their place, is the best means of preserving the remembrance of the gift of their family. That it may not appear that I am undervalueing the goods which I want to buy according to the common custom, let me quote what Monr. Michel says of those two Pictures of Rubens.[3] dans la seconde chapelle à la gauche de l'entree de l Eglise de Capucins representant l Adoration des Bergers, sa Composition est tres-revenante d'un Coloris vigoreux et savamment groupè, mais helas, un de ces frotteurs dont l'Univers abonde, a effacé la superficie de tout l'ouvrage; de maniére qu'il n'a laissè que le triste souvenir, qu'autrefois ce tableau fut du pinceau de le Rubens. Of the other Picture, St. Francis receiving the Enfant Jesus, he says likewise, ce tableau a encore passé le maniement décharnant du dernier, car les draperies de la Vierge, & le fond de tout l'ouvrage, est autant qu'emporté This printed account of the Pictures wil[l be a] sufficient apology both to the Capuchins [and the] family for placing good Copies in the [Church].[4] I calculate the Copies to cost me about £100. When a man is about an object that will upon the whole cost £400 it is not worth while to bogle at small things, if making the principal of the family a compliment of a present of a Gold watch or any English trinket of the value of about twenty Pounds I should be glad to do it I have not left room to make such an apology as I intended for the trouble which I have given to you and express my thankfullness for the great favour you have conferrd on me –

I am with the greatest respect Yours &c
Joshua Reynolds

a Monsr Monsr Cunynham[5] / Lille

1 Possibly William Burton Conyngham (1733–96), teller of the Irish exchequer, treasurer Royal Irish Academy, who had sat to JR in 1761 (Cormack, 114, 116; untraced; Mannings 401). Previously tentatively identified as the artist Edmund Francis Cuningham (Hilles 1929; *Journey* 1996, 203n18), but this was subsequently doubted by Hilles (Hilles, *Notes*). See also Letter 141n3.

2 Rubens, *Adoration of the Shepherds* (church of Ste Marie-Madeleine, Lille, in 1886) and Rubens, *St Francis receiving Christ from the Virgin* (now musée des Beaux Arts, Lille), see *Journey* 1996, 203nn 17, 18.

3 J.F.M. Michel, *Histoire de la Vie de P.P. Rubens* ..., Brussels, 1771, 198f. JR omits two phrases and changes the accents.

4 *Lacunae* due to a portion of the MS being torn off with the seal.

5 For this form of address, see Letter 9n24.

147

TO CHARLES, 4TH DUKE OF RUTLAND 14 DECEMBER 1785

Source: Belvoir Castle MSS

London Decr 14 1785

My Lord

Mr. De Gree[1] the bearer of this, was very desirous of the honour of being introduced to Your Grace, I therefore delayed my letter in order to give him this opportunity, besides being a very ingenious Artist in variety of ways, he is a very excellent Connoiseur, and was the means of my procuring some very excellent Pictures at Antwerp. He was the agent about the Pictures of Rubens and Vandyck[2] consequently he will be able to give your Grace all his information about them.

I am very glad the Picture of the Children[3] meets with Your Graces approbation, I am sorry to say the companion[4] is not yet finishd but I will endeavour to exert my self and set furiously about it.

The Portrait of Morilio[5] which I have seen, is very finely Painted & there is not the least doubt of its being an original of his hand, it will be a very considerable acquisition to Your Graces collection

The Poussins[6] I suppose I am not to expect for some time, when they arrive I shall certainly take all possible care of them

I am with the greatest respect

Your Graces most humble

and most obedient servant

Joshua Reynolds

1 See Letter 141n2.

2 See Letter 140.

3 See Letters 134, 141.

4 Of the Duke's children, John Henry Granby and the Ladies Elizabeth and Katherine Manners, see Letters 150, 154, 162, 164, 171; the picture was destroyed in the fire at Belvoir Castle in 1816 (Mannings 1209).

5 Unidentified. JR owned the Murillo *Peasant Boy at a Window*, now in a private collection attributed to Caravaggio (Broun 1987, II, 333–34).

6 See Letters 136, 143.

148

TO CUNNINGHAM 29 DECEMBER 1785

Source: Hilles 1929, XCVI

London Dec 29th 1785

Dear Sir

The great probability there is that the Pictures are beyond the powers of Art to restore,[1] I confess to you, made me repent offering so much as I did in my last letter. however as they have declined accepting it I am very well contented to be cleared of my engagement; When I offered three hundred pounds for the two Pictures, I meant I would give so much to have them safe in my house without further expence, except the carriage duty &c which I believe would amount to near forty pounds. According to their demand, the Pictures would cost me before I received them upwards of five hundred Guineas. I wish therefore now totally to decline being a purchaser unless they choose to part with them clear of all deduction for three hundred pounds. Tho we have not succeeded in this business I am not the less obliged to you for the trouble and attention you have given to it and should be very glad of any opportunity of shewing the gratefull sense I have of your kindness

I beg most respectfull compliments to the Ladies and am with the greatest respect

Your most humble

and most obedient servant

J Reynolds

In regard to the last supper of Lucas of Leyden, I have the same picture of a larger size.[2] I only wished to know the name of the painter. Neither of them I am certain are by Lucas of Leyden.

P.S. as you mentioned a intention of becoming a purchaser yourself, I beg leave to observe that tho I have offer'd so great a sum for the Pictures they are by no means worth half that sum to anybody else. I have in my Possession a Picture of Rubens as large as the Nativity[3] which I bought at a public sale in London for twenty five pounds, tho' it was not so much damaged as those pictures are. If both of them were in a sale in London I should ~~expect~~ to buy them both for fifty pounds – they are worth nothing, (as I observed in my former letter,) but to a Painter. I should be very sorry therefore if you bought them upon speculation, as I think you would lose considerably by it.

1 See Letter 146.
2 Probably the *Last Supper*, JR sale, 1795: J. Van Wingen 'a high finished antique in great preservation ... bt. Bryan, 20 gns; and Coxe's, 18 May 1798 (12), bt. in 10gns (Broun 1987, I, 25, 186). A *Last Supper*, formerly called Lucas van Leyden, but signed and dated 1524 by Pieter Coecke Van Der Aelst (1502–50), remains at Belvoir.
3 Unidentified, see Broun 1987, II, 172–73.

149

TO CHARLES, 4TH DUKE OF RUTLAND 4 JANUARY 1786

Source: Belvoir Castle MSS

London Jan 4th 1786

My Lord
I have begun the Copy of Lord Mansfield for Your Grace.[1] He called on me and spoke himself about it. It is thought one of my best portraits, but he should have sat eight or ten years ~~ago~~ before, his countenance is much changed since he has lost his teeth. I have made him exactly what he is now, as if I was upon my oath to give the truth and nothing but the truth. I think it necessary to treat great men with this reverence, tho I really think His Lordship would not have been displeased if ~~with~~ this strict adherence to truth <had been dispensed with, and> ~~and have~~ drawn ~~him~~ a few years younger, ~~but~~ however being told by everybody, what a good picture, and how like it is, he is perfectly pleased with it, and has orderd a Print by Bartolozzi to be made after it.

The next Picture I take in hand shall be Lord Granby with the Hussar.[2] but I fear it will not be finishd till the Spring as I am at present overpowerd with business however I shall allways take care not to neglect your Graces commands

I am with the greatest respect
Your Graces
most humble and most obedient servant
JReynolds

1 William Murray, 1st Earl of Mansfield (1705–93), Lord Chief Justice, who had sat to JR in 1776; the copy was completed in January 1787, see Letters 150, 154, 162, 171; it was destroyed by fire at Belvoir Castle in 1816 (Mannings 1319).
2 John, Marquess of Granby, see Appendix II; this posthumous portrait was destroyed by fire at Belvoir in 1816.

150

TO CHARLES, 4TH DUKE OF RUTLAND 20 FEBRUARY 1786

Source: Belvoir Castle MSS

London Feb 20th 1786

My Lord

I shall take care to obey your Graces orders about the Velasques and Vandermeulen when they arrive.[1] Lord Mansfield Picture is finished.[2] I mean your Graces Copy. I am now about Lord Granby with the horse and swiss servant, which I think will be finishd in a weeks time,[3] and if the Reumatism will give me leave, for I am very stiff and aukward at present I hope in about a fortnight after, to finish the Children.[4]

I forgot whether I mentiond in my last letter that I have received a Commission from the Empress of Russia to Paint an Historical Picture for her, the size, the subject and every thing else, left to me, and another on the same condition, for Prince Potemkin.[5] The subject I have fixed on for the Empress is Hercules strangling the Serpents in the Cradle as described by Pindar of which there is a very good translation by Cowley.[6]

My nephew Mr. Palmer[7] who is now with me, desires me to make an apology for him, as he came away whilst your Grace was on your tour in the Country, and had no opportunity of asking your Graces leave, which he was in duty bound to do. I am with the greatest respect your Graces most obedient humble servant

Joshua Reynolds

1 Apparently a version of Velazquez's *Innocent X*, see Letter 152. The van der Meulen is not identifiable.

2 Perhaps an exaggeration; see Letters 149 and 171.

3 See Letter 149.

4 See Letter 147n4.

5 Catherine II of Russia and Griegorii Alexandrovich, Prince Potemkin, see Appendix II.

6 *Pindaresque Odes*, 1669, 'The First Nemeaean Ode of Pindar'. According to Northcote (1818, II, 215) the subject was chosen ' as the most fit, in allusion to the great difficulties which the Empress of Russia had to encounter in the civilization of her empire, arising from the rude state in which she found it'. JR's picture remains in the Hermitage, St Petersburg (Mannings 2094).

7 Joseph Palmer, see Letters 124, 151 and Appendix I.

Joshua Reynolds, *The Infant Hercules*, 1788; engraving by James Walker 1792

151

TO CHARLES, 4TH DUKE OF RUTLAND 21 MARCH 1786

Source: Belvoir Castle MSS

London March 21st 1786

My Lord

Your Grace has made us all very happy by the dignitary which you have been pleased to conferr on my nephew,[1] and indeed the manner in which Your Grace has been pleased to communicate this intelligence so much enhances the obligation, that I dont know whether the kind expressions with which it is accompanied has not given me as much pleasure as the thing itself. I have not yet heard from Mr. Palmer, but I take it for granted he is the happiest of men.

The only news of Virtù at present is Lord Ashburnhams purchase of the Collection of the late Humphry Morris[2] for which he gave four thousand pounds. Out of forty Pictures he had reserved I think six only, the principle of which are two Salvator Rosa's a Landskip of Nic. Poussin,[3] and a Mola the remaining part were sold by Auction which amounted to only four hundred pounds, he has made in my opinion a very bad bargain.

I am with the greatest respect

Your Graces most humble and most obedient servant

Joshua Reynolds

1 Joseph Palmer; this must refer to a promise rather than an appointment, see Letters 157 and 162 and Appendix I.

2 Humphry Morice (1723–85), MP and collector, died at Naples on 18 October 1785. John, 2nd Earl of Ashburnham (1724–1812).

3 These may be identified as the *St John preaching in the Wilderness* (St Louis, Art Museum) and the *Philip baptising the Eunuch* (Walter Chrysler jr., New York) by Salvator Rosa, and the *Landscape with Pyramus and Thisbe* (Frankfurt-am-Main) by Poussin.

152

TO CHARLES, 4TH DUKE OF RUTLAND 23 JUNE 1786

Source: Belvoir Castle MSS

London June 23d 1786

My Lord

I am very much flatter'd by your Graces kind invitation to Ireland, and very much mortified that it is not in my power to accept of it this year, on account of the Picture which I am to paint for the Empress of Russia however I dont despair of accomplishing this visit to Ireland before your Grace leaves it.

In regard to the Augustus[1] I fear it is irretriveably gone. It was bought by the Duke of Portland for £125. The Duke of Marlborough told me he bid as far as – 120 – but the Duke of Portland was resolved to have it at any price. he made the same resolution respecting the Vase which he bought at 900 Guineas The Augustus would have been worth double what it sold <for> if it had been perfect, the lower part of the Chin and the neck was gone. what remaind was of the most exquisite Greek workmanship.

I suspect the Popes Head of Velasques to be the same as is in the Pamphili palace at Rome,[2] and not the Portrait of Leo Xth The same Pope who having disobliged Guido he made a Caracatura of him, or rather made a Devil of him and put him under Michaels feet.[3] At Chiswick there is likewise a head of the same Pope by Velasques but not equal to that which is at Rome which I think is one of the first Portraits in the world.

I have heard nothing of the seven Sacraments.[4] I hope no cross accident had happen'd. I wish they were safe landed.

I am with the greatest respect

Your Graces most humble and most obedient servant

Joshua Reynolds

1 From the Portland sale, Skinner's, 24 April–8 June 1786 (Lugt 4028). Both pieces mentioned by JR were then bought by the Duke of Portland and are now in the British Museum, a cameo head of Caesar and the celebrated Portland Vase.

2 James Byres, see Letter 136n2, wrote from Rome on 5 July 'I am glad that the Duke has got a fine Velasquez. They are very rare to be met with ... That you mention in Rome is in the Doria Panfili Palace. It is likewise a half-length sitting' (*HMC Rutland*, III, 326).

3 For JR's copy of Guido Reni's *St Michael*, see Letter 6n5.

4 By Poussin, see Letter 136n2.

153

TO JOHN, 2ND EARL OF UPPER OSSORY 10 JULY 1786

Source: Yale Center for British Art

London July 10 1786

My Lord

After a carefull examination of the Picture I am sorry to confirm Roma's opinion[1] that it has been much damaged and painted upon, and that too in places which can never be successfully repaired particularly in the back of the

Venus. I am at a loss what to advise, The Picture cleaners will only make it ten times worse. The best advice I can give is that we make an exchange, by which each of us may have a bargain. If there ever was an instance where an exchange may be may be[2] made by which both parties may be benefitted, it is the present.

The Picture is a copy by Titian himself from that in the Colonna palace,[3] I am confident I see the true Titian tint through the yellow dirty Paint and varnish with which the picture is covered.

If it was mine I should try to get this off, or ruin the picture in the attempt. It is the colour alone that can make it valuable. The Venus is not handsome and the Adonis is wretchedly disproportioned with an immense long body & short legs.

The sky and Trees have been painted over and must be repainted which I have the vanity to think nobody can do but myself, – at any rate it is better to let it remain at my house till your Lordship comes to town.

I am with the greatest respect

Your Lordships most humble and

most obedient servant

JReynolds

PS I am thinking what picture to offer in Exchange – what if I give Gainsboroughs Pigs for it, it is by far the best Picture he ever Painted or perhaps ever will.[4]

1 Spiridone Roma (c.1737–87), from Corfu, portrait painter, came to England c.1770, and built up a considerable practice as a picture restorer with the London City Companies (E. Croft-Murray, *English Decorative Painting 1537–1837*, II, 1970, 270).

2 The verb ends the first page and begins the second.

3 The *Venus and Adonis,* now in the National Gallery as Studio of Titian.

4 JR bought it at RA exhibition in 1782, see Letter 304; Gainsborough then wrote to him: 'it could not fail to afford him the highest satisfaction that he had brought his pigs to so fine a market'; now Castle Howard.

154

TO CHARLES, 4TH DUKE OF RUTLAND 13 JULY 1786

Source: Belvoir Castle MSS

London July 13 1786

My Lord

I have at last receiv'd from Mr. ~~Beye~~ Byres a Bill of lading for two Cases belonging to your Grace.[1] I sent immediatly to the Custom house to know if the good ship called the Earl of Sandwich was arrived, but it is not, as soon as it does I shall acquaint Your Grace and give my opinion of the Pictures.

I am ashamed that I have not been able to finish the Picture of the Children but I will soon and send them with Lord Mansfield.[2]

In regard to the Venus, the Duke of Dorset is to have it,[3] not for himself but for a French Marquis whose name I have forgot. He is to give me 400 Guineas for it. I have since done another with variations which I think better than the first but I am not fond of shewing it till the other is disposed off.

I hope in a day or two to be able to acquaint Your Grace with the good news of the arrival of the Picture.

I am with the greatest respect

Your Graces

most obedient humble servant

JReynolds

1 i.e. the Poussins, see Letter 136n2.
2 JR's portraits of the Duke's children (John Henry Granby and the Ladies Elizabeth and Katherine Manners) and his copy of Lord Mansfield; see Letters 147n4 and 149n1.
3 John Sackville, 3rd Duke of Dorset (1754–99), then ambassador at Paris; for the *Venus*, see Letter 134.

155

TO JOHN, 2ND EARL OF UPPER OSSORY 17 JULY 1786

Source: Hilles 1929, CIII (amended from a copy in the collection of R. Vernon, Taunton; Hilles, *Notes*)

London, July 17th 1786

My Lord

My mind at present is entirely occupied in contriving the compossition of the Hercules,[1] otherwise I think I should close with your Lordships proposal which I acknowledge is very flattering to me, There is another proposal which I beg leave to make, which I can execute immediately and which I think will be equally valuable to your Lordship and save me a great deal of time, which is to copy the ~~Venus~~ Nymph and Shepherd,[2] with many improvements which I wish to make and add to it a landskip to make it the size of the frame at Ampthill: depend upon it I shall make it the most striking Picture I ever did.

I am with the greatest respect
Your Lordship's most humble
& obedient servant
J. Reynolds

P.S. If I paint this Picture perfectly to your Lordship's satisfaction, I expect you will give me the shield to the bargain.

1 See Letter 150.
2 Lord Ossory appears not to have taken up this offer, possibly the *Nymph and Boy* which Ossory chose at JR's death (private collection; Mannings 2174) or/and *Venus and the Piping Boy* (Polesden Lacey; Mannings 2176).

156

TO SIR GEORGE BEAUMONT[1] 23 AUGUST 1786

Source: Yale Center for British Art

London Aug. 23 1786

Dear Sir
I am sorry I have not more time to recollect myself. It is near five o clock and I am engaged to dine out. At Ghent, in the Cathedral is a fine Picture of Rubens of St. Bavon and in St. Michaels Church the <once> famous crucifixion of Vandick, allmost destroyed.[2]

At Brussels a Mr. Orion[3] has some good Pictures, but are difficult to be seen Mr. Danoot[4] the Banker can procure sight of them, there are two fine sketches for the Ceiling at Whitehall. At Mecklin the last Supper by Rubens,[5] and at the Recollet, ~~the~~ a Crucifixion the most capital of all Vandycks works.[6]

At Antwerp I fear you will not be able to see Mr. Peters Pictures, as I hear he is dead.[7] You must see the Chapeau <de> poile in the Cabinet of Mr Van Haveren.[8]

At Amsterdam take particular note of a Picture by Vander ~~Els~~ Elst.[9] At Surgeons Hall – The Professor Tulpius with a dead Body by Rembrant the best of his works.[10]

At the office of the Commissary of the warfs is the Vandeveld.[11]

Adieu my most respectfull Compt to Lady Beaumont
Yours
J Reynolds

Sir George Beaumont Bart / Tunbridge Wells

1 Sir George Beaumont and his wife were then about to travel in the Netherlands.
2 In situ (*Journey* 1996, 5, 7).
3 J.B. Horion, a merchant; his collection sold posthumously, Brussels, 1 September 1788 (*Journey* 1996, 21–22, 155n92).
4 Danoot's collection was seen by Mrs Piozzi in 1787; a sale of Daniel Danoot's collection, probably the same, Brussels, 22–23 December 1828 (*Journey* 1996, 19–20, 154n76) see also Letter 140.
5 Now Milan, Brera.
6 In situ, Mechelen, St Romboutskathedral.
7 J.E. Peeters d'Aertselaer (1725–86), banker and collector (*Journey* 1996, 79, 164n325).
8 J.-M.-J. van Havre; the *Chapeau de paille* by Rubens now in the National Gallery, London (*Journey* 1996, 81, 165n337).
9 B. van der Helst, *The Banquet of the Civic Guard* (now Rijksmuseum) (*Journey* 1996, 169n453).
10 Now in the Mauritshuis, The Hague.
11 W. van de Velde the elder, *The Y off Amsterdam with the Golden Leeuw*; Historisch Museum, Amsterdam (*Journey* 1996, 169n462).

157

TO CHARLES, 4TH DUKE OF RUTLAND 29 AUGUST 1786

Source: Belvoir Castle MSS

London Augst 29 1786

My Lord

I have the pleasure to acquaint Your Grace that the Pictures are in the River,[1] and that I am expecting them in Leicester fields every hour. I should have deferred writing to Your Grace till I had been able at the same time to give some account of their merit, But my Nephew[2] setting out tomorrow morning for Ireland and being very desirous of bearing a Letter to Your Grace I thought it would be no bad news to communicate this intelligence, the bad part of the story is that I insured the Pictures for two thousand pounds which cost thirty pounds, I confess I insured them with an ill will, but as I had received Your Graces orders I had no business to consider about the propriety of it.

I beg Your Graces pardon for returning to the subject of my Nephew, If I can do nothing for him during Your Graces Administration I must give up all thought or rather he must give up all expectations from any advantage he is to receive from my interest with the Great. We are not so ambitious as to think of Bishopricks, but if ~~the~~ Dean Marly[3] succeeds to the next Bishoprick which according to report, is probable, if Your Grace would give to Mr. Palmer his leavings either his deanery or the living of Loughilly, Your Grace would make him at once what you was so good as to say you would do one time or another, an independent Gentleman and I shall never pretend to have any further demands on Your Grace on his account.

Your Grace some time since wished Marlow[4] the Landskip painter to come to Dublin, but he has, as I am told quitted business. I have met lately with a Painter of Landskips and buildings that I think excells Marlow Mr. Hodges[5] who went the first Voyage of Capt Cook and has since been in the East Indies,[6] he is now desirous of seeing Ireland and would embark immediatly if he was sure of Your Graces protection, he is a very intelligent and ingenious Artist and produced I think the best Landskips in the last Exhibition which were taken from Drawings which he made in the East Indies – I have not left room to subscribe myself Your Graces most –

J Reynolds

1 The Poussin *Sacraments*, see Letter 136n2, had reached London.
2 Joseph Palmer, then Chancellor of Ferns, see Appendix I.
3 Richard Marlay (d. 1795), Dean of Ferns 1769, rector of Loughgilly 1772, Bishop of Clonfert 1787.
4 William Marlow, see Letter 135n3.
5 William Hodges, see Appendix II.
6 Hodges was in India 1779–84.

158

TO JOHN, 2ND EARL OF UPPER OSSORY 5 SEPTEMBER 1786

Source: Hilles 1929, cv (amended from a copy in the collection of R. Vernon, Taunton; Hilles, *Notes*)

London, Sep 5th 1786

My Lord

I have sent the Picture, according to your Lordships orders to Mr. Vandergucht[1] which I was very sorry to do, and I hope my sorrow did not proceed entirely from a selfish motive, for I felt the same sensation when I saw the Picture of Vandyke at Wilton, and the Titian at Northumberland house,[2] after they had been cleaned and painted upon, from being

Pictures of inestimable value, they are now hardly worth the rank of good copies; however, this is so to Painters' eyes only.

Without any disrespect to Mr. Vandergucht who as far as I know may repair the picture as well as any other man of the trade in England, the value of the picture will be lessend in proportion as he endeavours to make it better; and yet much must be done. What I propossed I am still confident was a good bargain on both sides however it is now over.

I have received the Seven Sarciments of Poussine, which the Duke of Richmond[3] has bought out of the Boccapuduli Palace at Rome. They are an exceeding fine set of pictures in perfect condition having never been touched I believe not even washed ever since they were painted they are consequently very dirty, but it is dirt that is easily washed off they cost him £2000. I should be glad to give him 500 for his bargain.

I am / with great respect / Your Lordship's

J. Reynolds

1 Benjamin Vandergucht (1753–94) painter and picture dealer.

2 JR refers to Van Dyck's *Pembroke Family* at Wilton and Titian's *Vendramin Family* (now National Gallery). He perhaps exaggerated their condition, cf. C. Gould, National Gallery cat., *Sixteenth-century Italian Schools*, 1975, 284, although Farington and Benjamin West agreed with him (*Farington Diary*, 14 September 1809).

3 In error for Rutland.

159

TO CHARLES TOWNLEY 6 SEPTEMBER 1786

Source: Bodleian Library (MS.Eng.misc.d.240, f.1)

Leicesterfields Sep 6 1786

Sir Joshua Reynolds presents his Compts. To Mr Townley[1] and has returned the order Mr. Couts,[2] sign'd and thanks him a thousand times for the trouble he has given him he thinks it need not now be any longer a secret who is the purchaser.

Endorsed: Copy of the order for payment of Mr. Jenkin's draft on me, wrote by Mr. Coutts & Signed by Sir Jos Reynolds

1 Townley had acted as go-between (and later as mediator) between JR and Thomas Jenkins, see Letter 160n5, in Rome concerning JR's purchase of Bernini's *Neptune and the Triton*, see Letter 160.

2 This is written on the verso of JR's instruction to Coutts, see Letter 280.

160

TO CHARLES, 4TH DUKE OF RUTLAND 7 SEPTEMBER 1786

Source: Belvoir Castle MSS

London Sep 7 1786

My Lord

I have <the> pleasure to acquaint Your Grace that the Pictures[1] are arrived safe in Leicester fields. I hang over them all day and have examined every Picture with the greatest acuracy. I think upon the whole that this must be considerd as the greatest work of Poussin, who was certainly one of <the> greatest Painters that ever lived.

I must mention at the same time that (except to the Eye of an Artist, who has the habit of seeing through dirt) they have a most unpromising appearance being incrustated with dirt, there are likwise two or three holes which may be easily mended when the Pictures are lined, excepting this, which is scarce worth mentioning, they are in perfect condition, they are just as Poussin left them, I believe they have never been washed or Vanishd since his time. It is very rare to see a Picture of Poussins or indeed of any Great Painter that has not been defaced in some part or rather and mended by picture cleaners, and have been reduced by that means to half their value.

I expected but seven Pictures, but there are eight. The sacriment of Baptism is represented by Christ baptising St. John but that Picture which does not seem to belong to the sett[2] (thogh equally excellent with the rest) is St. John baptising the multitude.

I canculate that those Pictures will cost your Grace 250 guineas each, I think they are worth double the mony.

A few evenings since I met Lord Besborough[3] at Brooks, I told him of the arrival of the Pictures, and askd him (as he rememberd them very well) what he thought they might be worth, he said they would be cheap at six thousand Pounds.

I think Mr. Beyers[4] managed very well to get them out of Rome, which is now much poorer, as England is richer than it was by this acquisition

I have likewise made a great purchase at Mr. Jenkins,[5] a statue of Neptune and a Triton grooped together, which was a fountain in the Villa Negroni (formerly Montalto) it is near eight feet high and reckond Berninis greatest

Gian Lorenzo Bernini, *Neptune and the Triton*, c.1620 (Victoria and Albert Museum)

work it will cost me about 700 Guineas before I get possession of it, I buy it upon speculation and hope to be able to sell it for a thousand.[6]

The Boccapadulo Palace was visited by all foreigners merely for the sake of these Pictures of Poussine, for I do not remember there were any others of any kind, Those Sacriments are much superior to those ~~of~~ in the Orleans Collection which I thought were but feebly painted, tho equally excellent ~~in the~~ <for> Invention[7]

There is arrived in the same Case a Portofolio with Prints after the Works of Raffielle in the Vatican and some Colour'd prints after Antient Painting.[8]

I saw this morning a very fine Picture of Raffielle of a Madonna and Bambino which Lord Cooper [brought?] from Italy[9] which he carried back with him again he sets off for Italy next week and I understand does not intend to return.

I am with the greatest respect &c

J Reynolds

1 The Poussin *Sacraments*, see Letter 136n2.

2 *Baptism* (see also Letter 162) was sold c.1939 and is now National Gallery, Washington; *Penance* was destroyed by fire at Belvoir in 1816. (see *Poussin Sacraments and Bacchanals*, National Gallery of Scotland, 1981, 71–84; Broun 1987, II, 218–21).

3 William Ponsonby, 2nd Earl of Bessborough (1704–93).

4 James Byres, see Letter 136n2.

5 Thomas Jenkins (1722–98), dealer and antiquary in Rome, where he lived from 1751, see Ingamells 1997, 553–56.

6 Bernini, *Neptune and the Triton*, now in the Victoria and Albert Museum; JR had alluded to the cast of the head of Neptune by Bernini in his *Tenth Discourse*, delivered on 11 December 1780.

7 The Rutland Poussins were the earlier series, completed in 1642 for Cassiano del Pozzo, whose descendant had married into the Boccapaduli family at Rome. The second set, commissioned by Fréart de Chantelou and painted in 1644–48, was acquired in 1716 by the duc d'Orléans; it is now on loan to the National Gallery of Scotland from the Duke of Sutherland. The Chantelou set is overall graver in mood; Doric replaces Corinthian architecture and landscape and anecdote are repressed (see *Sacraments and Bacchanals*, at n2, 99).

8 The Raphael prints were doubtless those by Giovanni Volpato whose engravings of the frescoes in the Stanze and Loggie of the Vatican were published in 1785.

9 3rd Earl Cowper, see Letter 35n3, had bought Raphael's *Niccolini Madonna*, from Zoffany in Florence in 1774 (now National Gallery, Washington).

161

TO HENDRIK JANSEN 2 OCTOBER 1786

Source: Yale Center for British Art

London Oct. 2d 1786

Dear Sir

I have sent according to your direction all the Discourses since the year 1776.[1] I have likewise inclosed the translation of Fresnoy by Mr. Mason, to which by his desire I added notes.[2] Those notes I apprehend may be usefull to Artists as they ~~treat of~~ <enter more into> the detail of the Art than I allowed myself to do in my Discourses.

As I have no doubt there is already a translation in French of Fresnoy, you may possibly think it worth while to republish it and add those notes.

I intended finding the Volume of the seven Discourses but forgot to put it up with the rest. If you have <it> not ~~got~~ in your possession I will immediatly send it.

The first Discourse was translated into French in the year 1769 and it appeard to me very well done. It was printed de l'Imprimerie de Michel Lambert rue de Cordeliers au Collége de Bourgogne, but if it should not be easily procured I can find you one.

I find I have been guilty of a mistake in not directing the little Box to Mr. St. George[3] it is directed to yourself which I hope you will receive safe.

I have only to add that I am very much flatter'd that my Discourses have met with your approbation and think myself much honourd in having them translated into the French language by your hand[4]

I am with the greatest respect

Your most humble

and most obedient servant

Joshua Reynolds

A Monsr Jansen / Inspecteur General de l'Académie/ Royale de Musique Rue de Bondi/ No. 23

1 Jansen had written to JR from Paris on 11 September to say he had just completed a translation from the Italian of the life and writings of A.R. Mengs, in which Mengs described JR's *Discourses* as liable to lead 'youth into error, because it abandons them to superficial principles, the only ones known to that author' – 'puó condurre i giovani nell'errore, poichè su lascia ai principi superficiali che sono i soli noti a quell'autore' (French ed. 1787, I, 52); see also Letters 35n2 and 176. Having, consequently, re-read

JR's *Discourses*, Jansen now sought his permission to translate them into French that the French might judge for themselves 'la séverité un peu hazardée de M. Mengs' (Hilles 1936, 62–63). For Mengs's comments, see Northcote 1818, II, 317–20; Hilles 1936, 61–62; Steffi Roettgen, *A.R. Mengs*, exh. cat., Kenwood, 1993, 17–18. JR himself had been a little provocative, suggesting in his *Fourteenth Discourse* that Batoni and Mengs 'will soon fall into the rank of Imperiale, Sebastiano Concha ... and the rest of their immediate predecessors'.

2 JR sent Jansen further copies of both on 19 November 1787. For Mason's Dufresnoy, see Letters 101 and 109.

3 St George, Directeur des Messageries Royales à Paris.

4 The letter is annotated with the draft of Jansen's reply, dated Paris October 10th 1786. See Letter 167.

162

TO CHARLES, 4TH DUKE OF RUTLAND 4 OCTOBER 1786

Source: Belvoir Castle MSS

London Oct 4th 1786

My Lord

I am very well disposed to fill this Letter with expressing the happiness which we all feel from Your Graces kindness towards my Nephew,[1] but as I am sure you would rather hear about the Pictures,[2] I shall only say that we feel it with all the gratitude we ought.

Everything relating to the Pictures has hitherto turned out most prospirously, they have past through the operation of lining and cleaning, ~~wld~~ which has been performed in my own house under my own eye. I was strongly recommended to a Neopolitan[3] as having an extraordinary secret for cleaning Pictures, which tho I declined listening to at first I was at length ~~per~~ persuaded to send for the man, and tryed him by putting in his hands a couple of what I thought the most difficult Pictures to clean of any in my house, the success was so complete that I thought I might securely trust him with the Sacriments, taking care to be allways present when he was at work. He possesses a liquid which <he> applies with a soft sponge only, <and> without any violence of friction takes off all the dirt & varnish without touching or in the least affecting the Colours; with~~out~~ all my experience in Picture cleaning he really amazed me. The Pictures are now just as they came from the Easel. I may now safely cong<r>atulate Your Grace on being relieved from all anxiety, we are safely landed all danger is over.

The eighth Picture – the Baptism[4] of the multitude, does not belong to the set nor is it engraved as the rest are, the figures are not upon the same scale, they are of less dimensions. This Picture is the only one that has been in a Picture cleaners hands, is more damaged and has been painted upon but it is equally excellent with the rest.

As to their originality, it <is> quite out of all question, they are not only original but in his very best manner, which cannot be said of the set in the Duke of Orleans's collection,[5] those latter are really painted in a very feeble manner, and tho they are undoubtedly originals, have somewhat the appearance of copies.

Wellbore Ellis Agar[6] told me they were offer'd to him some years ago for £1500 but that he declined the purchase by the advice of Hamilton the Painter,[7] on account, as he said of their being in bad condition. It is very extraordinary that a man so conversant in Pictures should not distinguish between mere dirtyness and what is defaced or damaged Mr Agar dined with me a few days since with a party of Connoiseurs, but the admiration of the company and particularly of the good preservation of those Pictures, so mortified him, at having missed them, that he was for the whole day, very much what the vulgar call, down in the mouth for he made very little use of it either for eating or talking.

Lord Spencer[8] tells me, that he stood next and was to have had them if Your Grace had declined the purchase, One of the articles, he says, between Beyers & the Marquis[9] was that he should bring the Strangers as usual to see the Copies and which he says he is obliged to do, and I suppose swear they are originals. and it is very probable those copies will be sold again and other copies put in their place, this trick has been played to my knowledge with Pictures of Salvator Rosa by some of his descendants who are now living at Rome,[10] who pretend that the Pictures have been in the family ever since their ancestors death.

The Connoiseurs or rather Picture dealers who are better judges of the prizes of Pictures value the Sacriments at £5000 Vandergucht who is both a Painter and dealer[11] says that if had any Idea of those Pictures being to be sold he would have sat out for Rome on purpose to purchase them.

All these circumstances I think may help to make your Grace perfectly satisfied with your bargain.

Lord Mansfield copy is quite finishd, but I am sorry and ashamed to say the other of the Children is not,[12] however I am about it, and do every day a little to it, I hope within a fortnight to be able to send them both together.

I cannot conclude this long, and I am afraid tedious letter without again thanking your Grace for your last very kind and obliging letter.

I am with the greatest respect
Your Graces
most humble
and most obliged servant
Joshua Reynolds

1 Joseph Palmer, see Appendix I, was instituted Dean of Cashel on 22 June 1787.
2 Poussin's *Sacraments*, see Letter 136n2. On 19 October the *Morning Chronicle* announced that JR had purchased 'Nicholas Poussin's famous designs of the Seven Sacraments of the Romish Church ... The purchaser, we learn, is the Duke of Rutland', and on 18 October Rutland told his chaplain Thomas Thoroton (see Letter 283n10) that he had purchased Poussin's *Seven Sacraments* which 'after a certain time will be sent to Belvoir, there to remain, I hope, as long as the name of Manners and its splendour endures' (*HMC Rutland*, III, 350).
3 Presumably Biondi, see Letter 175.
4 *Baptism*, see Letter 160n2.
5 See Letter 160n7.
6 Welbore Ellis Agar (d. 1805), collector and commissioner of customs; his collection was bought by Lord Grosvenor in 1806 (*Farington Diary*, 16 April 1806).
7 Gavin Hamilton (1723–98) painter and antiquary, see Letter 9n9.
8 George Spencer, 2nd Earl Spencer (1758–1834), elected to the Club in 1778, who had been in Rome in November–December 1785.
9 i.e. James Byres and the owner of the Boccapaduli Palace.
10 The house in the Strada Gregoriana, built by Salvator Rosa belonged in 1779 belonged to his descendant Augusto Rosa who earned a precarious living by making cork models of Roman ruins; the walls 'covered with Landscapes painted in Water Colour by old Salvator's pupils, which, tho' not executed with much neatness & delicacy, partook of the Spirit of their Master' (Thomas Jones, *Wal. Soc.*, XXXII, 1951, 87)
11 See Letter 158n1.
12 See Letters 147n4, 149n1.

163

TO JAMES BOSWELL [18 OCTOBER 1786]

Source: Fifer 1976, 238

Wednesday

This being St. Lukes day, the Company of Painters dines in their Hall in the City,[1] to which I am invited and desired to bring any friend with me.

As you love to see life in all its modes if you have a mind to go ~~I will call on you~~ I will car[2] you about two o'clock, the black-guards dine at half an hour after.

Yours

J Reynolds

1 The Painter Stainers Hall; JR had been presented with the Freedom of the Company in 1784. The date of this letter is confirmed by the *Morning Chronicle*, 21 October 1786, which mentioned JR and Boswell attending the St Luke's Day dinner. See also Boswell's 'View of My Life [from 20 September] till 1 November 1786' where Boswell recorded that JR 'carried me to dine with the Painter Stainers in their Hall' (Fifer 1976, 238n1).

2 Perhaps a Devonshire usage, i.e. 'I will car' you' (as suggested by Frederick Pottle in an undated letter to Hilles).

164

TO CHARLES, 4TH DUKE OF RUTLAND 2 DECEMBER 1786

Source: Belvoir Castle MSS

Dec: 2d 1786

My Lord

I did not receive your Graces Letter till to day, tho dated so far back as the 13th Nov. kept back by contrary winds, ten packets arrived at the same time. The Picture[1] has been finished some days and waits only for the frame, which the frame-maker says will require eight days longer Mr. Burke gives me such an account of the young Ladies that I dread the the comparison of the original with my copy.[2] Mr. Burk is very much pleased with his Tour to Ireland and speaks much of Your Graces great politeness to him. The voyage did not agree so well with his son.[3] he was sea-sick in his passage over, and has continued ill ever since.

I sent to Mr. Hill[4] to enquire about the Prints and books[5] which I find were sent away some time since, he supposes they are arrived by this time. I looked at the Prints before they were packed up I was mortified to see such trifling ornaments publishd with so much pomp merely because they are antique or painted by some of Raffaels Scholars in the Vatican An indiscriminate admiration for every thing that is Antient, appears to me full as prejudicial to the advancement of Art, as a total neglect of them would be.

Prince Rezzonico[6] was much mortified he said to see the Sacraments of Poussine in England and for the same reason that you (speaking to me) may be glad, but I must write to my Brother, says he, who is Secretary of State, that he should reprimand the Inspectors for suffering those Pictures to come out of Rome, sometime after this Lady Spencer[7] told me that in consequence of this smugling [~~there~~] <it> is now Death to attempt sending Pictures out of Rome with out being first examined.

I am Your Graces most obedient
humble servant
Joshua Reynolds

1 John Henry Granby with the Ladies Elizabeth and Katherine Manners, see Letter 147n4.
2 Edmund Burke had been in Ireland for two weeks in October.
3 Richard Burke.
4 I.e. Joseph Hill, see Letter 281n1.
5 See Letter 160.
6 Carlo-Gastone della Torre di Rezzonico (1742–96), Neapolitan poet; his brother was presumably the Cardinal Carlo Rezzonico (1724–99), 'camerlingo di Sta. Chiesa', who authorised the export of works of art from Rome (copies of some *permessi* signed by him from the period 1783–94 are in the Brinsley Ford Archive in the Paul Mellon Centre, London).
7 Lavinia Bingham (1762–1831), daughter of Lord Lucan, m. 1781 George, 2nd Earl Spencer; she had been in Rome with her husband in November–December 1785.

165

TO JOHN BOYDELL 8 DECEMBER 1786

Source: Collection Frits Lugt, Fondation Custodia

Dec 8th 1786

Sir Joshua Reynolds presents his Compts to Mr. Alderman Boydell He finds in his Advertisement[1] that he is styled Portrait Painter to his Majesty, it is a matter of no great consequence, but he does not know why his title is changed, he is styled in his Patent Principal Painter to His Majesty.

Mr. Alderman Boydell / Cheapside

1 In Boydell's proposals to publish an illustrated Shakespeare, see Letter 171, JR was described as 'Portrait Painter to his Majesty and President of the Royal Academy'. JR received payments from Boydell of £500 in June 1786 for a *Scene in Macbeth* 'not yet begun' (Petworth; Mannings 2103); 500gns on 22 June 1789 for the *Death of Cardinal Beaufort* (Petworth; Mannings 2063), and 100 gns on the same day for 'the Fairy Puck or Robin Goodfellow' (private collection; Mannings 2142), see Cormack, 146–47. JR was not seen at his best in these pictures, see LT, II, 501–04; W.H. Friedman, *Boydell's Shakespeare Gallery*, 1976, 116–24. For the subsequent financial entanglements, see Letter 230.

166

TO EDMOND MALONE 15 DECEMBER 1786

Source: Hilles 1929, CXII

Dec.15, 1786

My dear Sir
I wish you would just run your eye over my Discourse,[1] if you are not too much busied in what you have made your own employment. I wish that you would do more than merely look at it, – that you would examine it with a critical eye, in regard to grammatical correctness, the propriety of expression, and the truth of the observations.

Yours,

J. Reynolds

1 The *Thirteenth Discourse*, delivered on 11 December 1786 and published in January 1787, see Lettters 167 and 171.

167

TO HENDRIK JANSEN 10 JANUARY 1787

Source: Yale Center for British Art

London Jan 10th 1787

Dear Sir
I have herewith sent the last Discourse,[1] The Printing of which was delayed on account of the Christmas holydays when the Printers men will not work.

I should be much obliged to you for an Impression when the Translation[2] is finished

I am with great respect

Yours &c

J Reynolds

Annotated: (in Jansen's hand) Rep. le 18 Janvier/1787

1 See Letter 161; the *Thirteenth Discourse*, see Letters 166 and 171, published in January 1787 (Hilles 1936, 143, 292–93).

2 See Letter 176.

168

TO CHARLES TOWNLEY II FEBRUARY 1787

Source: British Museum (Townley MSS)

Leicester fields Feb 11th 1787

Dear Sir

I have every reason to be perfectly satisfied with Mr. Jenkins[1] Conduct in regard to the Neptune,[2] except that what relates to this after-consideration, which distresses me very much, as I wish to act not only with propriety but am allways ready to do what any man of the most refined sentiments of honour should think right for to be done.

I took an opportunity a few days since to mention to a friend, whom I thought a very competent judge of propriety, the appeal which Mr. Jenkins has made to my honour for an advance price He observed that after the bargain was made however more valuable the statue might turn out, or however great the sum that he might afterwards be offered or on the other side, if I had repented my offer, ~~I was~~ we were obliged to abide by the agreement, and that in delicacy no advance payment should have been mentioned. I cannot avoid telling who was the person I applied to. It was Lord Ossory,[3] whose opinion in all cases has allways great weight with me. Mr. Jenkins he added has certainly acted fairly, and honourable, but it is no more than what you have a right to expect from a man of honour, and his reward is the character he establishes by such conduct.

If Mr Jenkins was a poor man I should really think it my duty to reward him for doing his duty, but it is the reverse he is the rich man and I am comparitively the poor man. He must therefore be contented with my acknowledgments and thanks; and I do not forget that I am under the greatest obligations to you for the attention you have given to this business, but indeed it appears to me that I should lay myself open to ridicule to pretend to make a present of mony to such a warm man as Mr. Jenkins.[4]

I am with the greatest respect

Yours &c

J Reynolds

1 See Letter 160n5.

2 Bernini's *Neptune and the Triton*, see Letter 160n6.

3 The 2nd Earl of Upper Ossory, see Appendix II.

4 Townley replied the same day (Townley MSS) that Jenkins had offered the *Neptune and the Triton* 'at the estimation which in the first hurry of his Negroni purchase he had confidentially mentioned to me in the general calculation of his bargains, [and] seems to me to deserve, if not a pecuniary gratuity, at least some flattering verbal gratification'; in a postscript he suggested how JR might write to Jenkins, a formula JR adopted in the following letter.

169

TO CHARLES TOWNLEY [12 FEBRUARY 1787]

Source: British Museum (Townley MSS)

Dear Sir

I have inclosed another ostensible Letter[1] which I hope will meet your Idea and am very glad you stopt the former.

Yours sincerely

J Reynolds

1 See Letter 170.

170

TO CHARLES TOWNLEY 12 FEBRUARY 1787

Source: British Museum (Townley MSS) copy in Townley's hand

Leicester fields Feb 12th 1787

Dear Sir

When you next write to Mr. Jenkins[1] I shall be much obliged to you, if you will express my warmest thanks and acknowledgments for putting in my possession this inestimable work of Bernini.[2] it is happy for me that tho' Mr. Jenkins has lived so long abroad he still preserves his affection to his native country, for I am convinced that if he had been indifferent to what country this great work was sent to, he might have had a much higher price than that which ~~he~~ he suffered me to pay for it, he has the satisfaction of acting contrary to his interest, for the sake of embellishing his own country with the greatest modern work of art, that it at present possesses, if Mr. Jenkins had demanded what I really think to be the value, it would be far above my power of purchasing it, I must leave it therefore to his consideration and candour whether in respect to us both, it is not most proper that the matter should end as it now stands, at the same time I hope to have some opportunity of shewing Mr. Jenkins that I am not insensible of his very honourable and disinterested conduct in this business.[3]

I am with the greatest respect

your most humble and most obedient

servant

J Reynolds

1 This letter was enclosed with the previous letter and sent on by Townley to Jenkins in Rome; for Jenkins, see Letter 160n5

2 Bernini's *Neptune and the Triton*, see Letter 160n6.

3 On 13 February 1787 Townley wrote to Jenkins describing himself as 'the promoter of this purchase'; 'your taking it [the Neptune] again, now that the public suppose it his [JR's] property, will, I think, be awkward, his keeping it, without your full concurrence, will also be awkward. In short I never felt myself more awkwardly situated and I wait yours with anxiety' (Townley MSS, annotated by Townley 'extract from my letter to Jenkins 13 February 1787 inclosing Sir Jos Reynolds's letter upon Neptune').

171

TO CHARLES, 4TH DUKE OF RUTLAND 13 FEBRUARY 1787

Source: Belvoir Castle MSS

London Feby 13th 1787

My Lord

I will not trouble your Grace with the various causes of the Pictures of the Children and of Lord Mansfield being delayed so long,[1] it would take up the whole Letter I can only say they were inevitable, however they are now on their way to Dublin. In regard to the Sacriments,[2] I hear <u>people</u> continually regret that they are not to remain in London, they speak in a general principle as wishing that the great works of Art which this Nation possesses, are not, (as in other Nations collected together in the Capital but dispersed about the Country, and consequently not seen by Foreigners so as to impress them with an adequate Idea of the riches in Virtù which the Nation contains. A thought is just come into my head, that if Your Grace is determined to send them to Belvoir to let them stand in the Academy, in a room by themselves during the Exhibition, to give an opportunity of their being seen by the Students as well as the Connoiseurs before they finally leave London. If Your Grace has no objection to this Scheme I am sure it would be of great service to the Artists both the young and the old.[3]

I have order'd very handsome frames to be made for them, at ten Guineas each, & very broad, which I think gives a picture a more consequential air.[4]

Mr. Locks Discobolus as I have been informed is not to be sold.[5] At a sale which he had last year of his Marbles and models he bought that Statue inn, and I am told since that he intends to keep it for the use of his Son[6] who is a youth of a most extra<o>rdinary Genius in our Art, and which his Father intends he shall practice tho he will have a very good fortune at his Fathers death.

I have lately arrived a modern statue of a Neptune with a Triton[7] which far exceeds Mr. Locks statue or any other in this Nation. Your Grace may form some Idea of it from the Print in Rossis statues,[8] if such a Book is to be found in Ireland. I bought it of Jenkins who purchased all the Statues in the Villa Negroni, formerly Villa Montalto, the subject is the Quos ego of Virgil.[9]

But the greatest news relating to Virtù is Alderman Boydels scheme of having Pictures and Prints taken from those Pictures of the most interesting scenes of Shakespear[10] by which all the Painters and Engravers find engagements for eight or ten years; He wishes me to do eight Pictures but I have engaged only for one he has insisted on my taking Earnest mony, and to my great surprise left upon my table five hundred pounds, – to have as much more as I shall demand,

I have enclosed Boydels proposals and my last Discourse[11] which I hope will meet with Your Graces approbation.

I am with the greatest respect
Your Graces most humble
and most obedient servant
Joshua Reynolds

1 The copy of Lord Mansfield and the portrait of John Henry Granby with the Ladies Elizabeth and Katherine Manners, see Letters 147n4 and 149n1.

2 The Poussin *Sacraments*, see Letter 136n2.

3 It was agreed, see Letter 172.

4 Cormack, 163.

5 William Lock (1732–1810) of Norbury; he had acquired his *Discobolus* (now at Duncombe Park) from Cavaceppi in Rome (F. Haskell and N. Penny, *Taste and the Antique*, 1981, 200, 202n10); JR had mentioned it in his *Tenth Discourse* (delivered on 10 December 1780). His sale was Christie's, 16 April 1785.

6 William Lock (1767–1847), amateur artist of unfulfilled promise.
7 The Bernini; JR had already told Rutland of it, see Letter 160.
8 Domenico de Rossi, *Raccolta di Statue antiche e moderne*, 1704, pl.71.
9 *Aeneid*, I, 135.
10 For JR and Boydell's scheme, see W.H. Friedman, *Boydell's Shakespeare Gallery*, Garland 1976, 116–24; Postle 1995, 248–59.
11 The *Thirteenth Discourse*, published in January 1787, see Letter 167.

172

TO CHARLES, 4TH DUKE OF RUTLAND 3 MAY 1787

Source: Belvoir Castle MSS

London May 3d 1787

My Lord

I was very glad to find by Your Graces Letter that you wished to have made some purchases in Lord Northingtons sale,[1] particularly Portraits of Vandyck. tho I have not bought any of those portraits I have bought by far the most curious and most valuable part of that Collection which is a sketch upon board in black and white of the procession of the Knights of the Garter.[2] This sketch authenticates a circumstance that is allways mentiond in Vandycks life, of a project of King Charles of employing him totally on this subject to the exclusion of all other business but that his demand of £80000 being thought exorbitant, whilst they were treating for a less sum the Kings troubles came on and put an end to the treaty, The sum demanded is incredible I suspect therefore ~~a nought~~ an o by some accident was added, which would bring it to £8000 and even that would be according to the value of mony at present £24000.

There were three or four portraits which were called Vandyck but were certainly not of his hand. I did not think it worth while to send a commision for them, There was indeed a true picture of Claude Lorrain, but not his best and had been much damaged.

The sketch which I bought with a view of offering to your Grace at the price it cost whether much or little was sold for sixty and some odd pounds I sent a commision for a hundred that your Grace may form some Idea of it I have spoilt a print by folding it, in order to accompany this Letter.

The King when I accompanyed him at the Exhibition took much notice of the Poussins,[3] more than I expected, as they are of a different [kind?] from what he generally likes. He asked many questions where they came from? out of what palace? what they cost? and whether there was any suspicion of their being Copies to all which questions I answer'd to the best of my knowledge.

I have been often angry with myself for having declined parting with the portrait of Albert Durer[4] as your Grace wished to have it in your collection. As it is a rare and curious thing it canot be better placed and fixed than at Belvoir I shall there<fore> take the liberty of sending it with the Poussins.

I am extremely sorry to hear of Her Graces indisposition, it maybe hoped that the change of season may be a serviceable towards the Establishment of Her Graces health as the Change of Climate to which she is so averse.[5]

I am unwilling to give up all thought of going to Ireland this summer but am in great doubt whether I shall be able to compass it, I am sure I am, as I ought to be very much flatter'd by Your Graces kind invitation
I am with the greatest respect

Your Graces most humble and
most obedient servant
Joshua Reynolds

Upon second thoughts I have just sent the Print roled up.[6]

1 Robert Henley, 2nd Earl of Northington (1747–86), lord lieutenant of Ireland 1783–84; he d. unm. in Paris, 5 July 1786. His sale is not listed by Lugt, *Dictionnaire des Ventes.*

2 The Van Dyck remains at Belvoir. Pasquin alleged that, shortly after 1760, JR had been asked to imitate this sketch by painting the procession of the Knights of the Garter at the Coronation of George III, but had asked a thousand guineas (Pasquin 1796, 69; Broun 1987, II, 96–97); the tale seems unlikely.

3 JR had asked Rutland if he might show them with the RA exhibition that year, see Letter 171.

4 Probably the portrait at Belvoir of Edzard I, Count of East Friesland, listed as Durer until 1891 but now attributed to Jacob Cornelisz van Oostsanen, see Broun 1987, II, 249–50. Two portraits by Durer owned by JR were sold after his death: a self-portrait (Christie's, 14 March 1795, lot 23) and an unspecified portrait (Phillips, 8 May 1798, lot 18).

5 She was recovering by early June (*HMC Rutland*, III, 393).

6 i.e. of the Van Dyck, presumably that by Cooper of 1782 (Broun 1987, II, 97).

173

TO JOSEPH BONOMI 2 JULY 1787

Source: Hilles 1929, CXVIII (LT, II, 561–62)

July 2nd, 1787

Sir Joshua Reynolds presents his compliments to Mr. Bonhomme, and is very sorry that his engagements have prevented him from calling on him since his misfortune.[1] He hopes to hear from himself that he is nearly recovered.

The business of this note is principally to desire that he would once more become a candidate to be an Associate of the Academy, when he hopes top be able to convince the Academicians of the propriety and even necessity of electing him an Associate, and consequently an Academician, &c.[2]

If he has not yet subscribed his name, he begs he would do it immediately, as the time for subscribing is nearly elapsed.[3]

1 Bonomi had broken his arm in a carriage accident (LT, II, p. 561n).

2 Bonomi had failed on two previous occasions; JR now wished him to be Professor of Perspective at the RA, a post for which he would have to be a full RA; he was duly elected ARA on 2 November 1789; see Letters 192, 194–97.

3 Candidates were required to post their names three months before the date of election, which in the present instance was 3 December.

174

TO BENNET LANGTON 31 AUGUST [1787]

Source: Yale Center for British Art

Friday, Aug 31

<u>I have no Children</u>. I therefore send the present, which I found on my return to town to <u>your</u> Children.[1] It is scarce worth acceptance, and my only apology is that my friend thought it worth while to send them to me, I suppose therefore they are eminently good.[2] I thought it necessary to be able to say I had tasted them, which makes a little deficiency is one of the pottles – Yours

JReynolds

Bennett Langton Esq

1 Langton had four sons and five daughters when this letter was written (a last daughter was born the following October).

2 JR had just returned from a visit to Ampthill, Lord Ossory's seat.

175

TO PHILIP, 2ND EARL OF HARDWICKE [BEFORE OCTOBER 1787][1]

Source: British Library (Add MSS 35350, f.51)

Sir Joshua Reynolds presents his Compliments to Lord Hardwick. Biondi[2] an Italian who lives in Oxford Road on the right hand side of the way, not far from Orchard Street, his name on the door Sir Joshua has seen some Pictures which he has cleaned for the Duke of Rutland[3] that were extremely well cleaned & mended better done than any he had ever seen before.

The Earl of Hardwick

1 Apparently written after Letter 162 and before the Duke of Rutland's death on 24 October 1787.
2 Presumably the Neapolitan restorer mentioned in Letter 162.
3 Presumably the Poussin *Sacraments*, see Letter 162.

176

TO HENDRIK JANSEN 19 NOVEMBER 1787

Source: Hilles 1936, 66

Dear Sir
I have here-with sent you, according to your desire, du Fresnoy's translation, and the volume of Discourses;[1] the second volume will not be completed till next year; that is, those quarto Discourses will not be collected into an octavo volume, till another Discourse is added; which will not be till december 10th 1788, when I shall certainly take care to have them bound in the same manner and sent you.

I return you many thanks for the copies of your translation very much:[2] my approbation is of no great value; but having put it into the hands of some of my friends who are better judges, they speak of it in the highest terms, particularly a french gentleman who resides here. A connoiseur, and equally a master both of the french and english language, says that it has so much facility and elegance that it has not the appearance of a translation, but reads like an original work; this I apprehend is the highest commendation that a translation can receive.

I confess I am very much flatterd by the attention you have given to this work, and very proud I am to see myself strutting in so elegant a dress.

I hope the french artists will think better of it than M. Mengs did.[3] That it has faults enough there is no doubt; but it appears very strange that M. Mengs should think <u>that</u> superficial which endeavours to fix the principles of art in the great and general principles of all other arts, and on the invariable conduct of nature.

I am, etc.

J Reynolds

London, Nov. 19th. 1787

1 See Letter 161.
2 *Discours prononcés a l'Académie Royale de Peinture de Londres, Par M. Josuè Reynolds, Président de la dite Académie. Suivis des notes du même auteur, sur le Poeme de l'Art de Peindre de Dufresnoy*, Paris, 1787 (see Hilles 1936, 293–94).
3 See Letter 161n1.

177

TO BENNET LANGTON 23 NOVEMBER 1787

Source: Hilles 1929, CXXI

Leicester fields 23 [1]

Dear Sir

I am going this Evening to the Academy to propose Mr. Gibbon to be Professor of Antient History in the room of Dr. Franklin.[2]

There is another Professorship vacant Professor of Antient Literature which was held by Dr Johnson.[3] If you have no objection to succeed our late friend I have no doubt but the Academy will accept my recommendation. There is no duty required, we desire only the honour of your name, for which you have the entrè of the Academy and we give you once a year a very good dinner, I mean that before the Exhibition and you see the Exhibition as often as you please <u>gratis</u>.

I have been writing in the dark and perceive now I have a candle that I have begun this letter on the wrong side.

Yours sincerely

J Reynolds

1 The sheet is torn, but the date is supplied by the elections cited below.
2 Edward Gibbon (1737–94) was duly elected on 23 November 1787, succeeding Dr Thomas Francklin (1721–84), professor of Greek at Cambridge. Gibbon later offended JR by declining to present him with a signed copy of the last volume of his *Decline and Fall of the Roman Empire* in 1788 (Farington Diary, 6 September 1805).
3 Langton was duly elected on 23 November 1787.

178

TO GEORGE, 1ST MARQUESS OF BUCKINGHAM 2 DECEMBER 1787

Source: John Waller, London, Catalogue 119, 1878 (as dated 1786)

London, Decr. 2 178[7]

My Lord

When your Lordship went last to Ireland[1] I took the liberty of recommending to your protection my nephew, Mr. Palmer, he has been since promoted to the Deanery of Cashel, which is but of small value.

If your Lordship, when an opportunity offers, will give him a remove that his income may be a little encreased,[2] it will be acknowledged with the greatest gratitude by

Your Lordship's most Humble and
obedient servant
Joshua Reynolds

1 Lord Buckingham had been lord-lieutenant of Ireland in 1782–83; he returned as lord-lieutenant in November 1787, arriving in Dublin on 16 December, succeeding the 4th Duke of Rutland, who d. in Dublin on 24 October 1787, aged thirty-three.
2 JR had received his answer by 7 December, see Letter 179.

179

TO JOSEPH PALMER 7 DECEMBER 1787

Source: Yale Center for British Art

London Dec 7 1787

Dear Nephew

I really condole with you on the loss of your Patron the Duke of Rutland you are not likely to find another with whom I have equal interest. I had even a demand upon him having made him a considerable present of a Picture, indeed two Pictures,[1] but so near his death that ~~he~~ I never receiv'd his thanks for them.

I wrote a letter to the Marquis of Buckingham[2] ~~of~~ <to> which he was polite enough to give an answer which I have enclosed tho it is of no great import Fitzherbert,[3] is an old friend of mine and I shall certainly speak to him, but My Lord being a man of business and who loves it for its own sake he is not like to leave much power in the hands of his Secretary For fear I should forget it I must mention now, that Mr. Conyngham[4] when he dined with me desired that he might know you. You must make it your business therefore to be introduced, or you may wait on him yourself without any further introduction.

The bearer of this Letter is no less than the Archbishop of Cashel,[5] he calld on me this morning to know if I had any commands to you, I declined troubling him but he pressed it in so polite a manner that I accepted. It was the first time I ever saw him. I asked him however to dine with me but he was engaged everyday he stayd in Town but that next time he came he certainly have that pleasure &c his appearance and manner prejudice one very much in his favour as much as his Character does. He speaks very handsomely of you you ~~mutt~~ will be the Hare with many friends if you not get something amongst all these great men

Miss Palmer is still in Devonshire Mr. Johnson has been the whole summer at Suaffam hunting shooting and dancing, he lives totally a life of pleesure and amusement[6]

I beg my most affectionate compts to Mrs Palmer[7] whom we hope to see this ~~su~~ next summer.

Yours affectionately

J Reynolds

1 See Letter 172 (portrait by Durer); the second picture may have been the Van Dyck sketch described in the same letter, or a panel by Jan van der Heyden, *Waterside scene with Bathers*, still at Belvoir, acquired by JR in 1781 (Broun 1987, II, 19–20).

2 See Letter 178.

3 See Letter 94n2; chief-secretary to the lord lieutenant of Ireland 1787–89.

4 Probably the recipient of Letters 146 and 148.

5 Charles Agar, see Letter 116n5.

6 Miss [Mary] Palmer, Richard Johnson (who had returned from Bengal by 1786), see Appendix I.

7 Joseph Palmer married Eliza Edwards in 1787.

180

TO JAMES, 7TH EARL OF SALISBURY 11 FEBRUARY 1788

Source: Pierpont Morgan Library

Feb 11th 1788

Sir

The liberty I take in requesting a favour from a person to whom I have ~~the~~ scarce the honour of being known,[1] requires some apology – I wish very much to hear Mr. Burk open the business of the tryal,[2] which he thinks will be probably on the first day, as my deafness debarred me from entertaining any hope of that kind, it prevented me from solliciting my friends for a Ticket.

I have been this minute offer'd a place in the Managers Box, provided I can procure to the person who thus accommodates me, a place in the Lord High Chamberlains Box.

I am conscious I have taken a great liberty but I still hope <you> will excuse it.

I am with the greatest respect
Your most humble and
most obedient servant
Joshua Reynolds

1 JR wrote to Lord Salisbury (1743–1823) in his official capacity of lord chamberlain.
2 The trial of Warren Hastings (see Letter 88) opened in Westminster Hall on 13 February 1788; Edmund Burke's opening address lasted four days.

181

TO RICHARD COSWAY 27 APRIL [1788][1]

Source: Unidentified sale catalogue, lot 124

27 April

Dear Sir

Could you manage so as to get Capt. Morris[2] to dine with us tomorrow. I know him but little, but as he has dined ~~at~~ <with> the Prince of Wales, many of his R. Highness friends must of course know him enough to bring him with them, the reason of my wishing him to dine with us, is

~~the~~ from our singers being obliged to leave us at eight o'clock <on account of the Antient Music> by which time our dinner will be scarce over. If you think the above scheme practicable, send to Mr. Newton[3] for a Ticket.

Yours

J Reynolds

I wish you would enquire what hour H.R.H. chooses to dine, as from the President & Council

1 The RA dinner of 28 April 1788 was attended by the Prince of Wales; Cosway had been appointed his Miniature Painter in 1785.

2 Charles Morris (1745–1838), song-writer and wit, known as 'The Sun of the Table' in the Prince of Wales's circle at Carlton House; *A Collection of Songs by the inimitable Captain Morris* was published in 1786.

3 F.M. Newton, secretary of the RA, see Letter 21n7.

182

TO ANDREW STRAHAN 1 JUNE 1788

Source: Pierpont Morgan Library

June 1 1788.

Dear Sir

I am extremely mortifyed that I cannot have the honour of waiting on you today. I yesterday receiv'd a message from a family that I cannot refuse, of their intention of dining with me at Richmond this day. I endeavourd to put their visit off till next Sunday, but they are going out of Town. I only beg you to believe that this does not proceed from a capricious disposition. I consider such engagements as I was under to-day with you, in a much more serious manner than the generality of the world, and nothing but such circumstances as I am convinced would satisfy you, had I time to explain them, make me now break my engagement[1]

I am with great respect

Your most humble

& obedient servant

JReynolds

Strahan Esqr / New Street

1 JR's pocket-book has on 1 June 1788 '5 Mr. Strahan'.

183

TO THE RT REVD SHUTE BARRINGTON 16 JUNE 1788

Source: Hyde Collection

Sir Joshua Reynolds presents his Compts to the Bishop of Salsbury. He has not yet receivd from Mr. Wyatt the Cloth, he promises to begin the Picture the moment he ~~has~~ receive~~d~~s it[1]

June 16

Annotated: Sir Joshua R June 16.1788.

1 JR did not complete this portrait of Bishop Barrington who had previously sat to JR in 1759 (private collection; Mannings 121), and to Romney in 1784–88.

184

TO JOHN, 2ND EARL OF UPPER OSSORY 2 OCTOBER 1788

Source: National Library of Ireland (MS 8012, f.111)

London Octr. 1788

My Lord

Having receivd a very fine Turtle about a fortnight ago, and having now eaten it, it appears to be high time to thank your Lordship for this opportunity of regaling my friends, and I think I made up for the purpose a very good party – Lord Mornington Sheridan Courteney Malone, and Mr Fizgibbon ~~and~~ Capt Jephson and the Bishop of Killalo from Ireland,[1] with two or three more in order to balance all this spirit with a propor-tion quantity of Caput mortuum, which I hold to be a necessary circumspection in making up a party, Mr. Jephson is a great treat, tho he did not on that day exhibit but I have heard him since with great delight.

I hear the Postmans Bell so must conclude tho I dont know whether I had any thing more to say, than thank you, except to beg my most respectfull compliments to the ladies.

I am with the greatest respect

JReynolds

1 Richard Wellesley, 2nd Earl of Mornington (1760–1842), cr. Marquess of Wellesley 1799, governor of Bengal 1797–1805; John Courtenay (1741–1816) MP and litterateur, elected to the Club 1788; John Fitzgibbon (1749–1802), cr. 1st Baron Fitzgibbon 1789 and 1st Earl of Clare 1795, lord chancellor of Ireland (see Letter 218); Robert Jephson

(1736–1803), dramatist, master of the horse in Ireland from 1769; for Thomas Barnard (Bishop of Killaloe), Edmond Malone and Sheridan, see Appendix II.

185

TO CALEB WHITEFOORD 26 NOVEMBER [1788]

Source: British Library (Add MSS 36595, f.208)

Wednesday Nov 26[1]

If Mr. Whitefoord is not engaged tomorrow Sir Joshua Reynolds requests the honour of his company at dinner at five o'clock

1 After JR's knighthood in 1769, November 26 fell on a Wednesday in 1777, 1783 and 1788; on 26 November 1788 JR notes he is 'at home' at 5 o'clock.

186

TO JOHN BACON 25 DECEMBER 1788

Source: Hyde Collection

Dec 25 1788

Dear Sir

I wish tomorrow morning you would take a Walk to Westminster Abbey and look at the vacant niche which I think is next to the Monument of Handell that space is destined for a whole length statue of Dr. Johnson the figure to be near naked in the manner of Pithagoras <of> which we have a cast in the Academy.[1] After which I shall be obliged to you for an estimate of the whole expence of such a Monument with all its acompanyments of Books &c

Yours

JReynolds

Mr. Bacon

1 Apparently the cast of *Demosthenes*, which remains at the Royal Academy. Baretti's *Guide through the Royal Academy*, 1781, 23, describes a 'Pythagoras. A fine Statue, supposed to represent the Philosopher, I know not on what Ground. The Original is in the Duke of Dorset's Collection, and the Cast was a present of his Grace to the Royal Academy'. The original statue, acquired from the Duke of Dorset's descendants in 1929 by the Ny Carlsberg Glyptothek, Copenhagen, is identified as Demosthenes; no classical statue of Pythagoras is otherwise recorded. I am most grateful to Nicholas Savage for his help with this identification.

John Bacon
Dr Samuel Johnson's Monument in St Paul's Cathedral 1796

Johnson's monument, an undertaking close to Reynolds's heart, took eleven years to negotiate. Reynolds had first mentioned it to the Duke of Rutland in May 1785 (Letter 134) and Westminster Abbey had then agreed to accommodate it. Public contributions were solicited by advertisement, but the response was abysmal.

The project was revived at a meeting of the Club on 23 December 1788. Reynolds approached John Bacon who named a fee of £600, which subsequently grew to over £1000 (Letter 218). There was a public meeting on 5 January 1790, chaired by Sir Joseph Banks, and a Committee was formed to raise support (Letters 193, 215, 220, 250). On 17 March 1790 Westminster Abbey renewed their agreement and by April 1791 £900 had been collected.

But by April 1791 Reynolds had decided that St Paul's was the better site (Letter 218), Westminster being 'so stuff'd with statuary' while St Pauls 'has hitherto Lain Fallow for the harvest of the Chisel'. He offered to supply any deficiency of funding himself, but his intended gift of £100 from the RA was vetoed by the King (Letter 227). In 1791 Reynolds approached Dr Samuel Parr (who had been black-balled at the Club 28 March 1786) for the Latin epitaph and a Greek inscription for the scroll (Letters 225, 226). The Monument was finally erected in February 1796, exactly four years after Reynolds's death (Boswell, IV, 464–72).

187

TO EDMUND BURKE 25 JULY 1789

Source: Sheffield Archives (WWM Bk P 1/2177)

London July 25 1789

Dear Sir

We – that is Mr. Malone, Mr. Courtney[1] and myself propose to have the pleasure of dining with <you> on Monday, the day after tomorrow.

I should have given this intelligence yesterday that you might have time to forbid us if you were otherwise engaged. If that should be the case perhaps you may have an opportunity of letting us know by some conveyance on Sunday or Monday morning as I take it for granted we shall not set out till twelve.

Turn over

Mr. Windham[2] has just called, and being made acquainted with our scheme desires to accompany us, but on condition that we change the day to Tuesday, so on Tuesday unless we hear to the contrary we are to make a noise in Beaconfield.[3]

I expect this Evening or on Monday half a Buck from Lord Ossory which I beg leave to send to you as soon as I receive it.

I am Dear Sir Yours sincerely

JReynolds

1 See Letter 184n1.
2 William Windham of Norfolk (1750–1810) of Felbrigg, MP 1784–1810; elected to the Club 1778; see Letter 131.
3 Burke had bought a house, 'Gregories' also known as 'Bolt Court', in Beaconsfield in 1768.

188

TO PRINCE POTEMKIN 4 AUGUST 1789

Source: Hermitage Museum

Monseigneur[1]

Je me suis acquitté de l'ordre que vous me fites donner par Milord Carisfort,[2] de peindre un tableau pour Sa Majesté Impériale, et un autre pour Votre Altesse. Ces deux ouvrages, auxquels j'ai donné tous mes soins, sont addressés à Monsieur Sutherland, et viennent d'être portés à bord du navire le Friendship qui doit incessament mettre à la voile pour St. Petersbourg.

Comme les sujets de ces tableaux ont été laissés à mon choix j'ai cru devoir éviter ceux qu'on a souvent traité; ainsi <pour> celui de L'Impératrice, que je commençai le premier, j'ai choisi le trait surprenant de la Valeur d'Hercules encore Enfant, parce que le sujet fait allusions (au moins une allusion éloignée) à la valeur non Enfantine mais si connue de l'empire Russe.

C'est Je crois Monseigneur, la premiere fois que ce sujet ait été traité du moins en entier et tel que le décrit Pindare: Je sais qu'il n'est pas iniversellement connu; ainsi Je vous envois ci-incluse la description de cet évènement.

J'avois intention que le tableau destiné à Votre Altesse, fût de la même grandeur que celui de Sa Majesté Impériale, mais je trouvai tout de difficultés et d'embarras à peindre sur une aussi grande toile, que crainte de faire mal, il me fallut renoncer à mon projet, et tacher de rachetter à force de soins et d'efforts, la nécessité où je me trouvais de peindre en une moindre espace le Sujet est la Continence de Scipion, histoire trop connue pour qu'il soit besoin de la décrire.[3]

Les ordres dont Limpératrice et Votre Altesse ont daigné me charger me font un honneur infini, et en feroient au plus grand peintre, ainsi pour ma réputation, Je sens le désir le plus vif qu'il ne soit pas ignoré, et mon ambition me presse à demander humblement une grace à Sa Majesté impériale.

Comme le premier Tôme des discours que j'ai prononce à L'académie Royale, en qualité de son Président, est dédié au Roi d'Angleterre, je supplie L'impératrice de vouloir bien me permettre de dédier le second Volume à Sa Majesté impériale

Je prens la liberté Monseigneur, de vous envoyer deux exemplaires du premier volume, et vous prie d'en accepter un. Je serai extremêment flatté si Sa Majesté impériale daigne condescendre jusqu'à faire mettre lautre dans sa bibliothèque.

Comme il se pourroit que Votre Altesse n'entende pas l'anglois aussi bien que l'italien et le françois, je lui en envoye en même tems, deux traductions en Chacune de ces langues. Les traduction françois n'a pas seulement fait imprimer le premier Volume, mais à eu aussi l'adresse de se procurer mes autres discours à mesure qu'ils ont été prononcés, et il en a publie le second Volume en france, avant que je n'aie pas le faire en Angleterre. Cest ce second volume auquel je joindrai mon dernier discours, que je demande la permission de dédier à L'impératrice; et j'aurai la plus grande obligation à sa Majesté impériale, si elle daigne me l'acorder.

J'ai l'honneur d'être avec le plus profond respect

Monseigneur de Votre Altesse

Le tres humble et tres obeissant serviteur

Le Chevalier Reynolds

Londres le 4 aoust 1789

Translation: I have now completed the commission given me by Lord Carysfort, to paint a picture for Her Imperial Majesty and another for your Highness. These two works, which have received my closest attention, have just been sent by sea on board *The Friendship* to St Petersburg, addressed to Mr Sutherland.

As the choice of subjects was left to me, I sought something out of the ordinary; for the Empress, whose picture I began first, I chose to show the remarkable bravery of the Infant Hercules, since the subject suggests (albeit indirectly) the acknowledged strength of the growing Russian Empire.

I believe this is the first time such a subject has been used, at least such as it was given by Pindar, and as he is not a well-known writer I send you herewith a description of the event.

I intended that the picture for your Highness should be the same size as Her Majestyís, but I became apprehensive before such a large canvas and, being anxious to succeed, I renounced the idea and turned all my efforts towards painting, of necessity, a smaller picture of the Continence of Scipio, a familiar story which needs no explanation.

The commissions which the Empress and Your Highness have deigned to give me bring me the highest honour, as they would the greatest of painters. For my own reputation I very much wish that such an honour should be recognised, and my ambition prompts me humbly to request a favour of Her Imperial Majesty.

As the first volume of the Discourses which I gave as President at the Royal Academy was dedicated to the King of England, I beg the Empress to allow me to dedicate the second volume to Her Imperial Majesty.

I take the liberty, Sir, of sending you two copies of the first volume and I beg you to accept one. I would be most flattered if Her Imperial Majesty would condescend to place the other in her library.

As perhaps your Highness does not understand English as well as Italian or French, I am also sending two translations in each of these languages. Not only has a French translation been printed of the first volume, but has continued with the other Discourses as they were given, so that the second volume has been published in France before the English edition. It is the second volume with my latest Discourse which I now seek permission to dedicate to the Empress, and I would be most deeply indebted to Her Majesty if she were to grant me this favour.[4]

1 This letter, in poor French, addressed to the favourite of Catherine II, is not in JR's hand. With it was enclosed a page describing the subject of the Hercules, 'tiré de la premiere ode némienne de Pindare' (see Letter 150).

2 John Proby, 1st Earl of Carysfort (1752–1828), was in Russia 1784–87 whence he wrote to JR (8 December 1785) confirming the commissions from the Empress and Potemkin (Postle 1995, 225). Carysfort commissioned from JR a copy of his *Venus and Cupid* for Prince Potemkin (Hermitage; Mannings 2127); paid by Carysfort on 14 June 1788, £100 gns.

3 JR's *Continence of Scipio* remains in the Hermitage (Mannings 2047).

4 She did, see Letter 207.

189

TO ROBERT GWATKIN 20 AUGUST 1789

Source: Private Collection

London August 20 1789

Dear Sir

I thank you for your kind information relating to my dear Ophy,[1] I beg my love to her and to my sister,[2] not forgetting little Ophy,[3] If my sister is still with you, I wish you would send little Ophy with her to Torrington and Mary[4] will bring her from thence to London where I hope we shall see you & Mrs Gwatkin next summer and then you may take her back if she wishes it and I can spare her.

I am forbid writing on account of my Eyes[5] so you must excuse the shortness of this Letter

Yours sincerely

JReynolds

1 Theophila (Palmer), Mrs Gwatkin, see Appendix I.

2 Mrs Mary Palmer (1716–94), Gwatkin's mother-in-law, see Appendix I.

3 The Gwatkins' little daughter Theophila.

4 Mary Palmer, later Marchioness of Thomond, JR's companion from 1773 and later housekeeper, see Appendix I.

5 On 13 July JR first noted (in his pocket-book) 'prevented [from painting] by my Eye beginning to be obscured'; gutta serena would soon deprive him of all use of his left eye.

190

TO JAMES BOSWELL [8] JANUARY 1790

Source: Beinecke Library (Boswell Papers), in Mary Palmer's hand

Sir Jos. Reynolds & Miss Palmer request the favor of Mr Boswells company this Evening if he is not engaged to play at Whist.[1]

friday Morn.

1 Boswell's Journal records he went by invitation to play whist, drink tea and dine with JR on 8 January 1790 (he did the same on 23 July 1790, but there was then no mention of an invitation), see Fifer 1976, 274n1. According to one of his nieces, JR had become 'violently fond of whist' at which 'he is not tied down to common rules, but has always some scheme in view' (LT, II, 586).

191

TO RICHARD BRINSLEY SHERIDAN 20 JANUARY 1790

Source: Yale Center for British Art

Leicesterfields Jan 20 1790

Dear Sir

I have according to your orders bespoke a very rich frame to be made for Mrs. Sheridans Picture[1] You will easily believe I have been often sollicited to part with that Picture and to fix a price on it, but to those sollicitations I have allways turned by deafest ear, well knowing that you would never give your consent and without it I certainly should never part with it

I really value that Picture at five hundred Guineas – In the common Course of business, (exclusive of its being Mrs.Sheridans Picture) the price of a whole-length with two children would be three hundred, if therefore from the consideration of your exclusive right to the Picture, I charge one hundred and fifty Guineas, I should hope you will think me a reasonable man.[2] It is with great regret I part with the best picture I ever painted, for tho I have every year hoped to paint better & better and may truly say – nil actum reputans dum quid superesset agendum.[3] It has <not> been allways the case however there is now an end of the pursuit, the race is over whether it is won or lost

I beg my most respectfull compliments to Mrs Sheridan

I am with the greatest respect

Your most humble

and obedient servant

Joshua Reynolds

1 Elizabeth Linley, Mrs Sheridan, see Letter 45n1. LT, II, 552, suggested it was 'impecuniosity' which had prevented her husband acquiring it before, although at the time it was painted Sheridan was at the height of his theatrical fame. JR also painted Mrs Sheridan in 1775 as the Virgin in the New College, Oxford, window, see Letter 70n5.

2 Sheridan duly bought the portrait for 150 gns. in February 1790 (Cormack, 164); when debt compelled him to sell it in 1815 he declared 'I shall part from this Picture as from Drops of my Heart's blood' (F. O'Toole, *A Traitor's Kiss*, 1998ed., 455).

3 Lucan, *Pharsalia*, II, 657; the motto of *The Spectator* ('thinking nothing done while anything remained to be done').

The following letter contains the first direct reference to the controversial RA elections of 10 February 1790 which led to Reynolds's temporary resignation both as President and RA. Reynolds had then wished for the election of Joseph Bonomi (see Letter 173) in order that he might become the Professor of Perspective. Bonomi had previously been elected ARA in November 1789 only through the President's casting vote. On 10 February 1790 the Council declined to appoint a Professor of Perspective, and proceded to elect Fuseli RA at the expense of Bonomi. Meanwhile Edward Edwards, ARA 1773, had offered himself as a candidate, although he had refused to submit the drawing considered necessary to support his election (Edwards is officially listed as Teacher, as opposed to Professor, of Perspective at the RA 1788–1806). Reynolds construed Edwards's candidature as an act of disloyalty and resigned both as President and as RA on 22 February. But, with the approval of the King, he resumed the Presidency on 16 March (see Reynolds's Apologia *in* Hilles 1936, 174–77, 249–76; LT, II, 559–85*).*

192

TO JOHN BACON [JANUARY 1790]

Source: Yale Center for British Art

Dear Sir
There is a report circulated by busy people, who interest themselves about what is going on in the Academy with which they have no business That you have declared your intention of giving your vote for Mr. Edwards whether he produces a drawing or not.[1] This <report> I have treated with the contempt such a calumny deserves, that neither yourself Mr. Hodges[2] nor any of the rest of the Council were capable of such duplicity of conduct I repeated to my informer, the Letter which was sent to Mr. Edwards That it was the unanimous opinion of the Council that he could not be a candidate unless &c.

The Gentleman still persevering in his opinion, I beg you would give the means of confuting him under your own hand

I am with great respect

Yours

J Reynolds

Mr. Bacon

1 Bacon had been commissioned to undertake Dr Johnson's monument, see Letter 186.
2 William Hodges, see Letter 241 and Appendix II.

193

TO JOHN NICHOLS 6 FEBRUARY 1790

Source: Beinecke Library (Hilles Collection)

London Feb 6 1790

Dear Sir

I do not know by what accident your name was omitted but shall make an Enquiry at the next meeting of the Committee which will be on Tuesday next.[1]

He has some faint recollection of having heard Mr. Malone say that the Booksellers intended a meeting for the purpose, and that their names were then to be inserted in a body.

Yours sincerely

J Reynolds

1 On 5 January 1790 a meeting of Johnson's friends was held to raise subscriptions for the his Monument. Joseph Banks presided and the elected committee otherwise consisted of Edmund Burke, William Windham, Edmond Malone, Philip Metcalfe, James Boswell and the two surviving executors, Sir William Scott, see Letter 209n1, and JR (*GM*, LX, 1790, I, 3). Nichols's name did not appear in an advertisement of March 1790 with a list of bankers and booksellers to whom subscriptions could be paid (Boswell, IV, 467; *Public Advertiser*, 3 March; *The Diary*, 4 March).

194

TO JOSEPH BONOMI 11 FEBRUARY 1790

Source: Hilles 1929, CXXXIII

Leicester Fields Feby. 11, 1790

Dear Sir

I am sorry for the ill-success we have met with in our business,[1] and that I have been the cause of giving you so much trouble needlessly. I can only say I did not think it possible, to have made such a combination against merit, but what can stand against perseverance? I suppose you may have been apprised that this infamous Cabal was begun when you was first proposed as a Candidate[2] and has been encreasing ever since.

However I may flatter myself in my vain moments that my leaving the Academy at this time may be some detriment to it, I cannot persuade myself any longer to rank with such beings, and have therefore this morning ordered my name to be erased from the list of Academicians.[3]

I should be glad to have in my house for a few days those two drawings[4] or one of them when it is convenient for you to spare it as a full vindication to my friends of the merit which I recommended.

Yours sincerely

J Reynolds

1 His failure to be elected RA at the meeting on the previous day had made him ineligible to be made Professor of Perspective, see Letter 192.
2 In the spring of 1786.
3 But his formal resignation is dated 22 February, see Letter 197.
4 Of the saloon in the house of Mrs Montagu in Portman Square, and of the library at Lansdowne House (LT, II, 572n).

195

TO SIR WILLIAM CHAMBERS [AFTER 11 FEBRUARY 1790]

Source: Royal Academy (REY/3/94)

Sir,

I find that the causes of my resigning the Presidency of the Royal Academy,[1] have been grossly, & as I conceive from very unjustifiable motives, misrepresented.[2] I am indifferent about the opinion of such people as I know to be as injudicious as the spredders of the Reports are malicious. But I should be deeply concerned, if my Sovereign, the Patron of the Academy under whose auspicious Patronage it has so long flourished could be prevailed on to conceive me for one moment or in one instance insensible to the gracious and condescending message which his Majesty has been pleased to send through you, I received it with the most profound respect and the warmest gratitude, as a consolation of my retreat & the greatest honour of my life His Majesty by expressing his desire for my continuance[3] has born a testimony to my good intentions for his service as President of his Academy. This is a full and final sentence on the representations of those [deletion] <who> described me as capable of abusing a very small portion of Authority, in comparatively small concerns in order to gratify my own irregular & feeble passions.

Lay me most humbly at his Majesty's feet, and assure his Majesty that in quitting the Presidency of the Royal Academy I felt the most sensible pain and that nothing could remove me from it but the certainty that it was absolutely impossible for me to perform my duty any longer. I thought that the Professors Chairs ought to be filled by Persons skilful in the branch of Art which they professed and by those only and not by [deletion] <men> less skilful in the particular branch though otherwise of high merit. With all my self partiality I should have given a decided negative to any proposition which should be made for appointing me to the professorship, of Anatomy or Perspective. But of one thing I am sure that a specimen of an Artists performance as a tittle to the Academick place and office he is Candidate for ought not to be refuced Admission Where such a precedent is established I cannot be any longer of use in that Academy. The Academy thought differently ~~for~~ from me and probably on better grounds I submitted to their judgemnt and I resigned. I am confident that his Majesty, a Sovereign equally distinguished for his Justice and his Benevolence will graciously condescend to receive the humble apology of any Person whose conduct is in question and who has the most inconsiderable relation to his service, and who has been all his life, and will be for what remains of it most dutifully sensible of all the distinctions and honours received from his Majestys goodness I have the honour to be

JReynolds

Annotated: Copy of Sir Joshua Reynold's letter to Sir William Chambers on his resigning the Presidency of the Royal Academy 1790

1 Chambers had written to JR on 3 February reprimanding him for having given 'a Charge to the Academicians' concerning the elections to take place on 10 February and expressing concern that JR had been influenced by 'undue applications': since the electors were competent judges 'a Charge from the president could hardly be deemed necessary' On 7 February Chambers told JR that the election of a Professor of Perspective was considered unnecessary, and JR immediately replied that it was necessary specially to elect an Academician to teach Perspective, since no Academician would accept it (Hilles 1936, 260–61).

2 JR probably refers to his letter of resignation of 11 February, see Letter 194.

3 The King had told Chambers that 'he would be happy in Sir Joshua's continuing in the President's chair' (Northcote 1818, II, 253).

196

TO SIR WILLIAM CHAMBERS [AFTER 11 FEBRUARY 1790]

Source: Royal Academy (REY/3/94)

Dear Sir I send you a letter which I had just written before you returned my last, I wrote that letter, which I now enclose[1] because I wished to express with more clearness, my motives for declining the Presidency, I request that you will do me the justice to lay it before his Majesty. Hitherto our correspondence related to the Presidency only your last letter to me coveys your desire that though I have been driven from the <Chair of> Presidentcy I may still continue a member of the Academy If I could be of no service as President as you know I could not, I am yet to learn what service I can do in the Character of a simple Academician, That Character too will be rendered still more ineffectual by the little attention paid to my wishes for the honour of the Academy, when I was in a situation of more importance you think it a sacrifice due to the Kings condescension & to my own character that it will please his Majesty obviate conclusions and aspersions which might prove disagreeable to me; the only one of these motives which could have any weight with me, is your opinion that it would please his Majesty. But if I think myself in honour and conscience obliged with all gratitude & humility to decline the honour of Presidency when His Majesty has most graciously condescended to desire I would continue in it, I beg you to consider what reasons I can have for continuing a private member of [it] In my opinion it must give his Majesty and the world a poor notion of my discretion and of my zeal for his service in my humble walk; that it will 'be a sacrifice to my Character' is extraordinary indeed, what my Character in any light will gain by declining the honours of the Academy and continuing in a subordinate station, you best under stand I do not, if you mean by character, my moral character I hope it stands in no need of sacrifices. 'That it will obviate aspersions' I must to satisfy you upon this point beg leave to remind you of what you have said, 'that you have known me for forty years', in that time you may have known (or you ought not to have continued my acquaintance so long) that I am in a state of reputation ~~to defy~~ unfounded aspersions and if I had no other reason for quiting the Academy than to prove to you and those who may join with you in this kind of threat, that I am not to be moved with fear of those aspersions I would instantly resign if I had not before resolved on it that this sacrifice will obviate conclusions which might prove disagreeable to me, cannot have much more weight upon my mind, if the natural conclusion be drawn it will be this, that I do not approve of the method of chusing members of the Academy to places in it, without the fair mode of competition, that I did not like the method of turning out with scorn & every mark of personal ill will & ill manners to myself, works that are the [*space*] of the Candidate to the place he sollicits, and which did honour to the Academy, If this conclusion be drawn it is a conclusion to which I can have no objection, It is the only conclusion I would have drawn from my retreat. I do not wish to remain in the Academy to countenance a direct opposite conclution, which is that my resignation of the Presidency was, as you are pleased to think this my present resignation from motives disrespectful to the Patron and revengeful Members of the Academy when in reality it was done on account of your departure from the most essential rules of the Academy, without the observance of which the choice to officers in the Academy & to the Rank of Academicians itself must in future become a matter of party and Cabal and not of open & honourable competition, I have the honour to be with great respect your most humble obedient &c

JReynolds

1 See Letter 195.

197

TO JOHN RICHARDS 22 FEBRUARY 1790

Source: Royal Academy (c/2)

Leicester Fields Feby 22d 1790

Sir

I beg you would inform the Council, which I understand meet this Evening, with my fixed resolution of resigning the Presidency of the Royal Academy, and consequently my seat as Academician.[1] As I can be no longer of any service to the Academy as President, it would be still less in my power, in a subordinate station; I therefore now take my final leave of the Academy with my sincere good wishes for its prosperity, and with all due respect to its members

I am
Sir
Your most humble
and most obedient Servant
Joshua Reynolds

P.S. Sir Wm Chambers has two Letters of mine, either of which, or both he is at full liberty to communicate to the Council[2]

1 As secretary to the RA, Richards officially received JR's resignation.
2 See Letters 195 and 196.

198

TO THE RT REVD THOMAS PERCY 13 MARCH 1790

Source: Yale Center for British Art

Leicesterfields March 13 1790

My Lord

I have put the little business that you intrusted me with, into the hands of Mr Boswell, who indeed desired it as he said he owed your Lordship a letter.[1]

I write or read as little as possible on account of my Eyes, and this Letter is only to ward off the appearance of inattention till I shall have the honour of seeing your Lordship which we are all glad to hear, will be soon

I am with the greatest respect
J Reynolds

1 Percy had asked JR to send him Burke's speech on the French Revolution; Boswell posted two pamphlets on 12 March which Percy acknowledged from Dublin on 19 March, together with 'Sir Joshua's kind but short Billet of the 15th [sic]' (Fifer 1976, 282).

199

TO THOMAS LAWRENCE[1] 25 MARCH [1790]

Source: Royal Academy (LAW/1/27)

March 25[2]

Dear Sir

Mr. Roth is the person whom I have employed in Painting Drapery,[3] but having had no business of that kind for him to do, have not seen him for more than a year past,

Whoever now employs him and keeps him employed is the person to be applied to, and I have no doubt will grant your request,

I am with the greatest respect Yours sincerely

JReynolds

1 JR was much impressed with the young Thomas Lawrence, for a time a near-neighbour in Leicester Fields. At the age of twenty Lawrence painted a whole-length portrait of Queen Charlotte (RA 1790; National Gallery); JR, supported by the King, urged his election as ARA in November 1790, but Wheatley was elected in his place. Lawrence was elected the following year and became RA in 1794. See also Letter 204 and Appendix II.

2 Dated 1790 by D. Goldring, *Sir Thomas Lawrence's Letter-Bag*, 1906, 16.

3 Presumably William Roth (b. 1754, RA schools 1771), the 'Roth' who was copying Royal portraits for JR in 1789 (*Farington Diary*, 17 April 1794). His father George Roth (fl. c.1742–78) had also been a drapery painter, working for J.B. Vanloo, Hudson and Ramsay.

200

TO BENJAMIN WEST 8 APRIL 1790

Source: Yale Center for British Art

April 8th

Sir Joshua Reynolds presents his Compliments to Mr. West. He has receiv'd an Invitation from Mr. Hankey to come & see his Drawings on Wednesday next.[1] This morning he has received the inclosed Letter from Mr. Hankey. If Mr. West accepts of the invitation, Sir Joshua will send his Coach to Mr. West's house at half an hour after one o'clock and accompany him there.

Mr West / Newman Street

1 Probably Joseph Chaplin Hankey (c.1754–1803), head partner of Hankey's banking house in London 1793–1803, MP 1799–1802; nephew of John Barnard (d. 1784), from whom he inherited a large collection of prints and drawings (*Farington Diary*, 22 August 1809).

201

TO MRS THEOPHILA GWATKIN 15 APRIL 1790

Source: John Rylands University Library of Manchester

London April 15 1790

My Dear Niece

Tho, as you very well know, I am but a bad Correspondent yet I would not neglect answering your Letter, It would be superfluous to tell you that we should be glad to see you, and it was with great pleasure I read the Post-script which informs me that little Offy comes with you I write as little as I can, so adieu – my Compts to Mr. Gwatkin.

Yours most affectionately

JReynolds

202

TO JAMES NORTHCOTE [BEFORE 24 MAY 1790]

Source: Beinecke Library (Hilles Collection)

Sir Joshua Reynolds requests the honor of Mr Northcote company of dinner next Monday the 24 of May 5 o'clock[1]

Annotated: (in Northcote's hand): 1790

1 Letter in Mary Palmer's hand. JR's pocket-book has 'at home – 5' on 24 May 1790.

203

TO JOSIAH WEDGWOOD 24 MAY 1790

Source: Hilles 1929, CXLI

May 24th

Sir Joshua Reynolds having been informed by Baron – that Mr Wedgwood was seeking for a medal of the King of Hungary, has taken the liberty of sending the inclosed which he received from him when he was Grand Duke of Tuscany, and hopes it will answer his purpose.[1]

1 Leopold II, see Letter 54n3. For Wedgwood's medallion, see R. Reilly and G. Savage, *Wedgwood, the Portrait Medallions*, 1973, p. 214.

204

TO COUNT SEMYON VORONTSOV 25 MAY 1790

Source: Vorontsov archives, St Petersburg

Leicester fields May 25 1790

Sir

In consequence of the conversation which I had the honour of having with Your Excellence on Sunday last[1] I have spoke to Mr. Lawrence[2]

He says his engagements are such that he could not be absent from England above one year, He wishes therefore to know whether that time would be sufficient, or whether it is expected that he should reside in Russia a longer time.

I am with the greatest respect
Your Excellencys
most humble and
most obedient servant
Joshua Reynolds

1 JR had dined with Vorontsov on 23 May 1790.
2 Thomas Lawrence, see Letter 199 and Appendix II.

205

TO CHARLES TOWNLEY 1 JUNE 1790

Source: British Museum (Townley MSS)

June 1st 1790

The bearer Mr. Versteegh a Gentleman of Amsterdam[1] is very desirous of seeing your collection of statues. I am very glad to have this opportunity of obliging him by giving him this introduction to you, as I received many civilities from him when I was in Holland and saw many things by his means which I should otherwise have missed seeing.

You will excuse this liberty
from
Your most obedient servan
Joshua Reynolds

1 Dirk Versteegh (1751–1822), Dutch collector of prints and drawings (*Journey* 1996, 175n612).

206

TO JOHN WILKES [4 JUNE 1790]

Source: Historical Society of Pennsylvania (Gratz Collection)

Sir Joshua Reynolds presents his Compts to Mr. Wilkes and returns him many thanks for the present he has made him, the value of which is much encreased in his estimation by the honour of receiving them from him[1]

He is very much flatterd by Mr. Wilkes polite attention to him.

Leicesterfields

1 Wilkes had sent JR a copy of his edition of Theophrastus, printed in 1790 solely for presentation to his friends. Nichols dated this letter 4 June, printing it with a number of similar notes of thanks written in 1790 (J. Nichols, *Literary Anecdotes of the Eighteenth Century*, IX, 1815, 68, 468f.).

207

TO THE EMPRESS CATHERINE II OF RUSSIA [6 AUGUST 1790]

Source: Yale Center for British Art (copy by Mary Palmer, dated 14 September 1790, for her cousin William Johnson)

The approbation which your Imperial Majesty has been graciously pleased to express of the Academical Discourses which I presumed to lay at your Majestys feet,[1] I truly consider as the great honour of my Life. That condescending acceptance of my attempts raises me in my own estimation & must of course advance my reputation in the Eyes of my Countrymen. Your Imperial Majesty has left nothing undone to give all possible lustre to this most gracious mark of your protection by the magnificent present which encloses it.[2] This I shall carry about me as my title to distinction & which I can never produce but with a sight of that August personage who whilst by her wise government she contributes to the happiness of a great portion of mankind under her dominion, is pleased to extend her favorable influence, to whatever may decorate Life in any part of the World, that whilst I endeavour to demonstrate my gratitude for the distinction I have received I may have further motives to such gratitude by receiving accessions to my reputation, & that Posterity may know (since now I may indulge the hope that I may be known to Posterity) that your Imperial Majesty has deign'd to permit me to sollicit the patronage of a Sovereign to whom all the Poets, Philosophers, & Artists of the time have done homage & whose approbation has been courted by all the Geniuses of her Age. With every sentiment of profound veneration and attachment I am your Majestys most humble & most devoted Servant

J Reynolds

1 See Letter 188. Her letter to JR of 5 March 1790 was sent through her ambassador, Count Vorontsov (see Letter 204); it was published in the *London Chronicle*, 8–10 April 1790, and in Northcote 1818, II, 217. The letter anticipated learning the price of the 'large picture', but it was to be left for JR's executors to recover payments for the *Infant Hercules* and Potemkin's *Continence of Scipio* (M. Postle in Allen and Dukelkskaya, 1997, 66).

2 She had sent JR 'a gold snuff-box, adorned with her profile in bas relief, set in diamonds; and containing what is infinitely more valuable, a slip of paper, on which are written with her Imperial Majesty's own hand, the following words: 'Pour le Chevalier Reynolds en temoignage du contentement que j'ai ressentie à la lecture de ses excellens discours sur la peinture' (Boswell, III, 370).

208

TO FRANCIS, 5TH DUKE OF LEEDS 4 OCTOBER 1790

Source: Private Collection

Leicesterfields Octr. 4 1790

My Lord

I may say, without much affectation of modesty that the Picture which I have the honour of sending by the bearer,[1] is, either as a subject, or as a Picture scarce worth hanging ~~up~~ however it is very flattering to me that Your Grace is of another opinion, and your being so, I seriously consider as the greatest honour of my life

I am with the greatest respect

Your Graces most humble and most obedient servant

Joshua Reynolds

Annotated: Leicester Fields. Oct. 4. 1790. Sir Joshua Reynolds. With His Picture.

1 A self-portrait. The Duke of Leeds owned a duplicate of JR's last self-portrait of 1788; the original, now in the Royal collection, belonged in 1798 to the Earl of Inchiquin (see Mannings 22–23).

209

TO [JOHN] TOWNLEY 29 OCTOBER 1790

Source: Huntington Library

Leicesterfields Oct 29 1790

Dear Sir

I return you a thousand thanks for the pleasure you have given me in sending Sir Wm. Scots speech.[1]

However high Sir Wm. Scots abilities were rated by myself in common with the rest of the world, this speech I really think will raise his character still higher. So much good sense, and knowledge of life, so much sagacity joined with so much elegance and simplicity of stile and manner, and we may add so much chastised wit and humour, I believe never met before, in a higher degree, in the same composition.

I read it out-right the moment I receiv'd it, which considering how little I read at present, is paying it a very great Compliment.

I beg my most respectfull Compts to Mrs Townly[2] and am

Dear Sir

Your most obedient humble servant

Joshua Reynolds

1 Sir William Scott (1745–1836) Kt., cr. Baron Stowell 1821, a distinguished advocate, MP 1790–1821; elected to the Club 1778 and, with JR, Dr Johnson's executor. The speech referred to was probably Scott's sentence, given on 2 July 1790, in the case of A. Evans, the wife, versus T. Evans, Esq., the husband, which was separately published in 1790.

2 Charles Townley the antiquarian and collector did not marry and JR's correspondent was probably his uncle, John Townley (d. 1813) of Chiswick.

210

TO MRS MARY ROBINSON 18 DECEMBER 1790

Source: Beinecke Library (Hilles Collection), contemporary copy

Leicester Square Decr 18th 1790

Dear Madam

I am quite as ashamed of not having returned my thanks before this time for the obliging notice which you have taken of me in your truly excellent poem:[1] it was my intention to have done it in person though I am not much in the habit of going out. I confess I am surprized at the wonderful facility (or handling, as we painters call it) which you have acquired in writing verse, which is generally the result of great practise. Were I to say all I think, even to yourself, it would, I fear, look like flattering, and perhaps to others, as proceeding from the high style in which I have been bribed. I shall comfort myself therefore with saying, that I hope what you intend to publish will not be inferior to this specimen. If so, you will long remain without an antagonist in the field of poesy.

I am with great respect Dear Madam

London Jan 1st 1791

Madam

I am just setting out for Beaconsfield ~~for to~~ with an intention to stay there all next week, which I am sorry to say will prevent me from waiting on Your Ladyships at Ampthill, I should have said, throwing myself at your Ladyships feet and expressing my thanks and acknowledgments for the honour conferred on me by this new mark of favour.

I really think, as it is the work

Letter to the Countess of Upper Ossory, London, 1 January 1791
(Yale Center for British Art, Paul Mellon Collection)

your most humble
and most obedient servant
J Reynolds

P.S. The picture is ready whenever Mr Burke calls for it[2]

1 JR was one of many distinguished subscribers to Mrs Robinson's *Poems*, published in 1791. In 1792 she wrote a Monody to the memory of Sir Joshua Reynolds. 'Ainsi va le Monde' (*Poems*, 1791, 198–209), in which JR is addressed for twenty lines, culminating in: 'As BRITAIN's Genius glories in thy Art, Adores thy virtues, and reveres thy heart, Nations unborn shall celebrate thy name, And waft thy mem'ry on the wings of Fame' (200–01).

2 JR's portrait of Mrs Robinson of 1783, now in the Wallace Collection (Mannings 1532), was engraved by Thomas Burke as the frontispiece for her *Poems*, 1791.

211

TO ANNE, COUNTESS OF UPPER OSSORY 1 JANUARY 1791

Source: Yale Center for British Art

London Jan 1st 1791

Madam

I am just setting out for Beaconsfield[1] ~~for to~~ with an intention to stay there all next week, which I am sorry to say will prevent me from waiting on Your Ladyship at Ampthill, I should have said, throwing myself at your Ladyships feet and expressing my thanks and acknowledgments for the honour conferred on me by this new mark of favour.[2]

I really think, as it is the work of Your ladyships own hand, it is too good to wear, I believe I had better put it up with the Letter which accompanyed it, and shew it occasionally as I do the Empress of Russias Box and Letter of her own hand writing.[3]

I will promise this at least than when I do ware it I will not take a pinch of <snuff> that day – I mean after I have it on,[4]

Such a rough beast with such a delicate wastcoat.

I am sorry I am forced to end so abruptly as the Coach is waiting Miss Palmer[5] desires her most respectfull Compliments, and I beg mine to Lord Ossory and the Ladies

I am with the greatest respect
Your Ladyships &&c
J Reynolds

The Countess of Ossory

1 i.e. to stay with Edmund Burke at Gregories [Butler's Court], whence the following letter was written.
2 She had sent JR a tambour-worked waistcoat.
3 See Letter 207.
4 'What a quantity of snuff Sir Joshua took! I once saw him at an Academy-dinner, when his waistcoat was absolutely powdered with it' (S. Rogers, *Table Talk*, 1856, 21).
5 Mary Palmer, see Appendix I.

212

TO ANNE, COUNTESS OF UPPER OSSORY 3 JANUARY 1791

Source: Private Collection

Beaconsfield[1] Jan 3 1791

Madam

Your eloquence is irresistable. I am resolved to set out next Monday, and call in my way at Woburn Abby[2] and from thence gladly accept of Your Ladyships kind offer of a conveyance to Ampthill.

Perhaps if I was cunning I should throw some difficulties in the way, and by that means procure more flattering Letters, and more good Verses,[3] but I have heard say that too much cunning destroys its own purpose, and I fear that my coyness in the present case would make you all so angry, that you would never more invite me or think me worth saying a civil thing to, which would break my heart.

My apprehension at present is, that when I come I shall not be able to hear a word. Young timid actors are not apt to throw their voices out sufficient for a deaf man, however I have an Eye which will be sufficiently gratified if beauty and elegance, if – I believe I had better reserve what I have further to say on this inexhaustable subject, till I come to Ampthill I am, with the greatest respect

Your Ladyships
Most humble and
most obedient servant
JReynolds

The Countess of Upper Ossory

1 From Edmund Burke's house; see Letter 211.
2 The seat of the Duke of Bedford.
3 She had enclosed with her invitation a copy of the prologue to a play by Richard Fitzpatrick (see Letter 30n6) which was to be acted at Ampthill.

213

TO EDMUND BURKE 25 JANUARY 1791

Source: Sheffield Archives (WWM Bk P1/2314)

London Jan 25 1791

Dear Sir

I have settled every thing with Bonomi relating to the Obelisk.[1] I represented to him the shortness and uncertainty of life, I cannot boast indeed that I said anything new on the subject, except what related to myself, that I wished to see it up,[2] and therefore beged it might be done as soon as possible. He promises ~~for~~ by May next to finish it. It is necessary it seems that the ground should be opend on the spot, about a month before the foundation is laid, in the mean time, merely from curiosity, it is wished that a little pit be now dug in order to ascertain the nature of the ground. They may stop when they come to a hard sandy soil.

The whole <stone cutting business> will be prepared in London. The obelisk will rest on the back of four cats <they> will inevitably appear like four Tigers which will raise their Characters not a little The Inscription, if any, must be cut <in town>; but there is no hurry for it.

I believe you will think it necessary to make a narrow gravel walk from the Wood, to the Obelisk and from thence round the ground to the east part of the house

Mr. & Mrs. Hatsell[3] dine with us on Sunday—it will make them very happy to meet you—possibly you make think it necessary to come to Town a few days before the meeting of Parliament.[4]

I am with the greatest respect

Your most obedient

humble servant

JReynolds

The report is that you are to have a Peerage and a Pension, however I heard from very good authority that the Chancellor[5] said at his own table that such a measure would be very proper and that he would support it whenever it was proposed.

Pray send <an impression of> your Crest

1 In memory of Juliana Burke, Mrs Patrick French (1728–90), Edmund Burke's sister (*Burke Corr.*, VI, 209).
2 A reference to his fading sight.
3 Probably John Hatsel (1733–1820) Clerk of the House of Commons, and his wife Mrs Hatsell (c.1731–1804), daughter of the Rev. Jeffery Ekins, widow of Maj. Newton Barton; see *Burke Corr.*, VI, 209n4.
4 Wednesday, 2 February.
5 Lord Thurlow, see Letter 99n3, then presiding over the trial of Warren Hastings in which Burke was the prosecutor.

214

TO EDMOND MALONE 8 MARCH 1791

Source: Bodleian Library (MS.Malone 26, f.147)

London March 8th 1791

My Dear Sir

In requires some apology to expect you to distribute the enclosed Books[1] – I believe the persons to whom they are directed are all your friends – I am sorry to hear Lord Charlemont[2] has been unwell, which gives real concern to all that know him, I am afraid to express my particular esteem and affection as it would have an air of impertinent familiarity and equality and for another reason shall say nothing regarding your self for fear of the suspicion of being a Toad-eater, a character for which We Gentlemen about town, have great abhorrence and are apt to run too much <on> the other side in order to avoid <it> however I will venture to say thus much ~~however~~ that you are every day found wanting and wished for back, and by nobody more than your very sincere friend and humble servant

J Reynolds

To day is Shrove Tuesday, and no Johnson.[3]

I beg my most respectfull Compts. Lord Sunderlin[4]

1 Probably copies of the *Fifteenth Discourse*, delivered on 10 December 1790, and recently published.
2 James Caulfeild, 1st Earl of Charlemont (1728–99), elected to the Club 1773; he had proposed JR's election to the Society of Dilettanti in 1766.
3 Boswell had hoped to publish his Johnson that day.
4 Richard Malone, 1st Baron Sunderlin (1738–1816), Irish MP, the recipient's brother.

215

TO SIR JOSEPH BANKS 15 MARCH 1791

Source: Yale Center for British Art

March 15 1791

Dear Sir
I shall be obliged to you if you would summons the Committee to meet any day that is most convenient to yourself, in order finally to determine about Dr. Johnson Monument[1] I should think the morning – about two o'clock would be the best time, From the number of engagements that every man has, it can scarce be expected we can meet to <a> dinner

I am with great respect
Yours &c
J Reynolds

Sir Joseph Banks Bart

Annotated: Sir Joshua Reynolds March 15 – 91 16.

1 See Letters 186 and 193n1.

216

TO JOHN, LORD HERVEY 19 MARCH 1791

Source: Hilles 1929, CXLIX

London March 19 1791

My Lord
Though I have not the honour of being known to your lordship, yet I trust shall be excused in the liberty I take of recommending to your lordship's patronage and protection the bearer of this – Mr. Howard, a young painter who is on his way to Rome.[1] He gained first prize of our Academy in December last, and I had the pleasure of telling him, when I delivered the gold medal, that it was the opinion of the academicians that his picture was the best that had been presented to the academy ever since its establishment.

To such merit I rest assured that an introduction alone is sufficient to procure your lordship's favour.

I am with the greatest respect
Your Lorship's Most humble and most obedient servant
Joshua Reynolds

1 Lord Hervey was then British envoy in Florence. Henry Howard (1767–1847) had won the RA gold medal with his *Caractacus recognising the dead Body of his Son*, a subject taken from Mason's *Caractacus*; he was in Italy 1791–94.

217

TO JAMES NORTHCOTE 26 MARCH 1791

Source: Hilles 1929, CL (original sold Sotheby's, 29 October 1975, lot 229)

March 26 1791

Dear Sir

Mr Desenfans[1] told me yesterday a most extraordinary story, that the Lord Mayor[2] should say to me that he had an intention of introducing whole-length portraits of Lord Mayors into the Mansion House, and that he added he intended to employ Northcote and Opie,[3] and that I advised him not to employ them but Mr. Lawrence.[4]

The reason of my mentioning this to you is in hopes that you will help me in endeavouring to trace this story to its fountain-head.

If my opinion is considered of any value, it is certainly your interests to detect this mischief-maker; I am far from thinking that the Lord Mayor is the author.

I am &c

Yours sincerely

J Reynolds

1 Noel Desenfans (1745–1807), the prominent picture dealer (see also Letter 219).
2 John Boydell, see Appendix II.
3 John Opie (1761–1807).
4 See Letter 199 and Appendix II.

218

TO EDMOND MALONE 9 APRIL 1791

Source: Hyde Collection

Leicester fields April 9 1791

Dear Sir

Boswell has been just sealing a letter to you, I beg'd before the wafer was dry that he would insert a paragraft, he says there is not room for a single word, All that I wanted was to beg you would get as many subscriptions as you can exclusive of the Club, such as The Chancellor[1] Secretary Hutchinson[2] &c As the Monument is to be in St. Paul's[3] and the figure Colossal it will require £1200 of this sum we can count only upon £900 the rest I have engaged to pay myself if it cannot be procured from others

I have receivd the bill of Lading for the two Hogsheads of Claret.

Yours sincerely

JReynolds

Edd. Malone Esq / Sackville Street / Dublin

1 Lord Fitzgibbon, see Letter 184n1.
2 John Hely Hutchinson, see Appendix II.
3 Dr Johnson's monument, see Letter 186.

219

TO WILLIAM CRIBB 14 APRIL 1791

Source: Collection Frits Lugt, Fondation Custodia

April 14 1791

Dear Sir

Go to my house & tell George to deliver to you the Picture[1] that is over the Chimney in the blue Bed Chamber, I wish you would get it lined & varnishd which I believe it wants very much as it has not been moved from the place these thirty years. It is a Copy after Claude Loraine, I am told if it was an original it would have been worth a thousand pound; as a Copy I should think it is worth half, at any rate I will not sell it under two hundred Guineas. If you cannot sell it at that price ~~order a~~ <let> the handsome frame ~~for it~~ <to be new gilt> and let it be hung up in the Parlour by the time I come to Town.[2]

Yours sincerely

~~J Reynolds~~[3]

P S. Dont let any body know to whom the Picture belongs

1 Willis's *Current Notes*, September 1857, explained that JR, irritated by Desenfans (see Letter 217) who constantly praised old masters at the expense of the contemporary, had Marchi copy the Claude *View near the Castle of Gandolfo* which was then dried, smoked and substituted for the original in the frame over the fire-place in the dining-parlour. This letter was then sent to his frame-maker Cribb, who was in the secret, and who 'accidentally' allowed it to be seen by Desenfans, who at once paid £200 for it. JR

returning the draft expressed surprise that a man of such discrimination should have thus been taken in by a contemporary work.

2 JR was then, apparently at Richmond, but he attended RA Council meetings on 11 and 18 April (LT, II, 606).

3 When this letter was sold at Sotheby's in 1905 the signature was said to have been obliterated by JR.

220

TO THOMAS CADELL 18 APRIL 1791

Source: Johnson Birthplace Museum

April 18 1791

Sir Joshua Reynolds presents his Compts to Mr. Cadell. and begs leave to acquaint him that the Committee for Dr. Johnsons Monument returns their thanks <to him and the rest of the subscribers> for their liberal benefaction of one hundred pounds which sum if Mr. Cadel will please to pay to the bearer (his servant Ralph Kirkley) Sir Joshua will transmit it to Mr. Metcalf[1] the Treasurer

Mr. Cadell

Annotated: April 18/ Sir Joshua Reynolds Order & Rect For £100 for Dr. Johnsons Monument Pd April 18, 1791

1 Philip Metcalfe, see Letter 94n1; treasurer of the committee responsible for Johnson's monument and one of JR's executors.

221

TO WILLIAM GILPIN 19 APRIL 1791

Source: W. Gilpin, *Three Essays: on Picturesque Beauty; on Picturesque Travel; and on Sketching Landscape*, 1792, 34–36

London April 19th 1791

Dear Sir

Tho I read now but little, yet I have read with great attention the essay, which you was so good to put into my hands,[1] on the difference between the beautiful, and the picturesque; and I may truly say, I have received from it much pleasure, and improvement.

Without opposing any of your sentiments, it has suggested an idea, that may be worth consideration – whether the epithet picturesque is not applicable to the excellence of the inferior schools, rather than to the higher. The works of Michael Angelo, Raphael, & c., appear to me to have nothing of it; whereas Reubens, and the Venetian painters may almost be said to have nothing else.

Perhaps picturesque is somewhat synonymous to the word taste; which we should think improperly applied to Homer, or Milton, but very well to Pope, or Prior. I suspected that the application of these words are to excellences of an inferior order; and which are incompatible with the grand stile.

You are certainly right in saying, that variety of tints and forms is picturesque; but it must be remembred, on the other hand, that the reverse of this – (uniformity of colour, and a long continuation of lines,) produces grandeur.[2]

I had an intention of pointing out the passages, that particularly struck me; but I am afraid to use my eyes so much.

The essay has lain upon my table; and I think no day has passed without my looking at it, reading a little at a time. Whatever objections presented themselves at first view,[3] were done away on a closer inspection: and I am not quite sure, but that is the cause in regard to the observation, which I have ventured to make on the word picturesque.

I am &c

Joshua Reynolds

To the revd. Mr. Gilpin, Vicar's hill.

1 Gilpin had sent JR a copy of his *Three Essays: on Picturesque Beauty; on Picturesque Travel; and on Sketching Landscape*, 1792.

2 These three paragraphs were quoted by William Blake in a letter to Thomas Butts, 22 November 1802 (G. Keynes, *Blake, Complete Poetry and Prose*, 1967, 856–57).

3 Gilpin, *op. cit.* [at Source above], 35, wrote that JR had been shown the essay, several years before, by William Mason; 'he then made some objections to it; particularly he thought, that the term picturesque, should be applied only to the works of nature.' See also LT, II, 606–07.

222

TO AN UNIDENTIFIED CORRESPONDENT 25 MAY 1791

Source: B. Altman, New York, 13 September 1986, lot 102 (as dated London, 25 May 1791)

. . . I think the last letter which I had the honour of receiving from you is dated so far back as February –89, I was then unable to answer it, I had lost one eye and was in danger of immediately losing the other which however has not happened, though it continues in a feeble uncertain state and obliges me to refrain from writing much as well as from painting . . . I shall not forget to send you the second volume[1] when it is printed, but my misfortune has so much retarded the publication . . . In regard to our Diploma I am sorry it is not in my power to send you one. It is given solely to the Academicians and Associates . . .

1 Presumably referring to JR's *Discourses*, the last of which was published in March 1791.

223

TO DR JAMES BEATTIE 28 MAY 1791

Source: Aberdeen University Library (AUL/MS 30/B24/4/3), in Mary Palmer's hand

If Dr. Beattie <and his son> should happen to be disengaged today and will take a family dinner in a quiet way with Sir Joshua Reynolds & Miss Palmer[1] – they will be very glad.

Sat 28th / Dr. Beattie

Annotated: Invitation from Sir Joshua Reynold's to dinner. Sat. 28th May 1791.

1 Mary Palmer, see Appendix I.

224

TO JOSEPH FARINGTON MAY 1791

Source: National Library of Scotland (MS 590, f.153, no.1625), in Mary Palmer's hand

Sir Joshua Reynolds presents his compts to Mr Farrington & would much be much obliged to him if he could find time to call in Leicester Square any hour this morning, as he wishes to speak to him on particular business.[1]

Mr. Farrington

Annotated: May 1791

1 Conceivably concerning the proposal that the RA should offer their services and advice over the erection of monuments in St Paul's, which was to be discussed by the RA Council on 5 May.

225

TO DR SAMUEL PARR 31 MAY 1791

Source: Hilles 1929, CLVIII

London, May 31st 1791

Dear Sir

I felt myself much flattered in receiving a letter from Dr Parr,[1] and still more by its being a long one, and more still by the confidence which you have been pleased to repose in me: I may add, likewise, that a man is most successfully flattered by being supposed to possess virtues to which he has the least pretensions.

My critical skill, alas! I am afraid is entirely confined to my own profession. It would be in me the highest degree of impertinence to speak of your superior qualifications for this business as from my own judgment: it is my learned friends who have universally pointed you out as the only man qualified in all points for this task. That is an arduous task I am well aware, and that you are alarmed at the difficulty is a presumption in favour of what may be expected from your head.

A blind horse starts at no precipice. I have heard you speak of Dr. Johnson, and am therefore confident that you have nothing to seek in regard to sentiment; and in regard to your ability of expressing those sentiments in Latin, nobody has any doubt. You have, therefore, nothing to do but 'skrew your courage to the sticking place, and we'll not fail'.[2] Since I have stumbled by accident on this passage in Macbeth, I cannot quit it without observing that this metaphor is taken from a wheel engine, which, when wound up, receives a check that prevents it from running back. The only check that I can imagine to prevent you from retreating from what I wish to consider as a private half-promise, would be its being publicly known that you had undertaken it. And then, as Dr. Johnson used to say, 'what must be done, will be done'.

I do not at all wonder at your being terrified at the difficulty: I am inclined to think that it is the most difficult of all compositions. Perhaps it is impossible to write an epitaph that shall be universally approved; or that shall not open to some objection on one side or the other: even men of the best and most refined taste, are often unreasonable in their demands, and require (as I have seen connoisseurs do) an union of excellencies incompatible with each other.

The simplicity which you intend to adopt, and which is perfectly congenial to my own taste, will be criticised that it is not the lapidary style, that it wants dignity and stateliness, and so vice versa.

Though I have great abhorrence of pertness or quaintness, either in the style or sentiment, yet perhaps an epitaph will admit of something of the epigrammatic turn. I remember once having made this observation to Edmund Burke, that it would be no bad definition of one sort of epitaphs, to call them grave epigrams. He repeated the words 'grave epigrams', and gave me the credit of a pun, which I never intended.

I have no doubt but that you are surprised to receive a letter in this form. The truth is, this was intended only as a rough draft, but the weakness of my eyes must prove my excuse in not writing it over fair.

I shall enclose, if it will not make too large a packet for the post, the list of subscribers.

I am, with the greatest respect,

Your most humble and most
obedient servant
Joshua Reynolds

Dr. Johnson / born Sept. 18 1709/ died Dec. 13 1784

1 Parr's undated letter to JR (printed in *Works of Parr*, 1828, IV, 678–81) had explained at length the difficulty of composing an epitaph for Johnson's Monument which would universally please; he sought JR's opinion (as a man of 'most elegant taste and most deep judgment'), as well as Johnson's dates and a list of subscribers to the monument.

2 *Macbeth*, I, VII, 60–61.

226

TO DR SAMUEL PARR 11 JULY 1791

Source: Hilles 1929, CLIX

London, July 11, 1791

Dear Sir

You may depend on having all your injunctions, relative to the inscription, punctually obeyed.[1] We have great time before us. The statue is hardly yet begun, so that the inscription will not be wanted for at least these twelve months: in the meantime, you will probably have an opportunity of seeing the monument itself, and the place which it is to occupy in St. Paul's.

There would be, I think, a propriety in having on the scroll a Greek sentence,[2] as it would imply at first sight that it is the monument of a scholar. Dr. Johnson was Professor of Ancient Literature to the Royal Academy. I could wish that this title might be on the monument: it was on this pretext that I persuaded the Academicians to subscribe a hundred guineas.[3] But I do not want to encroach on your department: you must ultimately determine its propriety.

I do not think that in any of my letters I have mentioned Mr. Windham's name,[4] which looks as if we did not see each other as often as we used to do, but this is not the case; I have shewn him all your letters, but as he expressed only general approbation, and the propriety of the whole being left to your judgment, I neglected telling you as much, which still I ought to have done.

I sent to Bacon the sculptor, to desire he would send me a sketch of the monument, which, if it comes in time, I will enclose it in this letter; if not, I will take the first opportunity of sending it to you.

I confess I am rather impatient to see the inscription; but still, not so much so as to wish in the least to break in upon any determination of yours. I must wait, likewise, for your orders respecting Mr. Seward;[5] as he has been active in this business, one would wish not to mortify him by neglect.

I am, with the greatest respect, your sincerely, J. Reynolds

1 JR is responding to two lengthy letters from Parr, of May 1791 and 23 June 1791 (*Works of Parr*, 1828, IV, 683–85).

2 This was duly incorporated.

3 But see Letter 227.

4 William Windham, see Letter 131n2, member of the committee in charge of the monument, see Letter 193n1. Parr wished JR to consult Windham alone on this business.

5 William Seward (1747–99), man of letters, who had first proposed that Parr should compose Johnson's epitaph (*Works of Parr*, 1828, IV, 678). In his answer Parr allows JR to take Seward into his confidence. See Boswell, IV, 469–70; H.B. Wheatley, 'Johnson's Monument and Parr's Epitaph on Johnson', *Johnson Club Papers*, 2nd series, 1920, 221ff.

227

TO THE RT REVD THOMAS BARNARD 19 JULY 1791

Source: Private Collection

London July 19 1791

My Dear Lord

I have inclosed Mr. West Letter which he sent to me immediatly after he had executed the commission with which he was intrusted <by> the

Council of the Academy.[1] He appears to have conducted this business with great propriety. He told the King that your lordship wished to be connected with an Academy to which His Majesty paid so peculiar an attention, and that ~~he~~ <you> would accept of the proposal which had been made to ~~him~~ you by the President and the rest of the Academicians, of being Chaplain to the Royal Academy if His Majesty thought there was no impropriety and approved of it, The King answered, he thought there was no impropriety, and that he very much approved of it, and added that it was a great honour to the Academy to have a person of your rank, a litterary Character and so agreable a man, for their Chaplain.

Your Lordship has been so lately to London, that I have nothing new to say, excepting that the paper acquainting the King that the Academy had subscribed out of their own fund 100 Guineas towards defraying the expences of Dr. Johnsons monument,[2] He <His Majesty I should say> was graciously pleased to draw his pen ~~his~~ across, that it might not be supposed <he said that> he gave his approbation to that measure when he signed the Election of Boswell to the Secretaryship,[3] both being on the same paper. I had unwittingly told the Academy that I had no doubt but that this donation would be very agreable to His Majesty as I had so often heard him speak with the highest admiration of the Learning and Piety of Dr. Johnson How inscrutable are the hearts of Princes.

Do you find it so My Lord that the longer you live the less confidence you have in your sagacity?

I am with the greatest respect

Your Lordships most humble

and most obedient servant

JReynolds

Annotated: Sir Joshua Reynolds Letter on my accepting the office of Chaplain to the Royal Academy in London July 19th 1791

1 Barnard was elected Chaplain to the RA in 1791.

2 See Letter 226.

3 Boswell was elected Secretary for Foreign Languages at the RA in 1791.

228

TO DR JAMES BEATTIE 7 AUGUST [1791]

Source: Aberdeen University Library (AUL MS 30/B24/4/2)

Dear Sir
I wish you and your son would dine with me to day, you will meet two or three of your friends pray come if you can – consider we have scarce seen each other

Yours sincerely
J Reynolds

August 7th / Dr Beattie / No. 3

Annotated: From Sir Joshua Reynolds asking Dr. Beattie to dinner August.7th 1791?

229

TO BENJAMIN WEST 10 NOVEMBER 1791

Source: Royal Academy (GA/1)

Dear Sir
I must request the favour of you to supply my place at the General Meeting held this Evening, I beg at the same time that You will acquaint the Academicians that however desirous I am & ever shall be to contribute every service in my power towards the prosperity of the Academy, yet as I feel myself incapable of serving the Office of President for the ensuing year, I think it necessary that this should be declared at the present Meeting, that the Academicians may have time to consider between this & the tenth of December of a proper successor.[1]

I am with great respect
Your most Obedt: Servt
Joshua Reynolds.

1 Following the receipt of this letter JR was attended by a deputation from the RA and was persuaded to remain in office. Although he last attended an RA meeting on 25 June 1791, he was re-elected President on 10 December. He died on 23 February 1792. The following (Royal Academy, REY/3/17) was apparently the first draft of the above letter, and the number of alterations suggest how difficult JR found the composition:

Tho my Eyes are much better than they have lately been yet I am afraid ~~to~~ put them to the severe tryal of ~~a~~ the business of this Evening as such interruptions <to a man> are likely ~~often to happen~~ to be more & more frequent I ~~thi~~ must beg leave to recommend to the Academicians at the next General Election that they would elect <for a> a President ~~it that is likely~~ less liable to such accidents

~~There~~ <it> is undoubtedly open to ridicule the declining an honour <before it> ~~that is~~ ~~not nor~~ can <is> ~~it be~~offerd, ~~nor am~~ but ~~it must be considered~~ as I have had had the [deletion] honour annually conferrd on me for these two and twenty years, it will not be considerd as too presumptious to suppose that the same favour would be continued <another year> ~~on the tenth of Dec next was I to wait for that Election before~~ <but> ~~I gave in~~/~~in order then to give in~~/~~my resignation it would be creating additional trouble to the Academy~~, I thought it ~~therefore~~ more elegible to run the risque of incurring the censure of <this> presumption rather than give ~~this~~ <on the> additional trouble <of another Election> to the Academicias of another Election I need not repeat the regret which I feel in parting with the Academy

230

TO JOHN BOYDELL 15 DECEMBER 1791

Source: Folger Shakespeare Library (not in JR's hand)

The Letter which Sir Joshua has had the honour of receiving from Mr. Boydell, dated Decr. 10th, begins in this manner "It is now so long since my Nephew or I had any conversation with you on the subject of the picture from Macbeth that we concluded you no longer thought of us as Purchasers" and concludes with desiring to know the price put on the picture and if it was anything near what their work could possibly afford they should certainly be happy to become the purchasers.

To speak so lightly of an Engagement in which 500£ was deposited as an earnest[1] that it should be fulfilled appears somewhat extraordinary; it seems to imply what (certainly Mr. Boydell can never mean) that he is under no more engagement relating to the picture of Macbeth than to any other unsold picture in Sir Joshua's Gallery; that it depended solely on the caprice of the minute whether he would or would not become a Purchaser. Mr. Boydell will himself be satisfied that this is not exactly the case when the whole transaction relating to this picture is laid before him.

This picture was undertaken in consequence of the most earnest sollicitation on Mr. Boydell's part, since after Sir Joshua had twice refused to engage in the business, on the third application Mr. Boydell told him that the success of the whole scheme depended on his name being seen amongst the list of the Artists. Thus flattered Sir Joshua said he would give him leave to insert his name, as one who had agreed to paint for him and that he would do it if he could, at the same time told him in confidence that his Engagement in Portraits was such as to make it very doubtful. He recommended to Mr. Boydell's consideration whether it would be worth his while to give so great a price as he must demand, that tho' his demand would not be in any proportion to what he got by Portrait painting yet it would be still more than probably he would think proper to give. To this it was answered that the price was not an object to them; that they would gladly give whatever Sir Joshua should demand, adding that it was necessary they should be able to declare that Sir Joshua was engaged and had received earnest. Bank Bills to the amount of 500£ were then laid on the table; to the taking this Sir Joshua expressed great unwillingness as it seemed to change his lax and conditional promise into a formal obligation. Sir Joshua however took the money, but insisted on giving a receipt that the money should be returned if the Picture should never be finished. A few days after this Mr. Boydell, suspecting Sir Joshua's delay, at his own expence sent to Sir Joshua's a Canvas, nine feet by twelve; the largest that had ever been in his house.

What was to be the price of this picture was never determined; Sir Joshua apprised him that it would be very high, desired him to recollect that his fixed prices for Portraits were double that of any other Painter; to this he was continually answered, the price was no object; Sir Joshua should have whatever he demanded: by which Sir Joshua understands whatever he can reasonably demand; of this neither Mr. Boydell nor himself are the judges. Sir Joshua therefore proposes that a select number of Artists or of Connoisseurs with the assistance of some eminent Counsellor shall determine the business by arbitration. The Question Sir Joshua apprehends to be whether he can make it appear that he could have got 2000£ if he had employed the time in portrait painting which was employed in that Picture though Sir Joshua's demand is only 1500 Guineas.[2]

1 For JR's payments from Boydell, see Letter 165.

2 A draft of this letter, almost entirely in JR's hand, with additional paragraphs dated 15 December, and a covering letter from Mary Palmer to Boydell, is in the Beinecke Library (c2360). After JR's death the matter was settled, with a payment of £1000, as he had wished by a committee which included Sir George Beaumont, Sir Abraham Hume, William Lock, John Thomas Batt and John Hinchliffe, the Bishop of Peterborough (see Hilles 1952, 160–64).

UNDATED LETTERS

ALPHABETICAL BY CORRESPONDENT

231

TO MRS. ABINGTON 26 MAY

Source: Yale Center for British Art

May 26

My Dearest Lady

As soon as I receivd the honour of your Note <on Tuesday Evening> of invitation for Sunday next,[1] I put it carefully down in my book but forgot that it was necessary to acquaint you that I will do myself the honour of waiting on you on that day – which neglect I hope you will excuse from

Yours most sincerely

J Reynolds

Mrs. Abington / No. 62 Pallmall

1 JR took forty places in the front boxes for her benefit performance on 27 March 1775 (Penny 1986, 246), possibly indicating the date of this letter. His celebrated portrait of her as Miss Prue of 1771 is now in the Yale Center for British Art, and his full-length of her as the Comic Muse of c.1768 (revised 1773) at Waddesdon Manor.

232

TO WILLIAM, 2ND VISCOUNT BARRINGTON 24 JUNE

Source: Hilles 1929, LII

Leicester Fields, June 24th

My Lord –

I am sorry that the hurry of business has prevented me from returning the pictures before. I have *endeavoured* to repair Mr. Barrington's[1] in the best manner I can. in regard to the Admiral's picture,[2] I could *scarce* believe it to be the picture I painted, the effect was so completely destroyed by the green sky. This was occasioned by a blunder of my colourman, who sent blue verditer (a colour which changes green within a month), instead of ultramarine, which lasts for ever.[3] However,

I have made such a background now as I think best corresponds with the head, and sets it off to the best advantage.

I am, with the greatest respect,

your most humble and obedient servant,

Joshua Reynolds

1 The recipient's brother, the Hon. Shute Barrington (1734–1826), later Bishop of Durham, who had sat to JR in 1759, see Letter 183.

2 The recipient's brother Admiral the Hon. Samuel Barrington (1729–1800); JR began his portrait on 18 November 1779 (National Maritime Museum; Mannings 120).

3 'Sir Joshua once bought, at a very considerable price, of some itinerant foreigner, I believe a German, a parcel of what he pretended was genuine ultramarine, which, in point of color, seemed fully to answer its title. Without bringing it to any chemical test, the artist ventured to use it, and by it spoiled, as he assured me, several pictures; for the fictitious pigment soon changed into a muddy green, which he was obliged to repair, by painting over it' (W. Mason, in Cotton 1859, 54).

233

TO JAMES BOSWELL

Source: Beinecke Library

Dear Sir

I have promised to call on a person in St. Pauls Church yard this morning at half past three, <to see pictures> The Caoch therefore will be at your door a quarter before three when I hope you will be ready.

Monday / James Boswell Esq

234

TO MR BURNEY[1]

Source: Beinecke Library (in Mary Palmer's hand)

Sir Joshua Reynolds presents his Compts to Mr Burney & begs leave to remind him of his engagement on Saturday next at 5 o clock

1 Possibly the son of Dr Charles Burney (see Letter 45), the classical scholar Charles (1757–1817), but there were also several nephews, including the artist Edward Francesco Burney (1760–1848).

235

TO MR BURNEY[1]

Source: Sotheby's, 15 July 1998, lot 72[2]

Sir Joshua Reynolds presents his Compts to Mr Burney and returns him many thanks for the present which he has been so obliging to send him of a Haunch of Venison

1 See Letter 234n1.
2 Sold with an invitation to JR's funeral.

236

TO THOMAS CADELL

Source: Princeton University Library (end of letter only)

I hope soon to send you the Discourse for the 2d Vol. but I must look over them first[1]

Yours sincerely
JReynolds

1 The *Second Discourse* was published as a pamphlet in 1770, by March, printed by William Griffin (Hilles 1936, 39–40, 280–81). Letter 81, of 18 May 1779, possibly relates.

237

TO SIR WILLIAM CHAMBERS

Source: Beinecke Library

Sir Joshua Reynolds presents his Comptts. to Sir Willm Chambers. He had company yesterday with him when he answerd his note co cerning the Kings Picture. Sir William is [*right*?], there is no doubt of his opinion that a formal application from a Company is necessary before this favour can be granted – an individual of that Company requesting to have the Kings Picture is certainly not sufficient.

Feb 6th[1]

1 Written after JR's appointment as Principal Painter to the King in September 1784. Possibly relating to JR's portraits of the King and Queen for Mr Weston at Dublin Castle, or for Lord Charlemont, when Chambers was working at Trinity College, Dublin (see Cormack, 168).

238

TO GEORGE COLMAN

Source: Beinecke Library

Sir Joshua Reynolds presents his Compts to Mr. Coleman and takes the liberty to mention that in one of the Rolos[1] which he receivd from him there was but twenty four Guineas.

March 17th.

1 viz. a *rouleau*, a number of gold coins in a cylindrical packet. George Colman jr., son of JR's correspondent, in a letter to an unknown correspondent of 10 September 1823 (Beinecke Library), said of this letter that 'there is an anecdote attached to the Rolos (as he barbarously spells them)'.

239

TO RICHARD COSWAY [?]

Source: Collection Frits Lugt, Fondation Custodia

April 22d

Dear Sir

If you will trust me with your sketch of Rubens of Jupiter & Venus,[1] for a few days, I shall take it as a great favour.

Yours sincerely

J Reynolds

1 Unidentified; for Cosway's addiction to Rubens, see S. Lloyd, *Richard and Maria Cosway*, exh. cat., Edinburgh/London, 1995–96, 73–82.

240

TO DR SAMUEL FARR

Source: Beinecke Library (in Mary Palmer's hand).

Sir Joshua Reynolds presents his compts to Dr Farr & if he happens to be unengaged to morrow will be very happy if he will eat his Christmas dinner with him at five o'clock

Leicester Square Thursday Decr 24

241

TO WILLIAM HODGES

Source: Beinecke Library

20th Feb.

Sir Joshua Reynolds presents his Compliments to Mr Hodges[1] and returns with many thanks the Prints from the Orleans Gallery[2] which he was so good to lend him.

The fourth Number is wanting which he has searched for in vain – If Mr Hodges has it not Sir Joshua will take care to procure that number to complete his set.

1 JR had 'lately met' Hodges in August 1786, see Letter 157.
2 The *Galerie du Palais Royal*, engraved by J. Couché and others, began publication in *livraisons* in 1785; a first volume was published in 1786, the third and last in 1808.

242

TO OZIAS HUMPHRY

Source: Beinecke Library

Sir Joshua Reynolds presents his compliments to Mr Humphry and desires the honour of his Company to dinner to morrow[1]

Leicesterfields Sept. 24

1 The letter is written in the hand of Frances Reynolds, who left JR in 1777; Humphry was in Italy 1773–77; Hilles dated this letter 1791.

243

TO MR JERNINGHAMI[1] (1789?)

Source: Huntington Library

Sir Joshua Reynolds presents his Compts to Mr. Jerningham and begs he would make use of his House as his own he has sent to the person who keeps his house at Richmond in his absence to receive his friend

1 Probably the poet and dramatist Edward Jerningham (1727–1812), who had met JR by January 1784; his poems included *Lines on a late Resignation at the Royal Academy* (1790) and *The Shakespeare Gallery or Subjects for Painters* (1791); in October 1791 he was staying with the Earl of Mount Edgcumbe at Richmond (L. Bettany, *Edward Jerningham and his Friends,* 1919, 9, 184, 315, 368).

244

TO SAMUEL JOHNSON

Source: Beinecke Library

Sir Joshua Reynolds's Compts to Dr. Johnson, ~~he~~ & has sent word that he will wait on Miss Monckton[1] on Saturday

Sir Joshua will send his Coach or call himself on Dr. Johnson a little before eight.

Leicester fields May 3d.[2] / Dr. Johnson

1 See Letter 87.
2 'Probably written in 1782' (Hilles 1952, 58).

245

TO THE REVD THOMAS AND MRS PERCY

Source: Huntington Library (in the hand of Frances Reynolds)

Sir Joshua & Mrs Reynolds present their compliments to Dr. & Mrs Percy,[1] and are sorry that they can only conditionally promise themselves the pleasure of waiting on them to morrow. Dr Johnson dines with Sir Joshua to morrow and if he leaves them early enough or will accompany them to Dr Percys they will be glad to do themselves the honour to wait on them to morrow. They imagine Thursday will not be equally agreable to Dr. & Mrs Percy.

1 Percy became DD of Emmanuel College, Cambridge, in 1770; he became a Bishop in 1782 when he would have been addressed as My Lord. 'Mrs Reynolds' probably Frances Reynolds who stayed with JR until 1777, see Appendix I.

246

TO THE REVD THOMAS PERCY

Source: Sotheby's, 18 December 1995, lot 134

Dear Sir

I wish you would be at the Club this [deletion] Evening in order to Ballot for Dr Warton[1] and dine with him tomorrow in Leicester fields

Yours

J Reynolds

Dr Percy

1 Thomas Warton was elected in 1777, Joseph Warton in 1782; both were Doctors.

247

TO [WALTER] RADCLIFFE

Source: Private Collection

Sir Joshua Reynolds presents his Compliments to Mr. Radcliff and desires the honour of his Company at Dinner to day at 5 o'clock

Thurs Nov 11[1]

1 Radcliffe was acquainted with Lord Boringdon, see Letters 23 and 24; on 11 November 1784 JR noted in his pocket book 'Lord Borringdon' at 5, possibly the date of this letter.

248

TO [WALTER] RADCLIFFE

Source: Private Collection

Sir Joshua Reynolds presents his Compliments to Mr. Radcliffe and desires his the honour of his company to dinner next Wednesday[1]
Leicester fields Nov. 17th.

Mr. Radcliffe / Duke Street St James

1 Possibly relating to Letter 247.

249

TO GEORGE SELWYN

Source: Society of Antiquaries of London (Cely-Trevilian collection)

Sir Joshua Reynolds presents his Compliments to Mr. Selwin, The Picture[1] is finished and will send it home tomorrow morning, he has taken the liberty of changing the dress of the head as every person disaproved of it as it stood before.

George Selwin Esq.

1 On the assumption this letter referred to the double portrait of Selwyn and Lord Carlisle of 1770 (Castle Howard; Mannings 947), it was dated March 1770 by Hilles, but JR appears to refer to a single figure. He painted Selwyn on three occasions, but only once on his own: a kit cat of 1766 (private collection), see Mannings 1601.

UNDATED LETTERS TO UNKNOWN CORRESPONDENTS

250

Source: Beinecke Library

April 28th

Dear Sir[1]

In the first place I am very sorry that this cursed business of the house of Commons will prevent us from having your Company to dinner to day but pray come in the Evening and have a game at whist.[2] In regard to the business of St. Pauls you said enough at our last meeting to shew that you wished to have done with it, and I considerd your suspending your vote as a delicacy towards me, whom you saw sanguine for the success of my Scheme, and for which I am much obliged. I shall push this business no farther and shall content myself in having endeavord support the interest of Sister Arts, which it is my duty to do however unsuccessfully. Upon the whole I am much obliged to you both for your conduct – and for your kind Letter

Yours sincerely

JReynolds

1 The correspondent is probably Sir William Scott, see Letter 209n1, and the subject the Johnson monument, see Letter 186.

2 JR had become addicted to whist by 1790, see Letter 190.

251

Source: Hilles 1929, CLV

Pray send me two volumes of the Discourses unbound[1]

1 Probably written after his last *Fifteenth Discourse* was published and addressed to the Academy's printer, Thomas Cadell.

252

Source: Fitzwilliam Museum

Dear Sir
If you can call on me any time this morning I can shew you a fine Picture
Yours sincerely
JReynolds
Friday.

253

Source: Hyde Collection

Dear Sir
If I had the mony in the house I should not make the least hesitation to send it to you but it is very extraordinary for me to say tho tis true, that I borrowed a hundred pounds yesterday of my Attorney in order to pay my bills the truth is I sent a week since every farthing I had to the funds as I thought they were so very low. If I receive any mony between this and the time you want it, I will send it to you
Yours
JReynolds

254

Source: Beinecke Library

Difficulty
My Lord
The truth is we do not, nor is it requird

LETTERS CONCERNING PAYMENTS AND RECEIPTS

255

ANTHONY EYRE 18 OCTOBER 1755

Source: photostat sold Sotheby's, 26 March 1975, lot 52 (with the original portraits)

London Oct. 18th 1755.

Sir

I ask pardon for my forgetfullness in not sending frames with your Pictures,[1] I have sent two this day by the York Waggon which sets out next Saturday, tis necessary to mention that therames are screw'd to the case, so that when they are unpack'd those screws must be first taken out

I remain with my comts. to Mrs Eyre your most humble and obliged servant

J Reynolds

	£ s
Pictures	50 - 8
Frames	10 -10
Packing cases	00 -15
	61 -13

To Anthony Eyre Esq / at Adwick near / Doncaster / Yorkshire

1 JR's three-quarter length portraits, painted at the time of the Eyres marriage in 1755, are in a private collection (Mannings 588–589).

256

JAMES BULLER 26 APRIL 1757

Source: Reynolds, exhibition catalogue, Birmingham, 1961, 20.

Sir

I received the honour of yours of April 22nd with a Bill of thirty two pounds for which I return you many thanks. My name is Joshua but I apprehend tis of no great importance the mistake.

I remain Sir your most humble & obliged Servant

J. Reynolds

April 26 1757

Received of Jas. Buller Esq. the sum of thirty two Pounds for his & Mrs. Bullers Pictures with Frames in full of all demands.[1]

by one J. Reynolds.

Jas. Buller Esq., At Kings Nympton, Near Chulmleigh, Devon

1 JR's sitter-book for the week 14–19 March 1757 had noted Buller's address (King's Nympton, Near Chulmleigh, Devon) and the weeks beginning 11 and 25 April 1757 had noted: 'Write to Mr Buller'. Buller had sat to JR in January and February 1757, but no sittings are recorded for his wife. Both portraits are in private collections (Mannings 271–272).

257

LORD BROWNLOW BERTIE 3 JUNE 1758

Source: Beinecke Library

June 3d 1758

Receiv'd of the Honble. Lord Brownlow Bertie the sum twelve Guineas being the remaining part of payment for his Lordships Picture[1] and five guineas for a Miniature[2]

by me

JReynolds

£17-17s-0

1 Sittings for JR's three-quarter length took place in March and April 1757 (Grimsthorpe; Mannings 162).

2 Unlocated.

258

SIR THOMAS HARRISON 18 JULY 1759

Source: GC, II, 443

Received, July 18, 1759, of Sir Thomas Harrison, for his and Lady Harrison's portraits,[1] the sum of sixty guineas in full of all demands by me, £63.
J. Reynolds

1 Sittings for the three-quarter length portraits (now Corporation of London; Mannings 852–853), took place in 1758.

259

CHARLES, 3RD DUKE OF RICHMOND 20 AUGUST 1759

Source: Goodwood, guide, n.d. [c.1972], 17 (illus.)

Receiv'd August 20th 1759 the sum of thirty Guineas for his Grace the Duke of Richmonds Picture[1] and six Guineas for a Miniature copy
Red. by me
JReynolds
37-16-0

1 JR's portrait, a three-quarter length of 1758, remains at Goodwood (Mannings 1113).

260

GERTRUDE, DUCHESS OF BEDFORD 19 SEPTEMBER 1759

Source: Woburn MSS

Receivd Sep. 19 1759 the sum of one hundred & twenty Guineas from her Grace the Dutchess of Bedford for three half-length Pictures by me[1]
JReynolds
126-0-0

1 Of Augustus Keppel, herself (Gertrude, Duchess of Bedford) and Lady Caroline Russell, afterwards Duchess of Marlborough; all three remain at Woburn (Mannings 1053, 1559, 1657).

261

MRS WILLIAM LEE 19 MARCH 1761

Source: GC, II, 570

Received, March 19, 1761, from Mrs. Lee, the sum of ten guines, being the first payment for her picture by me.[1]

£10. 10s.

J. Reynolds

1 Philadelphia (d.1799), dau. of Sir Thomas Hart Dyke, Bart., of Lullingston Castle, Kent, m. William Lee (d. 1778). She sat to JR in 1761 for a half-length, possibly the picture with Barbizon House, London, in 1929 (Mannings 1100).

262

JOHN, MARQUESS OF GRANBY 27 JANUARY 1762

Source: Yale Center for British Art

The Rt. Honble. Lord Granby[1] to J Reynolds Dr.

For his Lordships Picture, Kitcat size, given to Mr. Fisher[2]	18-18-0
Do. given to Mr. Shaftoe[3] the size between a whole and halflength	50- 0-0
Do. a halflength sent to Mr. Calcroft[4]	42- 0-0
Paid for a Miniature Picture of / Lady Granby[5]	06- 6-0
	117- 4

Receiv'd Jan 27th 1762 from Thomas Calcroft[6] Esq the contents of this Bill being in full of all demands by me

£	s		
117-	4	0	J Reynolds
			Witness Thomas Beach[7]

1 The Marquess of Granby sat to Reynolds for kit-cat and half length portraits in 1756–58 (see Mannings, p.323). Several replicas were made, including the three mentioned in this bill, for political friends.

2 Brice Fisher (d. 1767), MP for Malmesbury 1754–61, a racing companion of Lord Granby's and wholesale clothier; the portrait is in the musée Jacquemart-André (Mannings 1191).

3 Robert Shafto (?1732–97), MP for Durham County 1760–68, see Letters 275, 288; the portrait is in a private collection (Mannings 1192).

4 John Calcraft (1726–72), Paymaster of widow's pensions (War Office) 1757–62, MP for Calne 1766–68 & Rochester 1768–72; the portrait is untraced (Mannings 1195).
5 Lady Frances Seymour (1728–60) dau. of Charles, 6th Duke of Somerset, m. the Marquess of Granby in 1750; she sat to JR in 1757–59; one portrait was destroyed in the fire at Belvoir in 1816 (Mannings 1189), another remains untraced (Mannings 1190).
6 Thomas Calcraft (1738–83), lt.-col. 91st Foot, 1760, MP for Poole 1761–74.
7 Thomas Beach (1738–1806), painter, working in JR's studio 1760–62.

263

HENRY FANE 26 JUNE 1762

Source: Lawrence, Crewkerne, 25 May 1995, lot 575

Leicesterfields June 26 1762

Sir

I am extremely glad to hear your Picture[1] is arrived safe, in Compliance with your order I have sent your Account and remain

Sir / Your most humble / and obedient servant

JReynolds

The Remaining half payment	42 - 0 - 0
Packing Case	01 - 12 - 0
Porters	0 - 5 - 0
	43 - 17 - 0
Frame	13 - 13 - 0
	57 - 10 - 0

Annotated: Henry Fane Esq at Brympton near Yeovill Somersetshire

1 This letter is apparently addressed to Henry Fane, 2nd son of Thomas Fane, who suc. as 8th Earl of Westmorland on 26 August 1762, but it is not altogether clear which picture is referred to. It was probably the whole-length of Thomas, 8th Earl of Westmorland (Antony House; Mannings 596). A Mr Fane gave fourteen sittings to JR in 1761 and on 10 May 1762 JR noted: 'Send to Mr Fane a Bill'. There are two undated (but pre-August 1762) payments in JR's Ledger from Mr Fane of 40gn., annotated 'now Lord Westmorland'; the sums suggest a whole-length, and probably correspond with this invoice. In 1760–64 JR was also painting Thomas Fane's three children, for which payments have otherwise been identified: a whole-length of his second son Henry with his two guardians (Metropolitan Museum of Art, New York; Mannings 593), £200 on 18 February 1766; his eldest daughter Ann (untraced; Mannings 592), 20 gn. on 29 March 1763, and his eldest son John, later the 9th Earl (private collection; Mannings 594), 100 gn. on 26 July 1764.

264

MRS ALVIN 18 SEPTEMBER 1765

Source: British Museum (print room, copy inserted in J.H. Anderdon's copy of Edward Edwards, *Anecdotes of Painters*, 1808, II, 188–89)

Received Sept. 18, 1765
From Mrs Alvin the sum of twenty five guineas being the first half payment for Miss Alvin's picture[1] by me
J Reynolds

1 Unidentified (Mannings 48); the price indicates a kit-cat portrait.

265

MRS ALVIN 16 AUGUST 1766

Source: British Museum (print room, copy inserted in J.H. Anderdon's copy of Edward Edwards, *Anecdotes of Painters*, 1808, II, 188–89)

Received Aug 16 1766
from Mrs. Alvin the sum of twenty five guineas being the last half payment for Miss Alvin's picture by me[1]
J Reynolds
£26-5

1 See Letter 264.

266

JOHN PALMER 27 OCTOBER 1769

Source: Hyde Collection

Received the 27th. day of October 1769 of Mr. John Palmer the Sum of Three hundred and thirty pounds being part of the moneys devised by the Wills of the late Revd Joshua Reynolds and Mrs Eliz: ffield[1] deceased to the Children of the late Revd. Samuel Reynolds and Thomas Reynolds deceased
by me
Joshua Reynolds

1 JR's uncle and his sister-in-law, see Appendix I.

267

WILLIAM, 1ST BARON CLERMONT 6 MAY 1771

Source: National Library of Scotland (MS.5407, f.160)

Received May 6th 1771 from the Rt. Honble Lord Clarmount the sum of thirty five Guineas for Lady Ancrams Picture[1]

JReynolds

1 Elizabeth Fortescue (1745–80), niece of Lord Clermont, m. 1762 the 8th Earl of Ancram, later (1775) 5th Marquess of Lothian; she sat twice to JR, the portrait mentioned here is probably that painted c.1769, now at Blickling Hall (Mannings 1064).

268

[THOMAS PARTINGTON] 29 MAY 1771

Source: Devonshire MSS, Chatsworth (Compton Place MSS)

Leicesterfields May 29th. 1771

Sir

Lord Northampton has informed that you[1] are the Executor of the late Lord Northampton[2] and consequently the proper person to apply to for the payment for a Picture which I did for the late Lady.[3] I have inclosed the Bill and will take it as a great favour if you order the Payment[4]

I am Sir with the greatest respect

Your most humble and obedient servant

Joshua Reynolds

Her Grace The Dutchess of Beaufort[5] as Administatrix to the Late Earl of Northampton to JReynolds Debtor ———

For Lady Northamptons Picture wit

with hands	31. 10
A Frame	03. 13. 6
	35 3 6

1 Spencer Compton, 8th Earl of Northampton (1738–96); this letter was apparently sent to Thomas W. Partington, Northampton's agent, see note 4 and Letter 269.

2 Charles Compton, 7th Earl of Northampton (1737–63); both he and his Countess had died abroad, while he was ambassador extraordinary at Venice.

3 Lady Anne Somerset (1741–63), dau. of the 4th Duke of Beaufort, m. the 7th Earl of Northampton in 1759. She sat to JR in 1761 and 1762 for a half-length portrait (private collection; Mannings 399).

4 Partington replied to JR from Brook Street, the same day (Chatsworth, Compton Place MSS) explaining that he was not the executor of the 7th Earl of Northampton, whose estate had been administered by the Dowager Duchess of Beaufort (whose daughter the Earl had married): 'if you will be pleased to compleat the inclosed Bill by _______ ascertaining the time when the picture was drawn & if you can, adding any further circumstances of description I will take the first proper opportunity of writing to her on the subject'. See Cormack, 160 ('a bill delivered to Mr. Partington cancelled 35-3-6').

5 Elizabeth, Duchess of Beaufort (1719–99), widow of the 4th Duke; in 1771-74 she was travelling in France and Italy with her daughter, Lady Mary Somerset (1756-1831) and her orphaned grand-daughter, Lady Betty Compton (1760-1835), dau. of the 7th Earl of Northampton.

269

[THOMAS PARTINGTON] 17 JUNE 1771

Source: Devonshire MSS, Chatsworth (Compton Place MSS)

Leicesterfields June 17. 1771

Sir

I have not been able to ascertain the time when Lady Northamptons Picture was sent home; I know it was painted a little before he sat out for Venice,[1] finish'd and deliverd (as well as I remember) after his death.

whoever is in possession of the Picture will probably be able to give a better account of it than I can, of this I am sure that I was never paid for it.[2]

I am Sir Your most humble and obedient servant

Joshua Reynolds

1 The 7th Earl and his Countess had set out for Italy in May, see Letter 268n2.

2 The Dowager Duchess wrote to Partington from Paris, 6 July 1771 (Chatsworth: Compton Place MSS): 'I am surprized that Sr. Joshua Reynolds did not make his demands when all the other Creditors made their's; beg you will acquaint Mr Bag[ot?] with his late application concerns it. I found the Picture in Grosr Sqr. & it is unknown to me when it was sent thither, but supposed it was when Ld. Northampton was in England.'

270

JOHN GAWLER 24 APRIL 1778

Source: Beinecke Library

Dear Sir

A friend, whom I wish to oblige wants to borrow of me today more mony than I have in the house

If it is convenient to you will oblige me with the contents of Your Bill
For Mrs. Gawler[1] 36-15-0
For Master Gawler[2] 36-15-0
Do———— 36-15-0
— — 109- 5-0[3]

Receivd the Contents
J Reynolds

April 24 1778

1 Floors Castle (Mannings 710).
2 'Master Gawler and his brother' sat to JR in 1777 and payment of £73 10 0 was listed in April 1778; the picture is in Birmingham Museum and Art Gallery (Mannings 711).
3 Addition was evidently not his forte.

271

THOMAS CADELL 27 NOVEMBER 1778

Source: Houghton Library

Receiv'd Novr. 27.1778 of Mr Cadell Sixty two Pounds Nine Shillings in full for my moiety of the Profit on the first Edition of my Discourses (the Octavo Edition)

£62. 9. 0
JReynolds

272

SIR WILLIAM FORBES 6 AUGUST 1779

Source: See Letter 82.

The Bill which I sent to my Lord and which probably may be found amongst his papers the following is a Copy.[1]

For Lord Errol[2] -	£105-0
For Lady Errol[3] -	26-5
For a Copy[4] -	026-5
For Mending a Picture	005-5
For a packing case	- -5
	163-0

1 James Boyd, 15th Earl of Erroll (1726–78), had died on 3 July 1778; the items of this bill were first submitted in 1763, June 1764 and February 1769; see Letter 277 (Cormack, 118–19, 151).
2 His whole-length portrait by JR of 1762–63 is in a private collection (Mannings 867).
3 Isabella, Countess of Erroll (1742–1808); a half-length portrait by JR of 1759–61 is in the Worcester Art Museum, Mass., and a three-quarter length of c.1763 in Glasgow Art Gallery (Mannings 865–866).
4 Presumably the unspecified copy after Allan Ramsay first entered in JR's ledger on 2 June 1762 (Cormack, 118).

273

NEW COLLEGE, OXFORD 16 JUNE 1780

Source: New College, Oxford

Receiv'd June 16th 1780 from Harry Peckham Esq the sum of one hundred and forty seven pounds for Designs for the Window of New College, Oxford.

Joshua Reynolds

<u>147</u>

1 See Letters 62, 66n2 and 138 (Cormack, 160).

274

ROYAL ACADEMY [5 AUGUST 1780]

Source: British Museum (print room, copy in Sir William Chambers's hand signed by JR in J.H. Anderdon's copy of Edward Edwards's *Anecdotes of Painters*, 1808, II, 188–89)

Recd Aug 5th 1780 of the Rt. Honble the Lords of the Treasury by the hands of Sr W. Chambers the sum of thirty one pounds 10s being in full for a picture painted in the Library <u>Cieling</u> of the Royal Academy somerset House[1]

£31.10s.

Joshua Reynolds

1 *Theory*, now at Burlington House (Mannings 2168).

275

MISS CAMILLA SHAFTO 21 MAY 1781

Source: Private Collection

London May 21 1781

Madam

I receiv'd the favour of your Letter of the 2d of April, but deferred answering it till I should be able to inform you of the Pictures[1] being shiped, which I did not receive till this day, at the same time I receiv'd your second Letter. I am sorry it came too late to prevent Lord Granbys Picture being sent with the two others, They were all packed up together and according to your orders recommended to the care of Mr. Anderson at Newcastle The name of the ship is the Dublin Thomas Dale Master – bound for Newcastle

I am with the greatest respect

Your most humble and obedient servant

Joshua Reynolds

I beg leave to add that Mr. Shafto's Picture which is a half-length comes to twenty four Guineas,[2] after the rate of twelve Guineas for a head which ~~the~~ was the price I begun with when I came from Italy – I have at present one hundred Guineas for that size

1 See Letter 288; the three portraits, now in a private collection, were of Ralph Jenison (kit-cat; Mannings 1001); Robert Shafto of Benwell, Camilla's father, see Letter 262n3; and John, Marquess of Granby, a three-quarter length (Mannings 1192).

2 Cormack, 164: 'June 1789 Mr. Shafto painted about 20 years since 26 5 0'.

276

CHARLES, 2ND MARQUESS OF ROCKINGHAM 2 JULY 1781

Source: Sheffield Archives (WWM vouchers for works of art 95)

July 2d 1781[1]

Sir Joshua Reynolds presents his Compts. To Lord Rockingham. He finds on looking over his books that there was a head copied from the whole-length[1] with a memorandum that it made for His Lordships Sister.

There was a Copy likewise made of the late Duke of Cumberland which ~~I~~ he has no account of its being paid for but if His Lordship recollects any thing to the contrary he will please to strike it out of the Bill.

For a whole-length of the Marquis of Rockingham[2]	157 - 10 - 0
For a Copy[3]	036. 15
For the Duke of Cumberland[4]	052. 10
	246 - 15 - 0

Annotated: 157-10-0
36-15-0
194- 5-0

1 Rockingham had sat to JR in 1766 and 1768 for a whole-length (St Osyth's Prory; Mannings 1858) and a double portrait with Edmund Burke (unfinished; Fitzwilliam Museum; Mannings 1863).

2 Copies of the whole-length portrait are in the Mansion House, York (presented in 1783; Mannings 1860), and at Dalmeny (Mannings 1861). Lady Rockingham presented a posthumous (1781–83) copy to George IV (Mannings 1859).

3 A half-length of 1766–68 is in a private collection (Mannings 1862).

4 William, Duke of Cumberland (1721–65); a three-quarter length from Wentworth Woodhouse is in a private collection (Mannings 1888).

277

JOHN WAUCHOPE 18 OCTOBER 1783[1]

Source: Sotheby's, 31 March 1998, lot 93

Sir Joshua Reynolds presents his Compliments to Mr Wauchope and has inclosed according to his desire the receipt in full of his demand on Lord Errol[2] he begs leave to return his thanks to Mr. Wauchope for his attention in his business

John Wauchope Esq writer to the Signet Edinburgh

Annotated: Recd 18 [October?] 1783 Sir Joshua Reynolds with Discharge of the late Earl of Errolls Debt to him,
and in another hand: See Discharge within, £163.5=

1 Dated from JR's letter to Sir William Forbes of 18 October 1783, see Letter 115.

2 See Letter 272.

278

SACKVILLE, 8TH EARL OF THANET [JULY 1786]

Source: Beinecke Library

The Earl of Tenett[1] to Sir J. Reynolds	Dit
For Lady Tenet whole length[2]	157.10
Master Tufton wholelength[3]	52.10
Two Master Tuftons Do[4]	105. 0
Miss Obrien[5] ————	52.10
	367.10

1 Lord Thanet (1733–86) died on 27 March 1786 (near Nice), so that this account was dealt with by his executors, see Letter 279.

2 Mary, Countess of Thanet (1746-78), sat to JR in 1770-71 (private collection; Mannings 1775)

3 Hon John Tufton (1773–99), third son of the 8th Earl of Thanet, sat in 1776–77 (private collection; Mannings 1776).

4 This entry is endorsed 'pd' before and 'X' after. JR's sitter-book December 1766 has: 'Lord Tenet, Eldest boy 2/Youngest 1' implying these were children Thanet had by Nelly O'Brien.

5 Nelly O'Brien, see Letter 104n2.

279

SACKVILLE, 8TH EARL OF THANET 18 AUGUST 1786

Source: facsimile in an unidentified bookseller's catalogue of 7 May 1961

Receivd August 18th 1786 from — Woodcock Esq the sum of two hundred and sixty one pounds ten shillings for Pictures done for the late Earl of Tenet, in full of all demands[1]

£261-10 JReynolds

1 i.e. less two Master Tuftons, see Letter 278n4.

280

THOMAS COUTTS & CO. 6 SEPTEMBER 1786

Source: see Letter 159.

London 6 Sepr 1786

Messrs Thomas Coutts and Co.: Mr. Jenkins of Rome has drawn a bill upon Charles Townley Esq. For five hundred and thirty five pounds.[1] Which I desire you will accept on my account, and charge to my debit when paid or of Mr. Townley accepts the bill payable at your house you will pay it in when

due & charge it to my Account – I am your most obliged humble servant
Joshua Reynolds

The Draft is dated Rome 5 Aug last at usance to Jeffrey & Street of Poole will be due 8 Nov – endorsed only by them – T's bill

Annotated: Copy of the order for payment of Mr. Jenkin's draft on me, wrote by Mr. Coutts & Signed by Sir Jos Reynolds

1 For Bernini's *Neptune and Triton*, see Letter 160.

281

CHARLES, 4TH DUKE OF RUTLAND 10 OCTOBER 1786

Source: Hilles 1929, CVIII

Oct. 10th 1786

Dear Sir[1]

I must acquaint you that having accepted a draught for six hundred pounds for the Neptune which I bought at Rome,[2] which draught will be due in a few days, it will oblige me if you could discharge those Bills for mony which I have laid out for the Duke of Rutland.[3] It would still add to the obligation if you can pay me the interest due in the Dukes Bond which I hold. You may be sure I should not be sollicitous about this interest, if it was not for the reason I have mention'd, and now I would much rather endeavour to borrow it than put the Duke to the least inconvenience.

I am with great respect
Your most obedient servant
J Reynolds

1 This account was probably addressed to Joseph Hill (d. 1811), the Duke of Rutland's agent in London, a friend of the poet William Cowper and secretary to Lord Thurlow.
2 By Bernini, see Letter 160.
3 Between May 1782 and September 1785 JR's account-book shows £263.10.2 owing from the Duke, £247.15.2 for Dutch pictures and £15.15 for 'Paid duty', see Letter 282.

282

HON. CHARLES GREVILLE 23 DECEMBER 1786

Source: Hilles 1929, CXIII

Dec. 23. 1786

Sir Joshua Reynolds presents his Compts to Mr. Greville and begs leave to return his acknowledgements of the receipt of £157-10- for the Picture of Thais and his own Portrait[1]

1 Cormack, 153, as a second payment. *Thais* (RA 1781; Waddesdon Manor; Mannings 2167) modelled by 'Miss Emily' at the request of Charles Greville cost £105 (Penny 1986, 295-96); Greville was included in one of JR's *Portraits of Members of the Society of Dilettanti* 1777-79 (Mannings 510) and a separate half-length of c.1775 is at Cawdor Castle (Mannings 768).

283

CHARLES, 4TH DUKE OF RUTLAND [1787]

Source: Belvoir Castle MSS

His Grace the Duke of Rutland to J Reynolds[1]

The Nativity[2]	1200 - 0 - 0
The Flemish Pictures[3]	0247 - 15 - 0
Pd. Duty	0015 - 15 - 0
The Dutchess whole-length[4]	0210 - 0 - 0
Lord Granby & Lady Elizabeth[5]	0210 - 0 - 0
Paid Mr. Smirk for a Copy[6]	0021 - 0 - 0
The Infant Jupiter[7]	0105 - 0 - 0
Lord Chatham[8]	0210 - 0 - 0
Lord Robert[9]	0210 - 0 - 0
Mr. Thoroughton[10]	0052 - 10 - 0
Kitty Fisher[11]	0052 - 10 - 0
General Oglethorp[12]	0052 - 10 - 0
An old man reading[13]	0031 - 10 - 0
	2618 - 10 - 0

1 The Duke had died on 24 October 1787. On 22 May 1789 the 5th Duke of Beaufort, his father-in-law, ordered Messrs Deane & Co of Temple Bar to pay JR £7,802, 'the amount of two mortgages and interest and a separate account, and place it to the account of the executors of Charles, late Duke of Rutland' (MS: Belvoir Castle; *HMC Rutland*, IV, 245).

2 Destroyed by fire 1816; see Letter 124.

3 See Letters 134–35, 138–43 and 147 concerning possible purchases of Flemish pictures.

4 'For the Duchess of Rutland 150' June 1781 (Cormack, 162) whole-length, exh. RA 1781; destroyed by fire 1816 (Mannings 1212).

5 'Duke of Rutland, for Children £200' June 1781 (Cormack 162) RA 1781 (Belvoir Castle; Mannings 1208).

6 'Paid for the Duke of Rutland's Children to Mr. Smirk 20g' June 1781 (Cormack, 162; Mannings 1208a). Robert Smirke (1753–1845) also copied the whole-length of the Duchess of Rutland (Mannings 1212a).

7 'Duke of Rutland for Jupiter 100g' May 1782 (Cormack, 162); RA 1774; destroyed by fire 1816 (Mannings 2098).
8 'Duke of Rutland, for Lord Chatham £200' May 1782 (Cormack, 162); see Letter 124; destroyed (Mannings 1454).
9 See Letter 103; 'Duke of Rutland (for Lord R. Manners not in the above Bill.), cancelled' May 1782 (Cormack, 162); whole-length (Belvoir; Mannings 1215).
10 Thomas Thoroton was Rutland's private chaplain at Belvoir; he lived at Scriveton; 'For Mr. Thoroughts 50', June 1781 (Cormack, 162); possibly Robert Thoroton, Rutland's confidential agent who accompanied him to Ireland and took his own life shortly after the Duke's death; the portrait, exh. RA 1781, is in a private collection (Mannings 1748).
11 'Miss Fisher' May 1782 (Cormack, 162); destroyed by fire 1816 (Mannings 619).
12 Gen. James Edward Oglethorpe (1696–1785), colonist of Georgia and first Governor of Savannah, friend of Dr Johnson; May 1782 (Cormack, 162); destroyed by fire 1816 (Mannings 1359).
13 'An old Man reading a Ballad', May 1782 (Cormack, 162); destroyed by fire 1816 (Mannings 2137).

284

GEORGE BIRCH 22 APRIL 1788

Source: Hilles 1929, CXXII

Ap'l 22nd 1788

. . . I am so hurryed in preparing for the Exhibition that I have but just time to acknowledge the receipt of your obliging letter inclosing a draft for one hundred guineas being the first half-payment for Dr Ash's Picture[1] which Picture I hope to begin in two or three days and you may be assured that no attention on my part shall be wanting in the finishing it. I am with great respect, Your most obedient servant,

Joshua Reynolds

1 John Ash (1723–98) physician, organiser of the Eumalian Club to which JR belonged, and one of the founders of the General Hospital, Birmingham, of which Birch was a governor; JR's portrait remains there (Mannings 78). Sittings began on 28 April.

285

ROBINSON 22 APRIL 1788

Source: Royal Archives, Windsor (RA GEO 26793)

April 22d 1788

Sir Joshua Reynolds presents his Compts To Mr. Robinson.[1] The only Picture that he has finishd of His Royal Highness since the account sent in the last year, is a whole length with ~~the~~ <a> black servant which is still at his house, the price of that is two hundred Guineas.[2]

There is another whole-length of the same price which is not quite finishd.[3] Another whole length unfinished of Mrs. Fitzherbert, 200 Guineas,[4] and a Head of His Royal Highness intended for Count Kegeneck[5] – 50 Guineas Whether Mr. Robinson intended this account to be sent in he is in doubt but he has no other demand.

1 Accountant and sub-treasurer to the Prince of Wales (*Court and City Register*, 1788).
2 Exh. RA 1787; now at Arundel castle (Mannings 721).
3 Probably the whole-length of the Prince of Wales in Mansion House, York (Mannings 721a).
4 She sat to JR in 1786 and 1788. This whole-length was cut down in 1816, now with Tweed Investments Ltd (Mannings 627).
5 Count Kageneck, see Letter 139n1.

286

ROBINSON [APRIL 1788]

Source: Royal Archives, Windsor (RA GEO 26795)

Sir Joshua Reynolds presents his Comp to Mr. Robinson. The price of the whole-length (the head of which was copied from Mr. Bradyll's picture) will be two Hundred Guineas.[1]

1 Referring to an untraced portrait of George Prince of Wales (Mannings 722); 'Mr Bradyll's [Wilson Bradyll, 1755–1818] picture' is now in the Tate Gallery (Mannings 720).

287

ROBINSON 24 APRIL [1788]

Source: Royal Archives, Windsor (RA GEO 26794)

April 24th

There is another whole-length which is intended for Lord Charlemont which according to Sir Thos Dundass opinion ought to be copied from the Picture of H.R.H. with the black servant and to have one sitting to make it an original.[1]

1 An untraced version of the portrait now at Arundel Castle (Mannings 721b).

288

MRS ADAIR [CAMILLA SHAFTO] 16 JANUARY 1789

Source: Private Collection

Leicesterfields Jany 16 1789

Madam

In looking over my accounts I find the Pictures I sent some years[1] since according to your direction have not yet been paid for.[2]

I am with the great respect Your most obedient humble servant

JReynolds

To Mr. Jennison	18-18
Mr. Shafto	25- 4
Lord Granby	25- 4
	£69- 6

Mrs Adair / ~~Miss Shafto / Benwell Lodge / near Newcastle upon Tyne~~Newton / Durham

1 See Letter 275.

2 William Adair's answer, Newton, 26 January 1789 (private collection), explained that 'the picture of the late Lord Granby was a present from his Lordship to Mr. Jennison Shafto of the Wratting, and Mr. Jennison's Picture was sent by Mrs. Adair', and that, according to JR's letter of 21 May 1781, the outstanding amount is only for 'the picture of the late Mr. Shafto her father at 24 guineas ... which I intended to have called upon you last spring when I was in Town, but from hurry of business forgot to discharge it.'

289

ANTROBUS 27 AUGUST 1790

Source: Hyde Collection

Sir Joshua Reynolds's Compliments to Mr. Antrobus and has inclosed a draft of 100 Guineas and another of ten Pound. He would be obliged if he would buy Stock with what mony is in his hands reserving one hundred pounds

Aug 27th 1790

£35.18.3
500 Exes
435.18.3
105
540.18.3

UNTRACED LETTERS

290

1750

To Miss Weston (two) 1750–51 (see Letter 7)

291

1750–52

To Mrs Mary Palmer (JR's sister who, with her sister Elizabeth, see Letter 292, helped finance his stay in Italy; LT, I, 39, suggested JR must have written 'a dozen or two' of letters to them while he was abroad).

292

1750–52

To Mrs Elizabeth Johnson (see Letter 291)

293

1761, 5 July

To Joshua Sharpe (Beinecke Library: envelope only, annotated: '5th July, 1761 Reynolds'; to Mr Sharpe at his Chambers in Lincolns Inn).

294

1767 , Spring

To David Garrick ('Sir Joshua Reynolds, by a letter still in existence, appears to have brought [Goldsmith and Garrick] together'; Prior, *Life of Goldsmith*, 1837, II, 151). 'At the painter's house in Leicester-square, Goldsmith placed in Garrick's hands the manuscript of the *Good-Natured Man*' (J. Forster, *Life & Times of Oliver Goldsmith*, 1855, 56). By July 1767 it was agreed that Garrick would not put on the play, which was finally staged at Covent Garden on 29 January 1768.

295

1770

To James Brunton of Norwich (c.1751–72; a young artist whom JR encouraged to come to study in London; Gwynn 1898, 51)

296

1772?

To George, 4th Viscount Townshend, when lord lieutenant of Ireland, 1767–72 (requesting a living for Joseph Palmer; Northcote 1818, II, 41; cf. Letter 151)

297

1773

To Sir William Elford (advice on the hanging of JR's self-portrait which he sent to Plympton when elected Mayor; LT, II, 36)

298

1775, 15 April

To James Boswell ('there came yesterday a card to me [Boswell] from Sir Joshua Reynolds, that Mr Owen Cambridge [1717–1802, satirist and historian] would be happy to see me at dinner that day at his house at Twickenham with Sir Joshua and Dr Johnson' (Boswell's *Journal*, 16 April 1775; Fifer 1976, 52).

299

1775, July

To John Robinson (JR's nephew, Samuel Johnson, wrote to his sister Elizabeth, from London, Saturday, ?July 1775, that JR had written to Mr Robinson about their brother William, who had gone to India in April 1774; *Joshua's Nephew,* 150). John Robinson, who had been made DCL at Oxford at the same time as JR, had at that time close control over the affairs of the East India Company.

300

1777, March

To Prince Hoare (in March 1777 James Northcote took with him to Italy a letter of introduction from JR for the painter Prince Hoare; R.L. Lightbown, Introduction, n. p., to Northcote's *Life of Sir Joshua Reynolds,* [1818] facsimile reprint 1971).

301

1780, 29 September

To Mr French [possibly Edmund Burke's brother-in-law, Patrick William French] (thanking him for partridges; Sotheby's, 24 July 1929)

302

1780, 22 November?

To the Rt. Revd. Jonathan Shipley (congratulating him on election to the Club; Lord Teignmouth, *Memoirs of Sir William Jones,* 1804, 194)

303

c.1781

To George, 3rd Earl Temple (later 1st Marquess of Buckingham), when lord lieutenant of Ireland 1782–83 (soliciting for his nephew; see Letter 178)

304

1782, 19 April
To Thomas Gainsborough ('With the hundred guineas he paid for the picture [*Girl with Pigs*] Sir Joshua sent a long letter containing, in the words of Bate Dudley 'half as many compliments on the merit of the artist' (Whitley 1928, I, 378).

305

1783
To Ekaterina, Princess Dashkov (thanking JR for his congratulations on her inauguration on 21 October as the first President of the newly established Russian Academy, and for a volume of his *Discourses*). In 1784 the Princess wrote to JR saying that 'when you shall appear in our language, I shall take care that you shall appear in a garb not intirely unbecoming to you'; Cotton 1859, 71–72; Hilles 1970, 268–69).

306

1785, April
To Thomas Warton (concerning the vacant post of Poet Laureate; LT, II, 472)

307

1785, 10 September
To Pieter de Gree (see Letter 141)

308

1787
To Charles, 2nd Earl Cornwallis, governor general of Bengal (recommending William Johnson; Beinecke Library)

APPENDIX I

THE REYNOLDS FAMILY

Derived from notes from John Edgcumbe; Devon and Cornwall Notes & Queries, *1912, vii, 49–54; J.J. Alexander and W.R. Hooper,* History of Great Torrington, *1948, 185–95, 222–23;* Joshua's Nephew, *and J.L. Clifford,* Dictionary Johnson, *1980.*

Listed in order of age within each heading

PARENTS AND UNCLES

John Reynolds (1671–1758), uncle; fellow of Eton, and fellow of King's College, Cambridge; rector of Stoke Charity, Hampshire, and canon of St Peter's, Exeter, 1729; he published an edition of Pomponius Mela, 1711, and, with the encouragement of Stephen Weston, Bishop of Exeter, the *Census Habitus Nascente Christo,* 1738; he married a Miss Towers and left several children, of whom William (c.1705–50), was a fellow of Exeter College, Oxford. He was buried in King's College chapel. His Will was in favour of Mrs Elizabeth Field (d. by 1769), his sister-in-law (GC, 1, 302); his portrait by JR in 1757 is at Eton College (Mannings 1517). He founded six Exhibitions at Exeter College, one of which was later taken by Samuel Johnson, his great-nephew.

Joshua Reynolds (1675–after 1734), uncle; fellow and bursar of Corpus Christi College, Oxford, and rector of Stoke Charity, Hants, 1716, a College living; he married Mary Field (d. 1734), whose sister Elizabeth sat to JR in the 1740s (Sotheby's, 2 February 1966, lot 143; Mannings 605); godfather of JR, he lived in Exeter.

Samuel Reynolds (1680–1745), father; scholar of Corpus Christi College, Oxford, 1699, and fellow of Balliol College, Oxford, 1705; he was master of Plympton Grammar School 1715–45. He married in 1711 Theophila Potter. His posthumous portrait by JR is in the Cottonian Collection, Plymouth (Mannings 1519).

Thomas Reynolds (1682–before 1734), uncle; brother of Samuel, an Exeter goldsmith; he had a son, Thomas, and a daughter Elizabeth, who married a Mr Keys.

Theophila Potter (1688–1756), mother; daughter of Humphrey Potter, rector of Nymet Rowland and curate at Lostwithiel, and his wife Mary Baker.

APPENDIX I

BROTHERS AND SISTERS

Humphrey Reynolds (1713–40), baptised at Torrington, Devon; a lieutenant in the Royal Navy, he was drowned at sea.

Robert Reynolds (1714–87), an ironmonger in Exeter.

Mary ('Molly' or 'Polly') **Reynolds** (Mrs Palmer) (1716–94), occasional authoress, her *Devonshire Dialogue* first published posthumously in 1837; married John Palmer (1708–70), an attorney of Great Torrington, where he was mayor in 1752, 1758 and 1765, and where in 1752 he built Palmer House which was inherited by his second son, John Palmer. With her sister Elizabeth, she lent JR money to travel in Italy in 1750–52. Her memorial, with that of her husband, is in Great Torrington church.

Ann Reynolds (1718–20)

Jane Reynolds (b. 1719)

Elizabeth Reynolds (Mrs Johnson)(1721–c.1797), author of a commentary on *Ezekiel* (privately printed in four parts, 1781–85), married in 1747 William Johnson (c.1722–95) of Great Torrington, 'a bustling, ambitious man', merchant, mayor in 1757 and 1764, who deserted her in 1775 and moved to London in 1776, only returning to her in old age; his conduct particularly vexed JR who had lent him money; although Elizabeth, with her sister Mary, had previously lent JR money to travel in Italy in 1750–52, he declined to lend her £300 at the time of the separation: 'There is no comfort for you from this quarter. Your suppos'd Brother and you could never have had the same parents', her son Samuel told her in May 1775 (*Joshua's Nephew*, 123). Her portrait by JR of c.1747 is in a private collection (Mannings 1017).

Joshua Reynolds (1723–92)

Theophila Reynolds (1725–26)

Samuel Reynolds (1727– by 1740)

Frances ('Renny') **Reynolds** (1729–1807), amateur painter and essayist, publishing an *Essay on Taste* in 1781. Particularly admired by Samuel Johnson, her manuscript 'Recollections of Johnson', in the Hyde Collection, were published in part in 1836 and 1897. In 1752 she was a milliner in Plymouth; she lived with JR in London 1753–77, until she was supplanted by her nieces, Theophila and Mary Palmer. She exhibited at the RA in 1774–75. She lived 'in a habitual perplexity of mind, and irresolution of conduct, which to herself was restlessly tormenting, and to all around her was teasingly wearisome' (LT, I, 91); according to Mrs Nollekens she frequently reminded JR he was the son of a clergyman and should not paint on Sunday; latterly she lived alone in Queen's Square, Westminster. JR left her £100 a year. Her portrait by JR of c.1746 is in the Cottonian Collection, Plymouth (Mannings 1515).

Martyn Reynolds (1731–40)

NEPHEWS AND NIECES

Palmers:

Joseph Palmer (1749–1829), attended Exeter College, Oxford, 1766, proceeding MA 1772. He was 'minister' of the Temple church in London and had rooms in the Temple; in 1775 he went to Paris with William Salkeld and later wrote a 'four month tour of France'. A friend of Oliver Goldsmith, he wrote an unsuccessful play, *Zaphira*, in 1776, in which year he went to Ireland where, through the influence of JR, Lord Townshend made him the chancellor of Ferns, 13 March 1779, which position he held until 1801. The Duke of Rutland presented him with the Deanery of Cashel, 26 May 1787, in which year he married Eliza Edwards, who had posed for 'Prudence' in JR's New College window. After JR's death and during the Irish troubles, he came to England. Although his Deanery and Irish living amounted to £1000 per annum, his sister Mary said in 1799 he would probably not return to Ireland. He was made precentor of Waterford, 6 June 1801. Latterly he lived at Beam, 'a delightful country house near Torrington'. Farington was disparaging of his character, calling him 'an ordinary & conceited man' and 'a lad of dull parts' with a harelip. His son, Reynolds Palmer, a military cadet at Marlow in 1804, married in 1814 Constant-Grace Collins. JR omitted Joseph from his will, perhaps because he had already done so much to promote his ecclesiastical career. His monument is in Exeter Cathedral.

Mary Palmer (Marchioness of Thomond) (1750–1820), JR's favourite niece, who stayed with him at Leicester Fields 1770–73 and 1774–92. She was said to have had as many suitors as Penelope; the principal beneficiary of JR's will, she married in 1792 the 5th Earl of Inchiquin (1726–1808), cr. Marquis of Thomond [I] 1800, and Baron Thomond [GB] 1801, an Irish MP 1757–68 who later sat at Westminster 1784–1800; despite his age, he was described as being 'lively as a lark' and both 'handsome and not agreeable' (*Commons*). They lived at Taplow Court, Bucks and she died at Baylis, Bucks.

John Palmer (1752–1827), attended St John's College, Cambridge, 1774, proceeding MA in 1783; he was rector of Clannaborough, Devon, 1807–27, vicar of South Benfleet, Essex, curate of Frithelstock, Devon, and honorary canon of Lincoln. He was in London in 1775 and sat to Northcote in 1775; he married Jane Johnson (1772–1843) and there were five daughters and five sons. He lived at Torrington until his death in 1827. Like his brother, Joseph, John was not named in JR's will, but he inherited the bulk of Mary Palmer's fortune in 1820 (*GM*, 1827, I, 376, had in error that he was from St John's, Oxford).

Theophila Palmer (Mrs Gwatkin) (1757–1848), one of JR's favourite nieces, lived with him at Leicester Fields from 1777 until her marriage in 1781 to Robert Gwatkin (1757–1843) of Killiow, Cornwall, high sheriff of Cornwall in 1789. Their daughter Theophila (1782–1844), 'little Ophy', was painted by JR in 1783 (Waddesdon Manor; Mannings 788); she married Robert Lowe, spent much of her life in India, and died childless.

Elizabeth Palmer (1759–84), whose husband was presumably the William Salkeld, of Southampton Buildings, London, Fellow of Exeter College, Oxford, 1771–81. She died of consumption.

Johnsons:

Samuel Johnson (1754–78), left Oxford through lack of money in 1772 when JR had offered to train him as an artist. He sat to Northcote in 1775 and in 1776 attended Exeter College, Oxford, through an exhibition organised by his great-uncle; he was ordained in 1777 but died the following year of consumption.

William Johnson (1756–99), sailed to India in April 1774 and became, with the help of Robert Chambers, Clerk of the Crown at Calcutta; he married Mary, daughter of Lt.-Gen. Tolley.

Elizabeth ('Betsey') **Johnson** (Mrs Deane) (d. 1841), sat for the figure of 'Fortitude' in JR's New College window when she was staying with JR from March to September 1776. In 1782 she sailed to India with her sister Jane to join her brothers, returning in 1785 with Sir John D'Oyley and his wife. She married Rev. William Deane of Webbery, Devon (d. 1818).

APPENDIX I

Richard Johnson (b. c.1760), sailed in February 1778 to join his brother William in India, where he became an accomptant general to the revenue department; he had returned by 1786; he did not marry.

Mary Johnson (Mrs Furse), married in 1791 the Rev. Peter Furse (c.1756–1832) of Halsdon, Devon.

Frances ('Fanny') **Johnson** (Mrs William Yonge), married William Yonge (1753–1845) Chancellor and Archdeacon of Norwich 1782–1814, vicar of Swaffham 1799–1845, rector of Hilborough 1806–37, and rector of Necton with Home Hale 1838–45. Their daughter married Mr Motte in 1806.

Jane Johnson (Mrs Philip Yonge) (d. 1782), married before she was sixteen Philip Yonge (c.1755–88), the brother of her sister Fanny's husband, and a barrister in the Supreme Court, Calcutta; she died in India within a month of her arrival.

APPENDIX II

BIOGRAPHICAL LIST OF CORRESPONDENTS

References are made to Letter numbers

Abington, Mrs Frances (c.1737–1815) [**231**], *née* Barton, courtesan and actress, she married her music master, James Abington, and was educated by a Mr Needham (d. 1765), an Irish MP. JR greatly admired her, painting a whole-length of her as *Thalia* c.1764–68 (Waddesdon Manor; Mannings 28), as Miss Prue in Congreve's *Love for Love* 1771 (Yale Centre for British Art; Mannings 29), and as Roxalana in *The Sultan* in 1784 (untraced; Mannings 32).

Adair, Mrs Camilla, *see* **Shafto**

Alvin, Mrs [**264, 265**]

Ancaster, Brownlow, 5th Duke of, *see* **Bertie**

Antrobus [**289**]

Astle, Thomas (1735–1803) [**119**], antiquary and palaeographer.

Bacon, John (1740–99) [**186, 192**], sculptor; ARA 1770, RA 1778; his monument to the Earl of Chatham in Westminster Abbey, 1779, established his reputation and thereafter he enjoyed uninterrupted success. His exceptional monument to Johnson in Westminster Abbey, completed in 1795, attempted to combine 'magnitude of parts with grandeur of style', but was said to have the air of a tired pugilist.

Banks, Joseph (1743–1820) [**76, 215**], botanist and traveller; he visited Iceland in 1772 and sailed with Captain Cook 1778–81; President of the Royal Society 1778, he was elected to the Club 1778 and made a Baronet 1781. He sat to JR for a three-quarter length in 1773 (National Portrait Gallery; Mannings 106) and appears in one of the Dilettanti groups of 1779 (Society of Dilettanti; Mannings 510).

Barnard, Thomas (1728–1806) [**227**], Dean of Derry 1769, Bishop of Killaloe and Kilfenora 1780–1806, elected to the Club 1775 and Chaplain to the RA 1791–1806. He sat to JR for a small half-length in 1767, finished in 1773 (untraced; Mannings 109).

Barrington, Hon. Shute (1734–1826) [**183**], sixth son of the 1st Viscount Barrington, Bishop of Llandaff 1769, of Salisbury 1782, and Durham 1791–1826. He sat to JR in 1759 (private collection; Mannings 121).

Barrington, William Wildman, 2nd Viscount (1717–93) [**232**], eldest son of the 1st Viscount Barrington, secretary of war 1765–78. He sat to JR in 1762 (private collection; Mannings 122).

Barry, James (1741–1806) [**22**], querulous but gifted Irish history painter, protégé of Edmund Burke; he studied in Italy 1766–70; ARA 1772, RA 1773; he ceased exhibiting in 1776; decorated the Society of Arts hall in London 1777–83 with six huge canvases showing the 'progress of civilisation'; professor of painting at the RA 1782, but expelled 1799.

Beattie, James (1735–1803) [**39, 101, 223, 228**], Scottish poet and essayist, professor of natural philosophy at Marischal College, Aberdeen, 1760, and subsequently of moral philosophy; author of *Essay on the Immutability of Truth* 1770, and the poem, *The Minstrel*, 1771 and 1774; Hon. DCL Oxford 1773 (at the same time as JR), and received a pension from the King; JR esteemed him 'for his virtues rather than his talents', while he admired JR for his 'enlarged understanding, and truly philosophical mind'; in 1767 he married Mary Dun, who had become mentally deranged by 1774. He sat to JR for an allegorical portrait in 1773 (Aberdeen University; Mannings 138).

Beaumont, Sir George, 7th Bt. (1753–1827) [**156**], of Coleorton Hall, amateur painter, connoisseur and art patron; succeeding his father in 1762, he married in 1778 Margaret Willes and was MP for Bere Alston 1790–96; his gift of paintings to the Nation in 1826 helped to establish the National Gallery in London. He sat to JR for a half-length portrait in 1788 (Frick Center at Clayton, Pittsburgh; Mannings 144).

Bedford, Gertrude Leveson-Gower, Duchess of (1719–94) [**260**], daughter of the 1st Earl Gower, she married in 1737 as his second wife John Russell, 4th Duke of Bedford (1710–71). She sat to JR in 1759–62 for a three-quarter length, as did the Duke (Woburn; Mannings 1558–60).

Bertie, Lord Brownlow (1729–1809) [**257**], MP for Lincoln 1761–79, succeeded his nephew in 1778 as the 5th and last Duke of Ancaster. His portrait by JR of 1756 remains at Grimsthorpe (Mannings 162).

Birch, George [**283**], a governor of the General Hospital at Birmingham.

Bonomi, Joseph (1739–1808) [**173, 194**], architect, born in Rome; he first came in 1767 to London, where he finally settled in 1784 and maintained a good practice; he designed a monument to Edmund Burke's sister in 1791 (see Letter 213); ARA 1789.

Boswell, James (1740–95) [**92, 107, 118, 123, 136, 163, 190, 233, 298**], biographer, born in Edinburgh, where he qualified as an advocate; he met Dr Johnson in London in 1763 and travelled on the Continent 1764–66. Author of *Journal of a Tour to the Hebrides with Samuel Johnson* 1786 and *The Life of Samuel Johnson* 1791; JR, who met him in 1769, enjoyed his lively company; he was elected to the Club in 1773 and secretary of foreign correspondence at the RA in 1791. He sat to JR in 1787 for a half-length portrait (National Portrait Gallery; Mannings 214).

Boydell, John (1719–1804) [**165, 230**], engraver, print-seller and publisher, elected Alderman 1782, Sheriff 1785 and Lord Mayor of London 1790. In 1785 he lavishly commissioned leading British artists to paint scenes from Shakespeare for exhibition in his

Shakespeare Gallery in Pall Mall, and engravings of the paintings were published in 1803. The enterprise proved unsuccessful and, after Boydell had died in straitened circumstances, the Gallery was closed and the paintings sold in 1805.

Bristol, Corporation of [**122**]

Brunton, James (c.1751–72) [**295**], painter from Norwich; RA schools 1770, he died shortly after of consumpton.

Buckingham, George Grenville, 1st Marquess of (1753–1813) [**178, 303**], son of George Grenville, who was first lord of the treasury 1763–65. In 1779 he succeeded his uncle as 3rd Earl Temple; lord-lieutenant of Ireland 1782–83 and November 1787–October 1789; he was created Marquess of Buckingham 1784. JR painted him with his family in 1780–82 (National Gallery of Ireland; Mannings 763).

Buller, James (1717–65) [**256**], of Morval near Looe, Cornwall, MP 1741–65, Mayor of East Looe 1752; he married secondly in 1744 Jane, daughter of the 1st Baron Bathurst. He and his wife sat to JR in 1757 (private collection; Mannings 271–72).

Bunbury, Sir Thomas Charles, 6th Bt. (1740–1821) [**26**], of Barton, Suffolk, MP and patron of the turf, he succeeded his father in 1764; he married in 1762 Lady Sarah Lennox (1745–1826) who eloped with Lord William Gordon in 1769; they were divorced in 1776; elected to the Club 1774, he was a pall-bearer at Samuel Johnson's funeral. He sat to JR for a half-length in 1766 (untraced; Mannings 281) and Lady Sarah in 1762 with her nephew, Charles Fox, and cousin, Lady Susan Strangways (private collection; Mannings 678) and in 1764–65 (whole length, sacrificing to the Graces; Art Institute of Chicago; Mannings 279).

Burke, Edmund (1729–97) [**18, 94–98, 121, 131, 187, 213**], statesman, essayist and orator, born in Ireland; MP 1765–94, mostly in opposition, but he was secretary to Lord Rockingham in 1765 and paymaster of the forces under Rockingham in 1782; led the impeachment of Warren Hastings 1788–94; he married in 1756 Jane Nugent, and there was one surviving son, Richard; in 1768 he purchased an estate at Beaconsfield; Johnson considered his conversation without equal and he was a founder member of the Club in 1764. JR, a close friend, painted him in 1767–69 (private collection; Mannings 284) and 1774 (National Gallery of Scotland; Mannings 285) and with Rockingham in 1766 (unfinished; Fitzwilliam Museum; Mannings 1863).

Burney, Charles (1726–1814) [**45**], organist, composer and musicologist, he settled in London in 1760; Doctor of Music, Oxford, 1769, he travelled in Italy 1770 and in Germany and the Netherlands 1772, afterwards publishing *The Present State of Music in France and Italy* in 1771 and a *General History of Music* in 1776–89. A near-neighbour of JR in Leicester Fields and a close friend of Dr Johnson, he was elected to the Club in 1784; father of the novelist Fanny Burney. JR painted his half-length portrait in 1781 (National Portrait Gallery; Mannings 290).

Burney [**234–35**]

Cadell, Thomas (1742–1802) [**79, 80, 220, 236, 271**], a London bookseller and publisher who succeeded to the business of Andrew Millar in the Strand in 1767, partnered by William Strahan and then by his son Andrew Strahan; he was an intimate friend of Dr Johnson. Printer to the Royal Academy from 1778, he published the collected edition of JR's first seven *Discourses* in May 1778 and all the subsequent *Discourses* in quarto. He was elected an alderman of London in 1798 and sheriff in 1800.

Carlisle, Frederick Howard, 5th Earl of (1748–1825) [**52**], succeeded his father in 1758; Dilettanti 1767; he married in 1770 Margaret, daughter of Granville Leveson-Gower, 1st Marquess of Stafford; lord-lieutenant of Ireland 1780–82; KG 1793. A pall-bearer at JR's funeral, he sat to JR in 1757–58 (whole length), 1769 (whole length as Knight of the Thistle) and 1770 (with George Selwyn), all at Castle Howard; a fourth half-length portrait of 1767 is in a private collection (*see* Mannings 944–47).

Carmarthen, *see* **Leeds**

Catherine II of Russia (1729–96) [**207**] Empress of Russia 1762–96; born in Stettin, Pomerania, she married 1745 Peter, son of Charles Frederick, Duke of Holstein; her husband succeeded his aunt as tsar Peter III in 1762, but she seized power herself after her husband's assassination. She became a considerable collector of works of art for her palaces at St Petersburg and works by British artists were held in particular esteem.

Chambers, Sir Robert (1737–1803) [**81**], professor of law at Oxford 1766; he married in 1774 Fanny Wilton (b. 1758), daughter of the sculptor Joseph Wilton; elected to the Club in 1768. In 1774 he went to India, with his wife and mother, as judge of the Supreme Court in Bengal; he was knighted in 1778; he made a celebrated collection of Sanskrit MSS (now in Berlin). He sat to JR in 1773 for a half-length portrait (private collection; Mannings 343).

Chambers, William (1723–96) [**46, 195, 196, 237**], architect, founder member and first Treasurer of the RA. Born in Stockholm, son of a Scottish merchant, he settled in London in 1755 after study in Italy. In 1770 he was made a knight of the Polar Star by King Gustav of Sweden, George III allowing him the status of an English Knight. He designed Somerset House (built 1776–1801) in part of which the RA was housed from 1780; Surveyor General and Comptroller of the Royal Works from 1782; JR respected his administrative ability but their relationship was essentially formal. JR painted his three-quarter length portrait in 1756 (National Portrait Gallery; Mannings 344) and 1778 (RA; Mannings 346).

Clermont, William Henry Fortescue, 1st Baron (1722–1806) [**267**], Irish MP, created Baron Clermont [I] 1770, Viscount Clermont [I] 1776 and Earl of Clermont [I] 1777.

Collingwood, Thomas [**100**], secretary of the Foundling Hospital 1758–90.

Colman, George (1732–94) [**238**], a barrister before becoming dramatist and manager of the Covent Garden theatre 1767–74 and of the Haymarket 1777–89; elected to the Club 1768. JR painted his half-length portrait in 1768–70 (private collection; Mannings 396).

Cornwallis, Charles Cornwallis, 2nd Earl (1738–1805) [**308**], army commander; MP 1760–62, before succeeding as 2nd Earl; surrendered to American forces at Yorktown 1781; governor-general of Bengal 1786–93; created Marquess Cornwallis in 1792; lord-lieutenant of Ireland 1798–1801. JR painted his three-quarter length portrait in 1761 (private collection; Mannings 422).

Cosway, Richard (1742–1821) [**181, 239**], portrait painter, miniaturist and collector; he was appointed principal painter to the Prince of Wales in 1785.

Coutts & Co [**280**] the London banking house, founded by Thomas Coutts (1735–1822).

Crabbe, George (1754–1832) [**110**], clergyman and poet from Suffolk, protégé of Edmund Burke who introduced him to JR in 1781; domestic chaplain to the Duke of Rutland at Belvoir from 1782–87, in which time he published *The Candidate* 1780, *The Library* 1781, *The Village* 1783 and *The Newspaper* 1785; his later years were spent as vicar of Trowbridge, Wiltshire.

Cranch (or **Craunch**) [4], of Plympton, Devon, was instrumental in getting JR apprenticed to Hudson; he had 'a small independent fortune' which enabled him to lend JR money for his Italian visit in 1750–52. JR painted him in 1766–67 (private collection; Mannings 441) and had a silver cup made for him in gratitude for his early encouragement but Cranch died before the gift could be made. He was conceivably Richard Cranch (b. 1683), of Exeter College, Oxford, rector of Dipford, Devonshire, in 1721.

Cribb, William [219], JR's frame-maker; he attended JR's sale in April 1795 (*Farington Diary*, 15 April 1795). His son, William Cribb, modelled the Hercules in JR's picture for the Empress of Russia and the Robin Goodfellow for John Boydell (Mannings 2094, 2142).

Cunningham [146, 148]

Dashkov, Princess (Vorontsova, Ekaterina Romanovna) (1743–1810) [305], amateur artist and musician, and a pronounced Anglophile; she was in England in 1780 while her son received a British education at Edinburgh and she met JR who held a distinguished place 'in the confined circle of those I believe and call my friends'. She returned to Russia in 1782 and in 1783 Catherine II made her the first President of the Russian Academy.

Daulby, Daniel (d. 1797) [64], brother-in-law of William Roscoe with whom he helped to form the Society for promoting Painting and Design in Liverpool; he published in 1800 *A Descriptive Catalogue of the Works of Rembrandt and of his Scholars.*

Edgcumbe, Richard Edgcumbe, 1st Baron (1680–1758) [6], created Baron Edgcumbe of Mount Edgcumbe in 1742; he first introduced JR to Commodore Keppel and was the subject of one of the earliest of JR's portraits, a three-quarter length of c.1740 (destroyed, formerly Mount Edgcumbe; Mannings 559).

Elford, Sir William [297]. Presumably William Elford (1749–1837), MP for Plymouth 1796–1806 and Rye 1806–08, created a Baronet in 1800.

Evans, Thomas (1742–84) [85], bookseller.

Eyre, Anthony (1727–88) [255], of Grove Hall, Notts., MP for Boroughbridge, Yorks., 1774–84, he married Judith Letitia Bury in 1755. He sat to JR 1755 (private collection; Mannings 588).

Falconet, Etienne-Maurice (1716–91) [38], French sculptor, worked in Russia 1766–78 where he designed the equestrian monument to Peter the Great (unveiled in 1784); his marble *Baigneuse* and *Seated Cupid* of 1757 (both in the Louvre) attracted much notice.

Fane, Henry, [263] probably Henry Fane (1739–1802), MP for Lyme Regis 1777–1802, 2nd son of Thomas Fane, who succeeded as 8th Earl of Westmorland in 1762.

Farington, Joseph (1747–1821) [224], topographical draughtsman and diarist; ARA 1783, RA 1785; his *Diary 1793–1821,* remains an inexhaustible source of anecdote; he wrote *A Memoir of the Life of Sir Joshua Reynolds* 1819 which also appeared in volume I of Malone's *Literary Works of Sir Joshua Reynolds* 1819.

Farr, Dr Samuel (1741–95) [53], of Taunton, physician to the Bristol Infirmary 1767–80. His daughter Susannah (c.1763–1839) married the Revd. William Rose (c.1763–1844) vicar of Glynde (J. Hemlow ed., *Burney Journals and Letters*, XI, 1984, 387n7) and J.W. Croker, in his ed. of Boswell's *Life of Johnson*, IX, 1839, 252, described receiving anecdotes of Dr Johnson from a Mrs Rose, daughter of Dr Farr of Plymouth and daughter-in-law of Dr Johnson's old friend, Dr Rose (identified as William Rose, 1719–86, of Chiswick).

Fitzwilliam, Anne Watson-Wentworth, Countess (d. 1769) [10], daughter of the 1st Marquess of Rockingham, married in 1744 William, 3rd Earl Fitzwilliam [I] and 1st Earl Fitzwilliam of Norborough [GB].

Forbes, Sir William, 6th Bt of Pitsligo (1739–1806) [**71, 82, 89, 115**], Scottish banker and occasional writer, whose *Life of James Beattie* was published in 1806. An episcopalian, he was the friend and mentor of James Boswell, and as a banker he was frequently consulted by William Pitt. In 1792–93 he travelled in Italy with his wife. His half-length portrait by JR of 1786 is in the Scottish National Portrait Gallery and an earlier half length of c.1776 is in a private collection (Mannings 657–58).

French [301]

Fuller, Stephen [120], London agent for the Jamaica House of Assembly.

Gainsborough, Thomas (1727–88) [304], portrait and landscape painter, the most serious rival to JR, their styles being quite different; he worked in Bath 1758–74 and in London from 1774, exhibiting at the RA between 1769 and 1783; he found more favour with the Royal family than JR, painting a series of Royal portraits from 1776.

Gardiner, Luke (1745–98) [**34**], Irish MP for Dublin 1773–89, he was created Baron Mountjoy [I] in 1789 and Viscount Mountjoy [I] in 1795; he was killed at New Ross leading his regiment against insurgents. His half-length portrait by JR of c.1773 is in a private collection and another of 1784 is untraced (Mannings 697–98).

Garrick, David (1717–79) [**41–43, 294**], actor and author, manager of the Drury Lane theatre from 1747; he had been Dr Johnson's first pupil in Lichfield and they left for London together in 1737; his enormous success on the stage was carefully promoted through paintings and engravings. Elected to the Club 1773. JR painted him on several occasions,including *Between Tragedy and Comedy* in 1760–61 (private collection), as Kiteley in *Every Man in his Humour* 1767 (Royal Collection), the 'Prologue' portrait of c.1775 (Knole), and with his wife in 1772 (National Portrait Gallery), *see* Mannings 700, 703, 705, 707.

Gawler, John (1726–1803) [**270**], of Ramridge House, solicitor, married in 1760, Caroline Ker (d. 1802), 2nd daughter of the 3rd Lord Bellenden. He and his wife sat to JR for half-length portraits in 1777–78 (his wife's engraved) and their sons, Henry and John, sat together for a kit cat in 1777 (all in a private collection; Mannings 709–11).

Gilpin, William (1724–1804) [**221**], biographer, miscellaneous writer, educationalist and amateur artist; schoolmaster at Cheam, Surrey, and vicar of Boldre, Hampshire, from 1777; published a number of illustrated essays on his travels in Britain; in 1792 he sent JR a copy of his *Three Essays: on Picturesque Beauty; on Picturesque Travel; and on Sketching Landscape.*

Granby, John Manners, Marquess of (1721–1770) [**262**], eldest son of the 3rd Duke of Rutland, brother of the 4th Duke (see below); an outstanding army commander; MP 1741–70; sat to JR several times between c.1756 and 1770, *see* Mannings 1191–1206. *The marquisate of Granby was successively held by John, Marquess of Granby 1721–70, and Charles, 4th Duke of Rutland (q.v.) 1770–79.*

Grantham, Thomas Robinson, 2nd Baron (1738–86) [**30, 35, 40, 65**], statesman, MP from 1761 before succeeding his father as 2nd Baron in 1770; appointed ambassador to Madrid 1771–79, and foreign secretary 1782–83; elected to the Society of Dilettanti in

1763; he married in 1780 Mary, daughter of the 2nd Earl of Hardwicke. His half-length portrait by JR was painted c.1758 (private collection; Mannings 1542).

Gree, Pieter de (1751–89) [**307**], portrait and decorative painter, born in Antwerp, where JR met him in 1781; he came to England before settling in Ireland in 1785, helped by JR.

Green, Valentine (1739–1813) [**112–13**], mezzotint engraver, worked in London from 1765, exhibiting at the RA from 1774; appointed mezzotint engraver to the King in 1775 and Keeper of the British Institution 1805. He engraved a considerable number of portraits by JR.

Greville, Hon. Charles (1749–1809) [**281**], collector and roué, 2nd son of the 1st Earl of Warwick, MP 1774–90; he was the nephew of Sir William Hamilton, to whom he passed Emma Hamilton in 1786. He appears in one of JR's group portraits of the Dilettanti (Society of Dilettanti; Mannings 510).

Gwatkin, Robert [**189**], JR's nephew, *see* Appendix I.

Gwatkin, Mrs Theophila [**63, 93, 97, 114, 201**], JR's niece, *see* Appendix I.

Hamilton, Miss [**133**]

Hamilton, Sir William (1730–1803) [**21, 25**], KB 1772, diplomat, vulcanologist, antiquarian, amateur musician; MP for Midhurst 1761–64, British envoy 1764–67 and minister plenipotentiary 1767–1800 at Naples; elected to the Club 1784. He sat to JR for a half-length finished in 1772 (Toledo Museum of Art; Mannings 822) and a whole length in 1776–77 (National Portrait Gallery; Mannings 823); he also appears in one of the Dilettanti group portraits (Society of Dilettanti; Mannings 510).

Harcourt, *see* **Nuneham**

Hardwicke, Philip Yorke, 2nd Earl of (1720–90) [**36, 111, 117, 175**], of Wrest Park, Bedfordshire; he was an MP from 1741 until succeeding his father in 1764, and a Trustee of the British Museum from 1753. JR painted his three-quarter-length portrait in 1765–66 (private collection) and his two small daughters in 1760–61 (Cleveland Museum of Art), *see* Mannings 1956, 1960.

Harrison, Sir Thomas (1701–65) [**258**], knighted in 1754; he married in 1727 Dorothea Snow (1702–73) and both sat to JR in 1756–58 (Corporation of London; Mannings 852–53).

Hastings, Warren (1732–1818) [**88**], colonial administrator; he first went to India in 1750, and was in England 1764–69; returning to India, he became governor of Bengal 1772 and governor-general 1773–85; impeached for corruption and tried 1788–95, the action led by Edmund Burke, he was eventually acquitted. JR painted his three-quarter length portrait in 1766–68 (National Portrait Gallery; Mannings 861).

Hervey, John Augustus Hervey, Lord (1757–96) [**216**], 1st surviving son of the 4th Earl of Bristol (Bishop of Derry); British envoy in Florence 1783–93.

Hoare, Prince (1755–1834) [**300**], portrait and history painter; studied in Italy 1776–68 and exhibited at the RA 1781–85, afterwards giving up painting to write musical farces and studies of the fine arts; elected secretary of foreign correspondence at the RA 1799.

Hodges, William (1744–97) [**241**], landscape painter; he sailed with Captain Cook to the South Pacific in 1772–75 and was in India 1779–84; elected ARA 1786, RA 1787.

Humphry, Mrs Elizabeth (c.1710–90) [**11**], *née* Hooper, married 1735 George Humphry (c.1714–59) of Honiton, Devon, where she ran a business in Brussels lace; *see* Ozias Humphry.

Humphry, Ozias (1742–1810) [**99, 242**], portrait painter, essentially in miniature, born in Honiton, Devon, he first came to London in 1758 and settled there in 1764 when JR befriended him; in 1772 his eyesight became affected and he went to Italy 1773–77 taking up life-size portraiture in oils; he was in India 1785–87; ARA 1779, RA 1791; he went blind in 1797.

Hutchinson, John Hely (1724–94) [**90**], lawyer and statesman, secretary of state in Ireland 1777–94, provost of Trinity College, Dublin, 1774–94. He sat to JR for a three-quarter length in 1778 (National Gallery of Ireland; Mannings 981).

Jansen, Hendrik (1741–1812) [**161, 167, 176**], a Dutch musicologist and translator of writings on art into French; in 1786 he was *inspecteur général de l'Académie royale de musique* in Paris.

Jerningham [**243**]

Johnson, Mrs Elizabeth (1721–c.1797) [**292**], JR's sister, *see* Appendix I.

Johnson, Dr Samuel (1709–84) [**68, 87, 244**], writer and critic, author of the *Dictionary* 1755 and *Lives of the Poets* 1779–81; LLD Dublin 1765; JR was said to have founded the Club in 1764 as 'a vehicle for Johnson's talk'; they admired each other greatly: Johnson considered JR a man 'most difficult to abuse', while JR said that Johnson 'formed my mind, and brushed off from it a deal of rubbish'; elected professor of ancient literature at the RA 1770. The 4th edition of Johnson's *Dictionary* in 1773 included several examples from JR's *Fourth Discourse*. JR painted a series of portraits of him, including a three-quarter length in 1756–57 (National Portrait Gallery), and half-lengths in 1769 (Knole) and 1778 (Tate Gallery), *see* Mannings 1011–14.

Johnson, William (1756–99) [**91, 108**], JR's nephew, *see* Appendix I.

Keppel, Augustus (1725–86) [**80**], naval commander, second son of the 2nd Earl of Albemarle; he sailed round the world with Anson in 1740–41; commodore 1749 in the Mediterranean, when JR sailed with him to Minorca; served in the West Indies 1761–62 and promoted Rear-Admiral 1762 and Vice-Admiral 1770; in 1778 he commanded the Channel fleet in a series of inconclusive actions against the French resulting in his Court Martial in January 1779, but he was honourably acquitted amidst national rejoicing; first lord of the Admiralty 1782–83 and created Viscount Keppel in April 1782. JR painted his celebrated whole-length portrait of Keppel in 1753; others are of 1749, 1765 and 1779 (all National Maritime Museum), 1759 (Woburn), 1781–83 (Tate Gallery) and 1785 (Royal Collection), *see* Mannings 1036–49.

Kirby, Joshua (1716–74) [**19**], draughtsman and landscape painter, elected President of the Society of Artists on 18 October 1768. His election was followed by the resignation of eight of the original Directors (Whitley 1928, I, 224).

Langton, Bennet (1737–1801) [**105, 174, 177**], Greek scholar and founder member of the Club, he married in 1770 Mary, Dowager Countess of Rothes, and they had ten children; professor of ancient literature at the RA 1787 in succession to Johnson, of whom he had been a close friend. He sat to JR in c.1759–60 (Gunby Hall; Mannings 1085).

Lawrence, Thomas (1769–1830) [**199**], portrait painter; a child prodigy, he came to London from Bristol in 1787, and exhibited at the RA from 1787, in 1790 showing the whole-lengths of Queen Charlotte and Elizabeth Farren; he succeeded JR, who had much admired his work, as Painter in Ordinary to the King 1792; President of the RA 1820.

Lee, Mrs Philadelphia (d.1799) [**261**], daughter of Sir Thomas Hart Dyke, Bt. of Lullingston Castle, Kent, she married William Lee (d. 1778). She sat to JR in 1761 for a half-length (untraced; Mannings 1100).

Leeds, Francis Godolphin Osborne, 5th Duke of (1751–99) [**208**], statesman, ambassador to Paris 1783 and foreign secretary 1783–91; he succeeded his father in 1789 as 5th Duke; elected to the Club 1792, he was a pall-bearer at JR's funeral. He sat to JR in 1764 (private collection; Mannings 1367) and appears in one of the Dilettanti groups (Society of Dilettanti; Mannings 510).

Lennox, Mrs Charlotte (1720–1804) [**44, 57**], authoress, born Charlotte Ramsay in Gibraltar, she came to England in 1735 and married c.1748 a Mr Lennox. A friend of Johnson, she published novels, poems and translations from the French; according to Mrs Thrale 'everybody admired her, but nobody liked her'.

Lowth, the Rt Revd Robert (1710–87) [**74, 75**], divine, Hebrew scholar, professor of poetry, Oxford, 1741–50; Bishop of St Davids 1766–77, of Oxford 1777, and of London 1777–87; Dean of the Chapel Royal 1777; declined the Archbishopric of Canterbury in 1783; published *Lectures on Hebrew Poetry* 1753 and a translation of the book of Isaiah into English verse 1778; he believed Hebrew to be the language of Paradise.

Macartney, George, 1st Earl (1737–1806) [**58**], diplomat and colonial governor, created Baron [I] 1776, Viscount [I] 1792, Earl [I] 1794, and Baron Macartney [GB] 1796; envoy in St Petersburg 1764–67; chief secretary in Ireland 1769–72; governor of the Caribbean islands 1775–79, governor and president of Fort St George, Madras 1781–85, ambassador to Peking 1792–94, and governor of the Cape of Good Hope 1796–98. He was elected to the Club in 1786; JR painted his half-length portrait in 1764 (Petworth; Mannings 1164).

Malone, Edmond (1741–1812) [**132, 166, 214, 218**], literary critic and editor; born in Ireland, he finally settled in London in 1777; devoted admirer of Johnson; generous in helping Boswell and JR prepare their publications; elected to the Club in 1782, acting as treasurer. He was one of JR's executors and his first biographer (*The Works of Sir Joshua Reynolds*, 1797. He sat to JR for a half-length portrait in 1778 (National Portrait Gallery; Mannings 1180).

Montagu, Mrs Elizabeth (1720–1800) [**33**], authoress and literary hostess, originator of the Blue Stocking Club; born Elizabeth Robinson, she married in 1742 Edward Montagu (1678–1761), grandson of the 1st Earl of Sandwich; after his death she built Montagu House (22 Portman Square) to the designs of 'Athenian' Stuart. She sat to JR in 1775 (untraced; Mannings 1270).

More, Hannah (1745–1833) [**67**], poet, dramatist, religious writer and an accomplished linguist; fourth of five daughters of a schoolmaster; friend of Dr Johnson; her tragedy *Percy*, with prologue and epilogue by Garrick, first performed at Covent Garden on 10 December 1777.

More, Miss P. [**83**]

Morrison, Thomas (1705–78) [**14, 15, 28**], rector of Langtree, near Great Torrington, Devon, and prebend of Exeter 1736; with literary pretensions, he wrote two tragedies, *Otho* and *Clytemnestra*, neither accepted for the stage, and some verse, including *Pindarick Ode on Painting*, 1768, dedicated to JR.

Moser, George M. (1706–83) [**78**], enameller and engraver, keeper of the RA 1768–83.

Newcastle, Thomas Pelham-Holles, Duke of (1693–1768) [**12**], created Duke in 1715; statesman, secretary of state 1724–54, first lord of the treasury 1754–56 and 1757–62; despite his considerable authority he remained remarkably timorous.

New College, Oxford [273]

Nichols, John (1745–1826) [**193**], printer, antiquarian and author; succeeded to William Bowyer's publishing business in 1777; sole manager of the *Gentleman's Magazine* 1792–1826; author of *Literary Anecdotes of the Eighteenth Century*, 1812–15.

Northcote, James (1746–1831) [**56, 202, 217**], portrait and history painter, born in Plymouth; pupil and resident assistant of Reynolds 1771–75, and subsequently his biographer (1st edition 1813, 2nd expanded edition 1818).

Nuneham, George Harcourt, Viscount (1736–1809) [**27, 73**], of Nuneham, Oxford, he succeeded his father as 2nd Earl Harcourt in 1777; amateur landscape gardener and engraver; his father's resiting of the village of Nuneham may have inspired Goldsmith's *Deserted Village*. He sat to JR c.1753–54 and in 1780 with his wife and brother (both private collection; Mannings 832–33).

Oglander, Revd John (1737–94) [**69, 70, 138**], Warden of New College, Oxford.

Oliver, Miss [13]

Ourry, Paul Henry (1719–83) [**32**], of Plympton, Devon, naval officer 1742–57; MP for Plympton 1763–75, and commissioner of the Plymouth dockyard 1775–83. His three-quarter length portrait by JR 1748 is at Saltram (Mannings 1372).

Palmer, John (1752–1827) [**266**], JR's nephew, *see* Appendix I.

Palmer Joseph (1749–1829) [**116, 179**], JR's nephew, *see* Appendix I.

Palmer, Mary [**291**], JR's sister, *see* Appendix I.

Palmer, Theophila, *see* **Mrs Gwatkin**

Parr, Samuel (1747–1825) [**225, 226, 240**], classical scholar; he taught at Harrow before becoming headmaster, successively, of grammar schools at Colchester and Norwich; from 1785 he lived at Hatton, Warwickshire, as a scholar and country parson; a quick-tempered but generous man, he was once asked to write a biography of Samuel Johnson, whom he admired.

Partington, Thomas W. [**268, 269**], agent for the Earl of Northampton.

Pelli, Giuseppe (1729–1808) [**54, 55**], Director of the Royal [Uffizi] Gallery at Florence and secretary to the Grand Duke of Tuscany.

Percy, the Rt Revd Thomas (1729–1811) [**16, 17, 20, 29, 47, 60, 109, 198, 245, 246**], antiquarian, Dean of Carlisle 1778 and Bishop of Dromore 1782; he married in 1759 Anne Gutteridge (or Goodriche, d. 1806), nurse to Prince Edward 1771. In 1765 he published the *Reliques of English Poetry*. As domestic chaplain to the 1st Duke of Northumberland (of whom he was a remote kinsman) he had rooms in Northumberland House from 1765 to 1782; elected to the Club 1768. His half-length portrait by JR, engraved by W. Dickinson in 1775, was destroyed by fire at Northumberland House in 1780 (Mannings 1437).

Pocock, Nicholas (1741–1821) [**86**], marine painter; a merchant sea captain before turning to painting, first in water-colour then in oils; he exhibited at the RA 1782–1815.

Potemkin, Prince Grigorii Alexandrovich (1739–91) [**188**], Russian military commander, who succeeded as the favourite of Catherine II in 1775; JR gave him *Cupid untying the zone of Venus* in 1788 and *The Continence of Scipio* in 1789 (both in the Hermitage; Mannings 2127, 2047), the latter probably a tribute to his bravery as leader of the Russian armies in the second Russo-Turkish war.

Potter [**66**]

Pringle, Sir John (1707–82) [**51**], physician from Roxburgh; served with the army in Europe 1742–44, revolutionising medicine and sanitation; he settled in London 1746 and was appointed physician to the Queen 1761 and to the King from 1764; he was made a Baronet in 1766 and became president of the Royal Society in 1772. He sat to JR in 1774 (Royal Society, London; Mannings 1486).

Radcliffe, Walter (1733–1803) [**23, 24, 247, 248**], of Warlegh, Devonshire; he sat to Reynolds in October 1757 (Saltram; Mannings 1506).

Reynolds, Frances (1729–1807) [**98**], JR's sister, *see* Appendix I.

Reynolds, Samuel (1680–1745) [**1, 2, 3**], JR's father, *see* Appendix I.

Richards, John Inigo (1731–1810) [**197**], landscape and scene painter; foundation member of the RA and secretary; he exhibited at the RA 1769–1809.

Richmond, Charles Lennox, 3rd Duke of (1735–1806) [**259**], distinguished army officer, diplomat and a foundation member of the Society of Arts; he married in 1757 Mary (1740–95), third daughter of the 3rd Earl of Ailesbury, and succeeded his father in 1758 as 3rd Duke. He sat to JR in 1758 and his Duchess in 1764–67 for the portraits at Goodwood (Mannings 1113, 1119).

Robinson [**285, 286, 287**], accountant and sub-treasurer to the Prince of Wales.

Robinson, John (1727–1802) [**299**], MP 1764–1802; as joint secretary to the Treasury 1770–82 he undertook the political management of the East India Company; he married in 1758 Mary Crowe, daughter of a West India merchant.

Robinson, Mrs Mary (1758–1800) [**210**], born Mary Darby; a successful actress, mistress of the Prince of Wales 1778–79 and afterwards of Charles Fox; following partial paralysis in 1783 she turned to writing, publishing *Poems* 1791 and a *Monody to the Memory of Sir Joshua Reynolds* 1792. JR's half-length portrait of her of 1783–84 is in the Wallace Collection (Mannings 1532).

Rockingham, Charles Watson-Wentworth, 2nd Marquess of (1730–82) [**276**], statesman, succeeded his father as 2nd Marquess in 1750; leader of the Whig opposition and first lord of the treasury 1765–66 and 1782; JR painted him twice in 1766–68: a whole-length in Garter robes (St Osyth's Priory) and with Edmund Burke (unfinished; Fitzwilliam Museum), *see* Mannings 1858, 1863.

Roscoe, William (1753–1831) [**126, 127, 129**], historian and collector, born in Liverpool where he was first an attorney; later partner in a bank which collapsed and he was thereafter supported by his friends; MP 1806–07 and the first President of the Liverpool Royal Institution 1817; published lives of *Lorenzo de Medici* 1795, and *Pope Leo X* 1805; the better part of his collection of pictures was acquired for the Liverpool Royal Institution (now National Museums on Merseyside).

Royal Academy [274]

Rutland, Charles Manners, 4th Duke of (1754–87) [**106, 124, 134–36, 139–43, 147, 149–52, 154, 157, 160, 162, 164, 171–72, 281, 283**], son of John, Marquess of Granby; he married in 1775 Mary, daughter of the 4th Duke of Beaufort and succeeded his grandfather as 4th Duke in 1779; Lord Privy Seal 1783–84 and lord-lieutenant of Ireland 1784–87, his splendid vice-regal hospitality in Dublin contrasting with considerable political unrest. He was a notable patron of JR who advised him on his collection of paintings and painted him whole-length in Garter robes in 1784 (Belvoir Castle); there are half-lengths of c.1775 (private collection) and c.1778 (Belvoir Castle), *see* Mannings 1184–88.

Sackville [104]

Salisbury, James Cecil, 7th Earl of (1743–1823) [**180**], cr. 1789 Marquess of Salisbury, lord chamberlain 1783–1804.

Selwyn, George (1719–91) [**249**], wit and politician; MP 1747 and 1754–80, who never once spoke in the House, and an extravagant gambler. JR painted him on several occasions: in 1759 with Lord Edgcumbe and Gilly Williams (private collection; Mannings 563); a kit-cat in 1764–66 (Dalmeny; Mannings 1601), in 1770 with Lord Carlisle (Castle Howard; Mannings 947) and a half length of c.1782 (Thomson collection, Toronto; Mannings 1602).

Shafto, Camilla (1756–1827) [**275, 288**], of Benwell, Northumberland, she married in 1784 William Adair (1754–1844) of Newton Hall, Co. Durham.

Sharpe, Joshua (d. 1786) [**293**], a well-known conveyancer; his three-quarter length portrait by JR (coll. Viscount Cowdray; Mannings 1610) was exhibited at the RA 1786 in the month of his death (April).

Sheridan, Richard Brinsley (1751–1816) [**191**], dramatist and politician, born in Dublin; manager of the Drury Lane theatre 1776; his plays *The Rivals* performed in 1775 and *School for Scandal* in 1777; elected to the Club 1777; whig MP 1780–1812 and a confidential adviser to the Prince of Wales. He sat to JR for a three-quarter length portrait in 1788–89 (private collection; Mannings 1612). In April 1773 he married the singer Elizabeth Anne Linley (1754–92) who then renounced public performances; Lord North once suggested Sheridan should receive an honorary degree 'uxoris causa'. JR painted her as St Cecilia in 1775 (Waddesdon Manor; Mannings 1614).

Shipley, the Rt Revd Jonathan (1714–88) [**125, 128, 302**], Dean of Winchester 1760, Bishop of Llandaff 1769 and Bishop of St Asaph 1769–88; 'knowing and conversible', elected to the Club 1780. He sat to JR in 1776 (private collection; Mannings 1616); he had entertained JR in London in the spring of 1784.

Smith, Charles (1749–1824) [**59, 130**], Orcadian painter, nephew of Caleb Whitefoord; exhibited with the SA in London in 1776; he sailed to India on 12 March 1783, reaching Calcutta on 13 September, and returned to England in 1788.

Strahan, Andrew (1749–1831) [**144, 182**], publisher.

Temple, *see* **Buckingham**

Thanet, Sackville Tufton, 8th Earl of (1733–86) [**278–79**], he succeeded his father in 1753 as 8th Earl; he married in 1767 Lady Mary Sackville (1746–78), daughter of the 3rd Duke of Dorset; before his marriage he had been 'for some years' the protector of Nelly O'Brien.

Thrale, Henry (1729–81) [**50**], brewer; he married, against her wishes, Hester Salusbury (1741–1821), later Mrs Piozzi, miscellaneous writer and close friend of Dr Johnson; MP for Southwark 1765–80; he was an expansive host at his villa in Streatham but narrowly escaped bankruptcy in 1772, following which his wife and Dr Johnson successfully assumed a share in the brewery management. From 1777 JR painted a number of literary portraits for Streatham, including a half-length of Thrale himself in 1777 (private collection; Mannings 1749).

Thrale, Mrs Hester (1741–1821) [**72**], *née* Salusbury, authoress, *see* Henry Thrale; she married secondly in 1784 Gabriel Piozzi (d. 1809) with whom she was in Italy 1784–87; published *Anecdotes of the Late Samuel Johnson* in 1784. JR painted her with her daughter in 1777–78 (Beaverbrook Art Gallery, Fredericton; Mannings 1750).

Townley, Charles (1737–1805) [**159, 168–70, 205**], collector and antiquarian, a catholic, educated in France, he travelled extensively in Italy in 1767–68, 1771–74 and 1777, laying the foundation for his extensive collection of antiquities which, on his death, was bought by the British Museum; from England he continued to buy antiquities in Rome, principally through Thomas Jenkins, whose account he settled annually.

Townley, John (d. 1813) [**209**], uncle of Charles Townley.

Townshend, George Townshend, 4th Viscount (1724–1807) [**296**], distinguished army officer; MP 1747–64 before succeeding his father as 4th Viscount; he was created Marquess Townshend in 1787; lord lieutenant of Ireland 1767–72. He sat to JR in 1767 (private collection; Mannings 1762) and 1778–79 (Art Gallery of Ontario; Mannings 1764).

Upper Ossory, Anne, Countess of (1738–1804) [**211–12**], *see* **Upper Ossory, John** below

Upper Ossory, John Fitzpatrick 2nd Earl of (1745–1818) [**84, 153, 155, 158, 184**], succeeded his father to the Irish Earldom 1758; he was MP for Bedfordshire from 1767 until created Baron Upper Ossory [GB] in 1794; he married in 1769 Anne Liddell (1738–1804), the divorced wife of the 3rd Duke of Grafton and one of Walpole's favourite correspondents; elected to the Club 1777. He was a close friend of JR who painted him in 1767 (untraced; Mannings 633) and painted his daughters Lady Anne in 1775 (Lady Lever Art Gallery, Port Sunlight; Mannings 631) and Lady Gertrude in c.1777–78 as 'Collina' (Columbus, Ohio, Museum of Art; Mannings 632) and in 1787 as 'Sylvia' (Museum of Fine Arts, Boston, Mass.; Mannings 630).

Verelst, Harry (1733–85) [**61**], Governor of Bengal 1767–69, grandson of the flower painter Cornelius Verelst (1667-1728); brought up by his uncle the portrait painter Willem Verelst, he went to Bengal in 1750, returning to England in 1770; his later years were ruined by litigation.

Vorontsov, Count Semyon (1744–1832) [**204**], brother of the Princess Dashkov, Russian ambassador in London 1785–96 and 1801–06; he settled in England in 1806. In 1789–90 he unsuccessfully negotiated for a British portrait painter to work in St Petersburg.

Waldron [**145**]

Warton, Joseph (1722–1800) [**62**], poet, critic and miscellaneous writer, brother of Thomas Warton; he was travelling chaplain with the Duke of Bolton 1751, and an unsuccessful headmaster of Winchester 1766–93; he published essays on Pope in 1756 and 1782 and was elected to the Club in 1773. He sat to JR for a half-length portrait in 1777 (Ashmolean Museum; Mannings 1837).

Warton, Thomas (1728–90) [**102**], historian of English verse, professor of poetry at Oxford 1757–67, brother of Joseph Warton; appointed poet laureate in 1785, JR having urged his claims; he published successive volumes of a *History of English Poetry* in 1774, 1778 and 1781; elected to the Club 1782. He sat to JR in 1784 for a half-length portrait (Trinity College, Oxford; Mannings 1838).

Wauchope, John [**277**], writer to the Signet, Edinburgh; administrator of Lord Erroll's estate.

Wedgwood, Josiah (1730–95) [**203**], master potter; he worked at Burslem and at Etruria, Staffs., from 1769; famous for his creamwares, black basaltes and coloured jasperwares, and for his classical designs; supplied two dinner services to Catherine II of Russia in 1774; he and his wife sat to JR in 1782 (Wedgwood Museum, Barlaston; Mannings 1850–51).

West, Benjamin (1738-1820) [**37, 200, 229**], portrait and history painter; born in Pennsylvania, he came to London in 1763 after spending three years in Italy; became the favourite painter of George III (who was antipathetic to JR); foundation member of the RA, he succeeded JR as President in 1792.

Weston, Miss [**5, 7, 8, 290**], of Great Queen Street, Lincoln's Inn Fields; she died in Fulham between 1792 and 1796. She may have been related to Bishop Stephen Weston of Exeter, one of whose daughters married a Colonel and went to Bengal in 1775 (*Joshua's Nephew*, 35). The death of a Mr Weston, formerly a 'hosier in Holborne', was reported in the *St James Chronicle*, 20 October 1769. A Miss Weston, otherwise unknown, sat to JR in October 1757 (LT, I, 157). JR's three letters to her were first published in 1796 by Anthony Pasquin in *An Authentic History of the Professors of Painting, Sculpture & Architecture, who have practised in Ireland; involving Original Letters from Sir Joshua Reynolds which prove him to have been Illiterate*, 1796, 60–63 [reprint 1970]. Pasquin described having met, 'some time since', 'an elderly lady oppressed by penury', residing in the vicinity of Fulham; in her youth she was considered well educated and handsome; she had been in love with a man 'now no more' whose identity would be revealed by letters she had kept. Pasquin, who offered the original letters for inspection at Mr Richardson's, Printseller, of York House, in the Strand, stated that their literary style would 'totally remove the long received idea, that [Reynolds] was the author of the Discourses.' Northcote (1818, 34) used biographical information from the letters, but said that the 'elegant, grateful, and feeling mind' displayed in JR's letter to Lord Edgcumbe demonstrated the 'absurdity of imputing some others to his pen'. Farington (1819, 9), while not denying their authenticity, dismissed them as 'literary scraps'. The Weston letters were next published in *Willis's Current Notes*, no. 82, October 1857, as 'Sir Joshua Reynolds's Love Letters' (and described as having been given 'to a family which had befriended her') but Leslie and Taylor (I, 39–40) felt unable to vouch for their authenticity. Whitley (1928 I, 142–48) accepted the letters and they now appear to be beyond reproach.

Whitefoord, Caleb (1734–1810) [**48, 49, 185**], wit, diplomat and collector, was born illegitimate in Edinburgh; he worked in a wine merchant's office in London, where he was a neighbour of Benjamin Franklin; their friendship led to his attending the British mission in Paris which concluded the peace settlement with America in 1782. Johnson, Goldsmith and Walpole admired his political squibs, written under the name of *Papyrius Cursor*. His half-length portrait by JR of 1775 is in a private collection (Mannings 1876).

Wilkes, John (1727–97) [**206**], MP, demagogue and scholar; outspoken criticism of Lord Bute led to temporary imprisonment in 1762; further prosecution for an obscene poem, followed by a duel, led to self-imposed exile on the Continent 1764–68; elected MP for Middlesex 1768, but such violence ensued that he was again expelled from the House; as alderman (1769), sheriff (1771) and Lord Mayor (1774) of London he became the champion of the City and was returned to Parliament in 1774, thereafter pursuing a more settled course.

Wilton, Joseph (1722–1803) [**9**], sculptor; studied in Paris and in Italy 1746–55, spending most of those last five years in Florence where JR painted his half-length portrait in 1752 (National Portrait Gallery; Manings 1915); appointed Sculptor to the King by 1764, and a foundation member of the RA in 1768; he inherited a competence from his father in 1768 and subsequently lost interest in sculpture, high living resulting in bankruptcy in 1793; keeper of the RA 1790.

INDEX

INDEX